Moments of IMPACT

Thankyou so much for your support. Hope you enjoy my story!
Jillian Monitello

Jillian Monitello

ISBN 978-1-63885-386-2 (Paperback)
ISBN 978-1-63885-387-9 (Digital)

Copyright © 2022 Jillian Monitello
All rights reserved
First Edition

Cover art by Isabel Trujillo

All rights reserved. No part of this publication may be reproduced, distributed, or transmitted in any form or by any means, including photocopying, recording, or other electronic or mechanical methods without the prior written permission of the publisher. For permission requests, solicit the publisher via the address below.

Covenant Books, Inc.
11661 Hwy 707
Murrells Inlet, SC 29576
www.covenantbooks.com

"Jill! We are here. Wake up!"

I feel like I have been sleeping for an eternity, but it's only been an hour. I feel exhausted but manage to open my eyes. I unbuckle my seat belt and jump out our black Toyota four-runner truck. That New York City smell fills my nostrils. It's a strong mix of city bus exhaust and hot pretzels coming from the corner, but not for long.

We walk up Seventh Avenue and into a ten-story building. We approach the check in desk. My father sits down with all of my bags, and my mother takes my hand as we approach a desk that says, "Check in here." A woman asks me, "Young lady, what is your name?"

I respond, "Jillian M. Monitello."

"Jillian what is your date of birth?"

I answer, "May 4, 1990."

The woman smiles at me and places a plastic bracelet on my wrist. It is a bracelet like no other, one I have never seen before. It has my name on it. It is not a nameplate bracelet like my older family members have with their names in gold and iced out in diamonds. It is made of plain plastic with my full name on it including my date of birth, and it even has my doctor's name on it. Yes, my amazing doctor's name is on it. This is making me wonder why I have a bracelet with both my name and his name on it.

The woman proceeds to tell us to take the elevator up to the fourth floor and to wait at the nurses' station. The hallway leading to the elevator is dark, and we are the only ones walking down it. Out of the corner of my eye, I see a few kids playing in the playroom. I think to myself, *This looks like fun.* I see toys all over the floor and the room is very colorful with some of my favorite colors, lavender and green. The sunshine is beaming through the windows this morning but it is also a pretty cold winter day.

I notice there is a lot of chaos on this floor. There are a lot of people in white coats running around, and I hear other children crying on the opposite side from where we are standing. There are kids with tubing coming out of their arms and feet. Poles are being pushed around throughout the floor, and they have bags and tubing hanging from them. As my eyes follow the tubing attached to the pole, I notice the tubing runs from the pole all the way to the children. One of the boys is trying to run away from his mother as she does her best to hold him. This is when I think to myself maybe this is much more than just the fun I saw in the playroom when arriving. For me, this is a whole new scene and pretty scary for a five-year-old.

Before coming here, I was told I would spend the next fourteen days in a place called the hospital because I was sick. Mommy told me that the hospital is going to make me better. I saw my mother was upset as we were packing our stuff last night, and now I have an idea as to why she seemed sad. To be honest, I am a bit petrified, but I don't want my parents to know. I smile and make like everything is fun, just like that playroom. As my mind drifts, I think about being outside and the busy streets of Manhattan. I wish I was downstairs, asking Dad to get an ice-cream soda from the store across the street for me.

Mom says, "Jillian, let's go. They are bringing you to your room."

As we walk down the hall, there are a bunch of rooms on each side as well as against the back wall. My room is in the far-right corner. It is a pretty large room. It looks much different than I expected. It is plain and has a very clean and sterile smell. The bed is like nothing I have ever seen before. I am intrigued by all of its buttons and all of the different positions it can adjust to. The TV will take us some time to get used to, and we also have a pale-pink telephone on the nightstand.

My room is private, meaning it does not have to be shared with another patient. The only good thing about my room is the view of the busy Seventh Avenue. For as long as I can remember, I love the streets of Manhattan, but I would love to just be beyond this window. This is when I learn the meaning of the saying my dad always says, "Every day out of the hospital is a beautiful day."

After a few minutes of taking in my new surroundings, my nurse comes back in and says, "Jillian, we have to put an IV in your hand."

I turn to my parents and say "A what?"

They say, "An intravenous. It goes in your vein, and this is how you will be getting your medications."

I look at them and can't say much besides, "Okay."

My nurse introduces me to a nurse that specializes in putting IVs in. She is very nice and takes me into another room which is down the hall. She introduces herself, and I say, "It's nice to meet you too Colleen." I sit in a chair similar to the ones that they use when drawing blood. Daddy comes in with me, and Mommy hasn't gotten out of her chair yet. I ask Mom if she is coming too, and she tells me she is going to stay in the room. Mommy explains that she isn't going to come with us because it is going to be a lot for her to handle. She tells me that she will be staying with me and be by my side for the next fourteen days straight.

I understand, and as I walk down the hall, I think to myself how fourteen days is such a long time. This is longer than when we go on vacation. This will be the longest time I will be away from my own house.

Colleen begins the procedure by tying the tourniquet nice and tight, and the smell of alcohol fills my nostrils. She tells me that it will just be a pinch and asks me to try and stay as still as possible. Well, this pinch feels much worse, and I let out a very loud yell. The entire floor must have heard me. To a child, it hurts like hell, and tears come streaming down my little cheeks. Now I am starting to feel the same pain the other children on the floor feel, especially the kids I saw when I came off that elevator for the very first time.

After a few minutes, I realize getting an IV isn't too bad, but my life will be challenging, and this is just the beginning of what is to come for one living with cystic fibrosis. My nurse adds some tape to the IV to hold it in place, and she lets me pick out a few stickers from the hospital's sticker box. I choose the scratch and sniff ones that smell like grapes and oranges. She also gives me other stickers that say

"Great job! and "Awesome!" This is the first time I am introduced to scratch and sniff stickers, and I am obsessed with them.

I run back to my room as my dad follows behind. My eyes are still watery from crying, but I can't wait to show my mom my new stickers. I walk into my room, and Mom doesn't have the smile that I have on my face. I ask her, "Did you hear me crying and yelling?"

She tells me she did and that it is okay, and she then goes on to tell me how she is happy to see me smiling. I show her the stickers I was given and tell her to smell them. She smiles and says, "Those smell good." My parents are talking. I can't hear what they are saying to each other because I am so distracted by my new stickers. All I can think about is how I want to start my own sticker collection. I have never seen scented stickers before, and I wonder which stores carry them near our house. I think Mommy is happy to see that I am okay. and she realizes that the pain I just endured is temporary. I also learned that I will go through a lot of temporary pains, but in time, they will pass. After the storm usually comes the rainbow, and in this situation, the stickers are my rainbow.

Let's rewind back about five years prior. I was born on May 4, 1990, to Diane and James. I was born in Staten Island, New York. I have an older brother named Francesco. My first year of life was somewhat "normal;" however, my parents knew something wasn't right. I was a very fussy baby. and by the age of one, I was underweight. I weighed just seventeen pounds. I was always hungry and ate a lot but never gained any weight. I also had recurring bronchitis.

After having recurring bronchitis, my parents decided it was time to switch pediatricians. The new pediatrician mentioned he wanted to send me to a specialist to be tested for cystic fibrosis (CF). He said he doubted the test would come back positive for CF. He also said he had never had any of his other patients test positive for this disease. Some of my symptoms were matching up, and he would rather be safe than sorry. My parents asked him what CF was, and he said not to worry. He told them that he would explain it if necessary. He said no one had ever tested positive before that he had sent for testing. Well, I guess this is where the saying "There's always a first time" comes in to play. I happened to be that first time.

I was diagnosed by a test called a sweat test. A sweat test is when a small round pad is placed on the arm in which the pad causes the patient to sweat by stimulating the sweat glands. The pad absorbs the sweat, and depending on the amount of sodium in the person's sweat, that will determine if one has cystic fibrosis or not. People with CF have very high amounts of sodium in their sweat. As soon as my parents learned about the possibility of me having CF, they immediately began to research this horrifying disease. They learned as much as they possibly could have. It took two sweat tests before doctors could properly diagnose me.

During the first test, enough sweat wasn't absorbed. My parents had brought my winter coat and had me wear it in the office in hopes of making me sweat more. My sweat tests were done in the middle of the summer. The first one did not take, but the second one came back positive. So here is where my CF story begins.

On June 11, 1991, at thirteen months old, I was diagnosed with cystic fibrosis. To my parents and family, it was devastating, but there wasn't much time to sit around and think. From researching CF, my family already knew the severity of the disease, and it was time to put into action what had to be done to help get me on the right path. The doctor that diagnosed me was a pulmonologist.

After being diagnosed, my pulmonologist referred my parents to a CF specialist in Brooklyn, New York. At the time, it was the closest CF center to where we lived, but my parents found out early on that it was not the best center for me. My family learned to not be afraid to go outside of their comfort zone when it came to traveling for health care. Early on, we found out that I would need to take digestive enzymes when eating to help my body digest fats and proteins. I would also have to do nebulizer treatments to open up my airways in order to breathe. My mother and father also learned how to do chest physiotherapies by hand, to loosen the thick sticky mucus in my lungs.

After going to the first CF center for a few months, my parents did not see any improvements. They actually saw things going backward for me and knew I was becoming more sick. I went from eating everything in sight to not wanting to eat much at all. I even spent four days in the hospital under their care where I received IV antibiotics. When I was discharged, the doctor told my parents that I was perfectly healthy; however, later on, you will learn I was the complete opposite of healthy.

My parents were actually pretty infuriated at the way that doctor cared for me, and my father even yelled at him. When my parents returned home with me, my Grandpa Francesco called a family friend who had a relative with CF to ask them which CF care center he went to. They referred my parents to a new care center located in Manhattan. My parents scheduled an appointment immediately at the new center. This is when things turned the corner for the better.

The appointment was a very long one and very overwhelming. My parents came home exhausted but also very well-educated and ready to take CF on as best as they could. At the first appointment, we met with my new doctor, nurse, and many others such as the physical therapist who played a major role in my CF care. She taught them how to do proper chest physiotherapy to clear my lungs of the thick secretions. The way she taught them was similar to the way they had previously learned; besides. there was one new thing that was different. Well, the most important thing actually.

After each position, they were told to "make sure Jillian coughs out the mucus!" That day, they learned how to push on my trachea in order to get me to cough. They were sent home with a catheter to stick down my throat to cause me to cough if I wasn't able to cough on my own. Yes, it sounds like torture, and I don't think that is a method used anymore today. It worked, and it was also very effective!

After my parents did chest physiotherapy (PT) the proper way, I actually filled both of my mother's hands with mucus twice in a row and after that I ate solid food for the first time in many months. The first solid meal I had was scrambled eggs that morning for breakfast. I finally wasn't swallowing the mucus and filling up on it but rather spitting it up and leaving room for nutritious food. My mother could not believe it. This was the first of many proper chest PTs, and it was not an easy time for my parents.

Chest PT consists of cupping both hands and clapping on the chest and back as well as sides while alternating hands. Besides the clapping and cupping, it also consists of vibrations and a total of eight different positions. To get just one chest PT done, it would take them approximately two and a half to three hours. I would also get pretreated with albuterol inhalation using a nebulizer to open up my airways prior to the chest PT.

Each day, my routine consisted of two rounds of chest PT along with two albuterol nebulizers. When I would have a CF exacerbation, meaning a lung infection, my parents would do three to four chest PTs per day along with extra albuterol treatments. When I was an infant, my parents noticed I had some other issues regarding the digestion of food. From having experience as parents with my older brother, they noticed my bowel movements were abnormal when changing my diapers. My bowel movements were not formed and they were very greasy and loose. I can best describe it as if you have ever seen the oil on top of pizza; well, that is what you would see in the diaper as well as when I got older in the toilet bowl. This is due to foods not being digested properly.

I was malnourished for my age, and at the age of one, I only weighed seventeen pounds. Due to the thick sticky mucus being produced in my lungs as well as other parts of my body, the mucus also blocked the pancreas from putting out digestive enzymes into the intestines. Without digestive enzymes, my body couldn't break down foods; therefore, I was not absorbing vital nutrients. Therefore, whatever foods I would eat would go straight through my system. As a result, I would not be able to gain any weight.

In order to digest the fats and proteins that my body would take in, I had to take man-made digestive enzymes in pill form at each meal along with snacks throughout the day. Also due to malnourishment, I had rectal prolapse as a baby. My parents had mentioned this to my first pediatrician, and unfortunately, he didn't pick up on that as being a possible symptom of malnourishment. This could have helped lead to the diagnosis of cystic fibrosis much sooner.

You could imagine it is not easy to get a baby to swallow pills at each meal, so my parents would use baby food applesauce. They would open the capsules up and mix the medication in it, and I would swallow it one spoon after the other. Inside of the enzyme capsules are a bunch of small, little enzymes that resemble white sprinkles. Sometimes not all of them would make it down my throat. The enzymes that didn't make it into my body would wind up all around the kitchen floor since I would spit them out. It was always fun hearing the vacuum suction them up. This was the beginning of getting me on the right track and doing things the right way. This was also the beginning of understanding cystic fibrosis much better than before and learning that a life with CF would not be an easy one.

The new CF center that I went to was in Manhattan, located on Seventh Avenue, and they were top-notch. They treated both children and adults. There were many phenomenal doctors in this center, but there was no doctor like mine. He was one of a kind. Still, until this day, thirty years later, no one can replace him. Not only did my doctor treat CF, but he also lived it each and every day himself. He had cystic fibrosis, and that alone at his age was very impressive.

To my parents and myself, he was an angel on earth. I can say I was put in the right hands. We listened and did everything we were told, and we saw progress; however, it didn't happen overnight. It took a lot of hard work, time, and dedication. I can truly say my parents gave it their all and they taught me to give it mine.

Let me tell you a little bit about my mother. She was a drill sergeant when it came to CF care, and there were no cutting corners when she was around. I was taught that if I cut corners, I would have consequences. Pretty much cutting corners in CF meant I wouldn't live. Each day, my parents and I are fighting for my life. We aren't fighting a person, but we are fighting a demon, a disease that is persistent. From time to time, my mother would ask my doctor, "So how is Jillian doing?"

My doctor's response would always be, "She's doing okay." It wasn't until I was about three and a half years old that my doctor told my parents the truth after my mom asked him again how I was doing. His response was a bit different this time. He said, "Well, you actually brought me a very sick baby, and I was scared for her."

My parents were a bit shocked. The scary part about that situation is how my first CF specialist told my parents I was doing well and released me from the hospital within the same week that my parents took me to my new CF doctor. At that time, my parents knew something wasn't right, but I don't think they thought my failure to thrive was that severe. I'm sure my doctor didn't want to scare my parents back then, but two years later, he told my parents just how sick I really was.

Still to this day, I think back and I cannot believe that was me in that situation, but I thank God for leading us to our "angel" doctor. I am so beyond thankful that my parents followed their instinct and that Grandpa's friend sent us here. Switching doctors has been a true blessing. Without making that move, I definitely wouldn't be here almost thirty-one years later, sharing my story. My "angel" doctor always told me that the most important part of staying healthy was to make sure my chest PTs get done and to not skip them. This is a part of my daily routine that I will always carry with me and will always live by. As an adult patient, I cannot agree with him anymore. Even when I am exhausted and feel like skipping a chest PT, I hear his voice telling me, "Jillian, you have to do this. It's important to stay healthy."

Speaking of chest PTs, as I mentioned previously, each therapy used to take my parents over two hours to get done. When I was around the age of three, my parents had Hutch, an amazing RN (registered nurse) come into our house to do my chest PTs twice per day for a couple of years. This helped give my parents a break, and I also cooperated a lot better for him. Having to listen to a stranger's instructions is a bit more intimidating than my parents. Hutch was able to get my therapies finished in under one hour and he also made them fun for me.

In between each position, he would let me sit on top of my Little Tike's Playhouse and do my coughs. He was able to find a way to make it productive and fun for me. One thing I did often was talk a lot, and so Hutch always called me a *chiacchierone*. *Chiacchierone* in the Italian language means a chatterbox. He often reminded me to cough when it was time to and to stop talking. I know I made him laugh because he would call me a *chiacchierone* and then laugh and tell me how cute I was.

Hutch was more than my nurse and was, more importantly, my friend as well as my family's friend. We became close with him over the years and still keep in touch, which is really nice. A couple of years went by, and my parents were now able to get my therapies done in the same amount of time as Hutch did. Years went by, and Hutch didn't come any more to do my therapies, but we remained friends with him, and he always visited us for Christmas and made Francesco and I birthday and Christmas cards.

At the age of three, I also started seeing a chiropractor named Steve. A family friend had recommended him and thought that he could help, so my parents gave him a try, and I continued to go to him until my late teenage years. Steve helped with aligning my body, and in later years, he helped decrease the sinus headaches that I was having. I suffered with sinus headaches for many years due to mucus buildup in my sinus cavities, and he was able to help reduce them along with helping to avoid sinus surgery for quite a few years. He truly had miracle hands and believed in his work, and so did we.

Besides having health issues, I was a regular kid. I loved spending time with my family and friends. Some of the best memories I can think back on growing up were holidays and parties. In my family, we always celebrated each and every occasion. For the most part, I was a happy kid. I was always laughing. I wasn't a very serious person. Due to CF causing the mucus in my lungs to be very thick, my doctors encouraged exercise and movement. I will never forget the day my parents decided to put a swimming pool in the yard. I was so excited about going in the pool, and I loved swimming with my brother and having our loved ones over. I remember my aunts teaching my brother and I how to play Marco Polo in the pool and learning how to make a whirlpool.

When I turned four years old, it was time to start preschool, which I absolutely loved. My mother said I would be so excited to go that I would jump out of the car and forget to kiss her goodbye before entering the building. I was the type of kid that would always kiss my parents goodbye before leaving to go anywhere. Back then, it was only half days, and this was where I made my first few friends on my own that weren't the kids of my parents' friends. I enjoyed playing, coloring, having snack time, and learning the alphabet along with many other things. This was where I started to learn how to be responsible when it came to my health. I had to take my digestive enzymes on my own during snack time and had to carry my own inhaler in my backpack.

I went to private school, so we did not have a school nurse at that time. My mother had to speak with both my teacher and my classroom aide about having CF, and they were more than accommodating. For me, this was all new, and I didn't want to feel different from the other students, but I also had the attitude that this is me, and if the other kids couldn't accept me for who I am, then, oh well, but I was not changing who I was just to be accepted. My parents taught me to always be tough and to not let anyone walk all over me. They also taught me to respect everyone and that two wrongs don't make a right.

I remember having to explain to my friends and my other classmates what my medication was. As soon as I took my medications, everyone was asking me, "What is that, Jill?"

I simply said, "When I eat, I have to take medication to help my stomach or else I will get a stomachache."

Their response would just be, "Oh, okay," as they watched me swallow my pills with my baby food applesauce. The expressions on their faces were priceless, and they would say, "Wow, how do you swallow them like that?"

I would say, "It's easy." I would then explain to them how the applesauce is smooth and helps the capsules slide right down my throat.

Once the kids saw the applesauce was actually baby food, they would smirk and say, "Why baby food? That's for babies."

I would then have to explain again how it's smooth and how regular applesauce is too chunky. If I were to use regular applesauce, then water would be a better choice.

The most fun part about it all was getting the jar open. Our classroom aide and I would take turns trying to get it open, and most of the time, I got it open first. Baby food jars could sometimes be a challenge to get open. If you have ever tried opening a Beech-Nut

Stage 2 jar, then I am sure you can relate. I'm pretty sure she must have loosened it for me, but I was strong for a four-year-old.

Speaking of getting the jars open, when I went to my grandparents' house, which was mostly every weekend, Nanie would buy every type of jar opener that existed, and we would see what worked best. We would have fun trying different openers. It would always give us some of the best laughs, and it made for some memories to look back on that I will never forget. Laughing was also a great form of airway clearance for me. As I would laugh, the mucus in my lungs would loosen and start to make its way up as I would start coughing nonstop. Little by little, the mucus would make its way out of my airways.

Of course, I didn't get all of it out of my lungs, but something was better than nothing. I always had a great sense of humor. I literally could crack myself up, laughing at the dumbest things for hours upon hours. You would think I was in a room with other people, but many times, it was me, myself, and I. One thing my mom always said is that I can entertain myself, and she is so right. My dad and I also do a lot of laughing together. Humor is what helped get me through some of my toughest times in life, and I always found it to be healthy to laugh. I also knew when it was time to be serious; well, most of the time, at least. I could just imagine something that I pictured to be funny and start laughing. Weird, I know, but that is me.

Besides having a good sense of humor, I was always a thinker. My mind was always going, and I could just sit and think for hours. I think CF has a lot to do with the way my mind worked from such a young age. In certain aspects, children with CF sort of have to grow up faster than others their age. Our responsibilities as a child are to do normal things like go to school, study, play sports, socialize with family and friends, and then do our daily medical regimen in order to stay alive. Along with our therapies and medications also comes a lot of doctor's appointments.

CF always kept my mind going; it is a very time-consuming disease. I was always thinking about what I had to do next in order to stay healthy. From a young age, my mother made sure to do her best to keep me on a schedule. Keeping me on a schedule would allow for me to have pretty much a "normal" life for a five-year-old. It would also allow me to have enough time in a day to do my therapies and take my medications.

When one has a disease as time-consuming as CF, you have to think ahead and plan your day, and sometimes, for me, it meant not always being able to do everything everyone else my age was doing. When I started kindergarten in September of 1995, reality hit me. This was the first year that I would go to school five days per week, and I was now going to the same school as my brother. Francesco transferred to my school so that we could be in the same school and have the same days off. We were both leaving the house at the same time and coming home the same time.

Our mother would drop us off at 8:30 a.m. and pick us up when school let out at 3:30 p.m. In order to be ready to leave my house by 8:15 a.m., I would have to be up by 6:00 a.m., so that way, my morning chest PT and inhaled medications could be completed. I would then eat a high-calorie, high-fat breakfast, get dressed, and off to school I would go.

For me, this was a very long day, and I hated going. I cried every single morning as we approached the front doors of the school. It probably took me a couple of months to get used to this routine. This was a pretty intense schedule. Although things weren't the easiest, I was learning a lot in many different subjects.

We started our day off with prayers to God. This was new for me. My parents didn't teach me to pray at home, and it is not something we did before dinner. We also prayed before lunch as we thanked God for his blessings and for blessing us with the food we were getting ready to eat. I never thought about those in the world not having food before and realized just how lucky I was. I can't imagine not eating when my stomach is growling. I thought everyone had food since you need to eat to stay alive.

We were also taught about the poor and how not everyone had a place to live or clothes to wear. There is a lot more to this world than my small Staten Island town. I have a lot to learn. The priest and nuns also started coming into our classroom and teaching us stories from the Bible, and I found this to be a very peaceful time in school. We learned about creation and how God created this world. I am blown away how God created all of this on his own. He must be very smart.

We are also taught that God sees everything we do. Even when we think no one is watching, he is. I guess there are no secrets kept from God. This puts a bit of fear into my class, but we are also taught that Jesus loves us and that God and Jesus are the same being. Kindergarten wasn't the easiest when it came to my nutrition and calorie intake. I went through a time where I didn't want to eat my lunch, and my mother would have to come up to the school each day. If she didn't come up to the school during lunchtime, I would take my lunch and put it back in the brown bag and throw it in the garbage.

When I think back, I was most likely not feeling well from a lung infection. The last thing I wanted to be doing when I was sick was eating in a large cafeteria with hundreds of other children as they screamed and yelled across the lunch tables. Lunchtime in school was a bit hectic. This truly was a huge adjustment for me, and from time to time, my teacher would go across the lunchroom to get my brother to try and cheer me up in hopes to get me to eat my lunch. What the teacher didn't understand was that I wasn't purposely not eating my lunch and that I was happy in school. Seeing Francesco wasn't going to get me to eat, though it made me happy to see him. My mom would tell me if I didn't eat, then I couldn't play with my friends at recess, so I would do my best to force my lunch down. Most of the time, I felt like I was going to vomit.

If you were wondering how my classmates adjusted to me having CF, well, my CF doctor had given me a book that was geared toward children and written in a way that kids can understand CF. My mother had shown the book to my teacher and thought it would be a great way to explain CF to the other kids. A couple of days into the school year, she read the book to the entire class. Everyone was very accepting, and they even asked me questions and made me feel comfortable. A bunch of my friends from preschool were also in my kindergarten class which was so awesome, and that helped me feel as comfortable as possible.

So as you all know my brother, Francesco, is three years older than me. He was born in Staten Island, New York, on December 3, 1987. He was born perfectly healthy. Francesco does not have CF, but he is actually a CF carrier, meaning he has one copy of the CF gene. In order to have CF, you need to have two copies of the CF gene. When I was a baby, he was truly my favorite person. My parents would always explain to me how excited I would get as an infant when I would see him. My eyes would just light up when I saw him come in the room, and I would put on the biggest smile. As I got older, I always wanted to do whatever I saw my brother do, and truthfully, I couldn't always do everything he did. Let's face it: he was a boy, and I was a girl, but I tried!

When Francesco was in kindergarten, he joined Boy Scouts. Francesco and my dad would go away with the Boy Scouts on a camping trip. I would ask my mother where they went and why we couldn't have joined them. She would have to explain to me that it's just for boys.

The year I started kindergarten, my parents signed Francesco up to play soccer. That was the first year he played on a sports team. After going to Francesco's soccer practice and games, without hesitation, I immediately said, "I want to play too." So you guessed it. Jillian was signed up and playing on the team called the Fireflies. I truly looked up to my brother and always wanted to be like him. My soccer season ran during the fall and then picked up again in the springtime, just like Francesco's.

Sometimes our games would overlap so our parents would have to split up, but it was rare when they did. Luckily, our fields were at the same park majority of the time. This was my newfound love. I loved to run and chase the ball while trying to score in the opponents' net. What I didn't do was keep score or time. The clock would run, and so would I.

As my games came to an end, I would shake the other teams' hands and always smile. After the game, I would run over to my parents and ask, "So did we win?"

My parents would laugh and most of the time say, "No, you guys lost."

My brother would laugh and say, "You guys got crushed. How don't you know you lost?"

To me, time and winning or losing didn't matter. That was my sweet escape from what was really important in life. The soccer field was a place where I could run without a care in the world for an hour and a half each weekend. I would leave everything else in the dust as it kicked up from my cleats. I was one of the fastest and smallest players on the field. I enjoyed using my speed to its advantage. I was also not aware that I was helping my lung function at the same time. I didn't fully understand what CF was yet, and at age five, during my first soccer season, I didn't understand lung function either. All I knew was that I had to do therapies in order to stay healthy, and it was important to cough out that thick and yucky yellow and green mucus that made breathing difficult.

My parents always told me that running was good for me, but I didn't know why. I knew I had to take pills or else I would have a really bad stomachache and spend hours in the bathroom. I knew my friends didn't have to do what I had to because I saw that my brother had a normal life. I noticed my friends were like my brother and were able to hang out with their friends whenever they wanted to. I especially noticed how my life was different when my friends would invite me over their houses after school, and I would either have to decline the invite or only go over their houses for one hour. The rest of my friends would be able to stay much longer than I can.

I also had a few friends who were just like me. They also had cystic fibrosis. My parents were part of a support group which was formed in the early 1990s on Staten Island. It was made up mostly of the CF families that participated in the Great Strides CF Walk to raise funds toward funding research, and one day, God willing, a cure for CF. My parents and family had been participating since 1992, and we had met some great people through the walks and support group.

The CF families would get together a few times per year at our annual summer picnic and the Christmas party. I would have a great time playing with the other CF kids that were just like me. Knowing they did nebulizers and therapies each day along with taking pills made me feel less alone. Just knowing I wasn't the only person living this life made things a bit easier. Unfortunately, as time went on and more research was done, CF doctors and researchers learned that people with CF shouldn't be around each other due to the harmful bacteria that our lungs harvest.

Through studies, we found out that these harmful bacteria are easily spread and overtime can lead to infection, and in time, lung damage along with loss of lung function. To clarify cystic fibrosis itself is not contagious, and the bacteria that patients carry are not contagious to a non-CF person. However, people with CF should not be in contact with each other since we can spread those bacteria among each other.

Well, I started getting used to normal life, school, sports, socializing, and balancing my medications and therapies. I was living a "normal" life for a kid with cystic fibrosis. At the age of five, things started balancing out for me health-wise, and I was doing okay.

It was January 1996, and it was time to go to my CF clinic checkup. I went for a checkup every two to three months. My checkup consisted of measuring my height, weight, and doing a pulmonary function test to check my lung function. I would be more excited about growing than gaining weight whereas my parents and doctor wanted to see the weight gain. My doctor would listen to my lungs and do a physical examination. I would also have to cough out mucus into a cup that way they could test the sputum (mucus) to see what kind of bacteria or possible fungus was growing. It wasn't always easy for me to cough out the mucus, so sometimes, my doctor would have to put a catheter down my throat, which I hated.

In the beginning, I would cry and try to push him away. He knew I was tough and would have to hold my feet and knees down toward the table. I must admit he was a pretty strong doctor, and I am glad he never let me have my way. It is very important to know what is growing in the lungs of a CF patient. This helps the doctors know how to treat an infection as well as choose what kind of antibiotics or medications would be best to attack the bacteria or fungus.

By age five, I was already growing a bacteria called Pseudomonas Aeruginosa (PA), which most people with CF grew by an early age.

This was common in the nineties and years prior. Nowadays, with all the amazing medical advancements, children don't always grow PA, and if they do, it can possibly be fought off with antibiotics. There are cases where it may not return for quite a while from my understanding. For myself, PA will always grow in my lungs and not go away. It will most likely cause lung disease to progress as I get older.

Unfortunately, most people my age and older will always grow PA and other nasty bacteria. At my appointments, I would also be sent for blood work a few times per year as well as chest X-rays of my lungs. As I try and think back to twenty-five years ago, I cannot remember if I missed school that day or if it was a half day for me, but it was a CF clinic appointment day. Those days were always a little nerve-wracking. My parents and I always hoped for good results.

CF is a disease where you could bust your behind and do everything right and still not get the results you are looking for, even at a very young age. Well, this day was one of those days where I would learn just a little bit more about the reality of this disease.

As we arrived at my appointment, the secretary greeted us as always. We waited in the large waiting room, and the best part about it was that they had a Super Nintendo hooked to a TV that was on wheels. I always wanted to play it as we waited, but my parents always said, "No, don't even think of it. There are a lot of germs on it, and it's better if you play Francesco's when we get home."

The funny part about that was my brother never let me play because, truthfully, I wasn't very good at it. Every time I played, I always made us lose and have to start from the beginning again. The only time I was able to play was when he wasn't home. I would have to sneak into Francesco's room and play his Nintendo. I would make sure I put everything back away into his cabinet just the way I found it. Mom always taught us to respect each other's belongings and to put things back the same way we found them.

At the CF clinic, I would always see other kids playing the Nintendo game and even other kids playing together at the same time that weren't related. Come to think of it, there were definitely a lot of germs circulating on that game system. My nurse would be the first person to call me into the back room. As we went to the back, we passed a bunch of rooms on the right and left, and those were all of the doctor's rooms. After having my nurse take my height, weight, pulmonary function, and oxygen, we would then turn the corner and enter my doctor's room.

My doctor's room happened to be the last door all the way in the right-hand corner. My nurse took my height and weight, and I always struggled to keep my weight up which is an issue with CF. Maintaining a healthy body weight helps maintain higher lung function as well. On this day, my weight was down, and after my doctor went over my pulmonary function test (PFT), he informed us that my lung function was down as well. Still, to this day, I am not sure what my overall lung function was, but I know that my lower airways were 40 percent, and that was down for me. He explained to my parents that he would have to admit me to the hospital for a two-week stay to start IV antibiotics. I just remember not even listening, and everything becoming hazy to me. A part of me didn't want to hear it all, and I figured since I wasn't going into the hospital until the next day, I would deal with it all then.

We went home, and I remember just relaxing on the couch as my mother was going up and down the steps a lot with bags and clothes and all kinds of things that we would need for the next two weeks. Still, I was in denial. I remember my parents explaining it to my brother, and he just stared at me. He may have been a bit confused himself. He was only eight years old at the time, and I could imagine that had to be a bit much to process.

My mother was also packing his things because after he got out of school that day, he would go to stay at my grandparents' house for the two weeks. The next morning came quickly, and Francesco hugged and kissed me goodbye and told me he loved me. My parents explained that Francesco would be able to visit soon.

Let me explain my parents' background a little bit. My parents were hard workers. My mom used to work in the World Trade Center in the eighties. After my brother was born, my mom became a stay-at-home mom. My father worked two jobs. He worked for the City of New York's Department of Transportation. My dad also owned a company with his father building custom homes. On this day, my father had taken off of work. He took Francesco to school, and then before we knew it, it was time for us to leave for my two-week stay!

Knock! Knock! It is my nurse at the door. "Come in."

"Hey, Jillian, I have this cool scale to take your weight. Can you take off your shoes for me, please?"

"Yes!" I untie my sneakers and jump onto the scale. "What is my weight?"

"Your weight is a bit down from yesterday."

I look over at my parents, and they aren't smiling. I see the worry come over their faces. I turn my head and look out the window. My mother looks extremely worried as she takes out her black and white marble notebook and records today's date and next to it my weight. My mom's notebook comes to every doctor's appointment, and she writes down everything that happens that day. She has an entire record of my health. Within her notebook includes all of my heights, weights, and lung function numbers. She also writes down all of my medications and whether or not my lungs sound clear to my doctor. She records my chest X-ray results and if there are any issues with my blood work.

There is another knock on our door, and it is a man with a clipboard. He approaches my parents, asking, "Would you like the telephone and TV turned on? The price will be ten dollars for both each day."

My father responds, "Yes, please." Dad goes into his pocket to gives the man the money. I am shocked that we have to pay for the phone and TV, but I am happy that we will be able to call our family when we want and watch our favorite shows, especially TGIF tomorrow night.

As the next couple of hours go by, my nurse returns with a medication that I have never seen before. It is in a small bag with tubing attached, and she hangs it up on the IV pole. The medication is a white milky color. She says, "We are going to hook this up to your IV to make you feel better." She then tells me that it may burn in the beginning as it goes into my hand, but after a couple of minutes, I will feel better.

She was right. It was burning and stinging at first, but then after a few minutes, it felt normal again. As my nurse pushes the buttons to program the IV pump. I am amazed at how quickly she does everything. I watch the IV bag drip and count the drops—one, two, three, four, and so on. Eventually, I lose count and ask my mother to get the blanket from the bottom of my bed. My mother covers me, and I doze off for a nap.

*****

It's 4:00 p.m., and I am woken up by my nurse who now has my albuterol nebulizer. She tells me after my nebulizer is complete that a woman will be in to do my chest PT. I am still drowsy from the IV infusion, and my mother straps the nebulizer mask around my head. She tightens the elastic, and it is squeezing my head. It is a brand-new mask, and so the smell of plastic is strong. Mom tightens the metal part of the nose clip attached to the mask. This way, the medication doesn't escape through the top of the mask. With everything being unfamiliar to me, the nebulizer is a comforting feeling, and the sounds makes me doze off again. I noticed the nebulizer wasn't attached to a compressor like mine was at home. The tubing was attached directly to the wall, and a small green knob was turned on in order to get the nebulizer running. It had a different smell than my regular nebulizer at home. Almost like a clean sterile smell which seemed to be a trend at the hospital.

My albuterol is finished in ten minutes, and it opens up my airways as I am opening up my eyes again. I am able to breathe a bit better already. A woman comes in and asks me to sit up straight in the bed, and she begins raising the bed off the floor, high enough so she could reach my shoulders to start my chest PT. I wish we had this type of moving bed at home. I wouldn't have to lay in difficult positions on the carpet at home and change positions so much. I must admit this lady reminds me of when I first met Hutch, but she intimidates me a lot more than he did. She is a little more firm, and I can tell she means business.

She pretty much gives me a beating. Her hands are so strong, but I don't want to tell her she is going too hard. I want to become strong and see how much I can tolerate, so I withstand the force of her hands. We rotate and do my back and sides, totaling eight positions.

The therapy takes about forty-five minutes to finish. She makes me cough in between, and when she does the vibrations, I am told to breathe in a certain pattern and to hiss while I exhale. She also does not let me move onto the next position until I have completed five full coughs after each position. She does not lose count either so I can't cheat, but in the end, I would be cheating myself. Then I remember that God sees everything and that he knows everything. I am becoming a bit more aware of my conscience and how things weigh on my heart.

My mom just sits there and smiles, and I can tell that she approves of how they do my chest PT here. She is happy to see that I am not getting off easy and that I am receiving the care I need. We all know if I am going to get better, then my treatments need to be done properly. I thank her for doing my therapy as well as Mommy, and she says she will be back in four hours. Oh gosh! Another beating later.

As I sit in my bed, relaxing, there is a strong smell of food coming from the hallway. It smells like a cafeteria, a mix of many different hot foods being cooked at once. My mother informs me that it is dinnertime, and at this point, I am a bit hungry. If that food tastes anything like the smell, I may puke after the first bite. The smell isn't very pleasing to me. I don't have a strong stomach, and the tiniest of things will make me heave. A woman is outside of my door with a big cart with metal doors on the front of it. As she gets closer to my door, the smell of food gets stronger. She says, "Jillian Monitello?"

My mother and I both respond, "Here."

She walks into my room, carrying a tray with what I am hoping has something yummy on it that I will enjoy. As she places the tray down on my table, my mother uncovers it, and I stare at the food. My mom says, "Jillian, you are not going to eat this."

My eyebrows raise as I ask, "What is it?"

"They gave you beans and white rice and some type of meat."

As I am staring at the beans and rice, I also notice there are two slices of white bread and milk on the tray. I am not a milk drinker unless I have Oreo cookies to go along with it. As far as the bread goes, I like bread as long as it is with a sandwich. I am a picky eater.

My father is still with us, and he says that he can go and get me anything that I would like to eat. I ask my parents for a bologna sandwich, and within a few minutes, my dad is back with my favorite cold cut sandwich. As he walks in my room, I can smell the sandwich in the brown paper bag. I will admit bologna doesn't have the most appetizing smell, but it is delicious, and I am thankful to have my parents here with me. As I came into the hospital, I noticed not every child had a parent with them, and the thought of not having my parents with me would upset me and make me feel nervous. I wish my parents could help the other kids too, but due to having CF, we have to be careful who they are around.

After dinner, we put the TV on for a bit before my mom and I head to sleep. It was a long day for all of us, and after my mom and I are settled, my dad kisses and hugs me goodbye and tells me that he will be visiting over the weekend. I don't want my dad to leave the hospital and go home, but I understand that he has to go to work and provide for our family. I'm sure he also wants to spend time with Francesco. I often think about Francesco and what he is doing tonight. This is the first time that the four of us will be separated from each other for this amount of time.

When I was a baby, Francesco had gotten sick, and I was sent to stay at my grandparents' house for a few days, so I wouldn't pick anything up from him. This is nowhere near equivalent to that time, but that was the last time we were separated due to sickness. I am a few years older now, and I am old enough to understand the separation.

It's my second day in my new surroundings, and it is not starting out the way I was hoping for. After all, my bed at home was much more comfortable, and when I was finally in my deepest sleep, I was woken up by the bright room lights at 6:00 a.m. to have my vitals taken followed by a blood draw. The lights are so bright I cannot even open my eyes fully. All I hear is noise coming from the hallway.

The wheels on the cart are screeching as the woman pushes it into my room.

She takes my vitals, and I am happy I can rest again, but she tells me the man who draws blood is coming in. Do they really have to draw blood this early? This is by far not the first time I had my blood drawn, but it is most definitely the earliest that I can remember. The phlebotomist begins by tying the tourniquet nice and tight, and I feel him cleaning my arm. I flash back to just yesterday when the IV was put in, but I know this isn't as painful. The smell of the alcohol pad has woken me up. He has four tubes, and he says, "Ready? It will just be a pinch."

A pinch doesn't sound bad. The needle pierces my skin, and it feels different from the other blood draws. I am in pain. "Ouch, ouch, ouch!" I yell. "You are hurting me."

My mother jumps up from her recliner and tells him, "Please stop fishing in my daughter's arms and get me someone else that can get the blood from her without fishing!" My mother is angry, and I am upset, but exhaustion takes over a couple of minutes later. I am having a hard time staying completely awake.

The phlebotomist says, "I will take the needle out. I am close to getting it."

My mother looks at him and says, "My daughter isn't a pincushion, and I would like someone more qualified and competent!"

He leaves my room, and another phlebotomist comes in and introduces himself. His name is Dwayne, and within a couple of seconds, he has all of the blood tubes filled. This time, I barely feel anything besides the pinch from the needle. I thank him, and the lights are out. I return to resting until breakfast.

My mother helped me pick my meals for today from the choices on the paper that the food service provided us. I am looking forward to enjoying the food that I picked.

I hear Mommy opening the shades, and she says, "Good morning, Jill."

I open my eyes, and the sunlight is in my face. I look over, and my breakfast is waiting for me on my tray. My mother asks if I am hungry, and truthfully, I am not, but I don't want my food to go to waste, so I try my best to eat as much as I can. My breakfast consists of cereal, which is my favorite, and scrambled eggs which I also like. Mom's eggs are my favorite, so I take a couple of bites, and I cannot finish them. They don't taste like the eggs I am used to, and they are dry and very flat. Rather than the eggs go to waste, my mother eats them. I eat my cereal, and my mother tells me she can get me anything I want from the stores outside. After all, we are in Manhattan, but I am not too hungry.

My appetite has little by little gotten worse over the past month. My routine at home is different from here. At home, I do my therapy first, and then I eat breakfast, but here, it is reversed. After breakfast, my nurse comes in with all of my pills as well as my nebulized medications. After I finish albuterol, the lady is back again for chest PT. This time, I don't feel as intimidated by her, and I am ready to do all of the positions and coughs after getting a good night's rest. My lungs are more productive with mucus in the morning, so I think this therapy will help me a lot.

The rest of my day continues with three rounds of IV antibiotics. I am hooked to the IV pole most of the day, mostly to receive IV hydration, meaning saline. I also get two more chest PTs for the day because when people with CF are sick and have a lung infection, they usually increase their chest PTs from twice per day to three times per day. My favorite part of the hospital stay is going for walks in the hallway with my mom and dad. I enjoy riding on the IV pole and using it like a scooter.

Before you know it, it's the weekend, and my family is on their way to visit. It is a beautiful Saturday winter morning, and the sun is piercing through the shades. It is breakfast time again, and as I eat, I stare out the window into the sun and daydream. I think of everything I would love to do when I am out of here. I think about the days when I feel bored at home and wonder how I could get bored at home compared to what I am doing now.

After my morning chest PT, my mother asks my nurse if it is okay if she gives me a bath. My nurse says, "Yes. I just have to wrap her IV with a plastic bag and tape it so it can stay dry. Just don't submerge it into the water."

My nurse comes back with what looks like a Ziplock bag with the word *Biohazard* written on it and what I like to call "hospital tape." She wraps the bag tightly. The tape is wrapped so tight that my fingers are getting cold, and the tape is pulling on the hair of my arm. She then shows us where the bathtubs are, which are down the hall. My room doesn't have a bathtub. It only has a shower. I will have a pretty difficult time showering with one hand without saturating my IV.

My mom tells me to wait in my room as she goes down the hall to clean the tub with bleach cleaner. It is now time to take a bath, and I don't want to go in a bath that other kids were in. I find the hospital to be filled with many germs, especially the bathtub. Mom puts a towel down for me to sit on in the tub, and she tells me to hang my arm out with the IV. She tells me to make sure it stays dry as she washes me. She tells me not to touch anything and to stay on top of the towel. I do my best to listen and do as she says. I don't want to have a new IV put in because I got it all wet. We do a good job at keeping it dry, and I now feel nice and clean.

Mom brushes my hair, and we let it air-dry since the hospital room is so warm. I am now ready for my visitors. With the heat going, it is too warm in the hospital to wear long-sleeved shirts and pants. Dad is bringing up more short-sleeved T-shirts and shorts for me.

As I sit in bed, relaxing while my IV drips, my family members begin to show up. First, my dad arrives, and then Nanie and Francesco walk in. My aunts and my uncles arrived a little bit later. It is nice to see everyone, and it makes me happy. For a little while, I forget why I am here at this place called the hospital. It is nice to see familiar faces in an unfamiliar place.

My family members hand me cards, candy, and goodies that I can enjoy while I am here. My aunt tells me that besides the card and goodies, she also bought me a special pen that she forgot at home. She explains to me that the pen has an angel on it and that I have a guardian angel watching over me. I am amazed and feel special, knowing I have my own angel who is watching me. She also tells me that besides having a guardian angel that I am also loved by Jesus and that he is watching over me also. I wonder why I can't see them and wish I could, but I know they are there. I believe one day I will look up in the sky and see my angel and Jesus, but I am not sure when that will be.

After seeing my family for a few hours, they leave, and it is just my parents and my brother with me. As Francesco and I talk while sitting in my bed together, we see the Nintendo game system being wheeled around just outside my door. I ask my parents if we can play it, but they aren't too thrilled about the idea. Their facial expressions say it all, but we are bored sitting here all day. We continue to beg them, and they finally agree to it. They say that we cannot touch it until it is completely washed down.

My mom goes outside and asks my nurse about the game system. She tells my mother that it has to be reserved and that we can have it next, which will be in an hour. She tells us the girl next to my door has it for the next hour. After the hour is up, my parents thoroughly clean down the game system, and my brother and I begin to play Mario Brothers together. Francesco is Mario, and I am Luigi. Of course, he is beating me, but I am having an amazing time. I am a little sick of hearing the "Game over" tune every time I lose, but we are laughing together. I think he is laughing at how terrible I am at this game.

A half hour goes by, and I am getting tired from the IVs. I think Francesco may be a bit tired too. It's been a long day. We begin arguing over the Nintendo game, and I get upset and put my controller down. I roll over to one side of the bed and start dozing off to take a nap. Francesco is annoyed, but after a few minutes, he realizes that I am tired and out of energy. I hear my dad telling him to stop arguing and that I am tired. Francesco also takes a nap beside me.

My parents and brother agree to give the game system back before the hour is up and bring it back to the nurses' station. This way, someone else can use it and enjoy it. It is late, and my dad and Francesco are getting ready to head home. It was great seeing everyone, but I am worn out. In between my visitors, I still had to complete two additional chest PTs along with IV antibiotics, nebulizers, and take a bunch of pills.

*****

The week goes on, and it's four days in the hospital. My daytime nurse knocks on the door. I say, "Come in!"

"Jillian, it is time to change your IV."

I reply, "What do you mean? Why do we have to change it?"

She then explains to me that the IV that I have can only last for three to four days, and then they have to put a new one in. I am starting to get used to the routine here, but having to get a new IV is not making me happy. I realize it's something that must be done. I put my shoes on and go with my nurse, Coleen, to the special IV room down the hall. I am happy to see the nurse Coleen that specializes in doing IVs. She is very sweet, and this time, I don't cry.

Within a couple of minutes, I have a new IV, and I walk back to my room, smiling. My mother says, "I didn't hear you cry this time."

I respond by saying, "That is because I didn't."

The day goes by like the rest of the hospital days so far, and it is almost time for bed. *Knock, knock.* A man pokes his head in the doorway and says, "May I come in?"

My mother says, "Of course."

It is my nighttime nurse. He comes over to my bed and introduces himself. His name is Jay, and he is very nice. As he sets up one of my nighttime IV doses. He tells me that he also has cystic fibrosis. I am in shock to have another adult with CF be a part of my care team.

I enjoy speaking with Jay. It is nice to talk to someone older with CF, and it makes me realize that I can also reach his age someday if I do what I am told to do. The first person of my health care team with CF is my amazing doctor and now nurse Jay. As I stare at him in amazement and watch him program the IV pump, he then goes on to tell me that he is actually my doctor's brother. I am taken back by this, and all I can think is, *Wow.* I put on a big smile and thank him for his help.

He also listens to my lungs with his stethoscope and asks if I am in any pain. I do mention that I am having some chest pain when I take a deep breath and that my IV is feeling sore. He reassures me that everything I am feeling is normal and that if the chest pain persists, then another chest X-ray will be done. When we arrived, my doctor had them do a chest X-ray of my lungs to make sure everything looked okay.

When my nurse leaves the room, I tell my mother I can't believe that he is my doctor's brother and how they both have CF. My mother says, "Yes." She then tells me that she knew he had a brother who also has CF and that he is a nurse at this hospital. She also tells me my doctor had a sister with CF that passed away when she was a kid. Hearing the second part of that makes me a bit sad, but there is nothing I can do. I take a minute to process the fact that a kid so young can pass away. I wonder what happens to them and also where they go once they leave this world.

This thought quickly fades away as I become more tired from the medication and can't think about it for too much longer. I still can't believe that this family has three siblings with CF. Wow, their parents must have had so much to do to care for them. I see how hectic things can be in our household with only me having it. Both my mother and I feel so blessed, and we sleep peacefully tonight, knowing I am in the best hands possible.

*****

The next morning, I wake up, and I still cannot get over how cool that was to have him as my overnight nurse. It must be tough for him to get his therapies done and work overnight, caring for sick people in the hospital. I hope to have him as my nurse again tonight. I begin to eat my breakfast that is on the tray next to my bed, and I can hear my mom just outside the door, speaking to someone. I hear them talking about how wonderful my doctor is and what an amazing nurse his brother is.

I listen a little longer, and I can tell the girl that Mom is speaking to is also a CF patient. I can tell that she is also much older than I am, and she seems very sweet. I turn on my TV, and Channel 7 has the usual morning show on, *Live with Regis and Kathy*. As I eat my Cheerios and listen to the TV playing in the background, I start to shift my attention toward the window. It is hard to concentrate on just one thing at a time here. I wonder what my classmates are getting ready to learn right now. I know that today, I will be learning more about the hospital IVs and meeting new nurses and possibly new doctors. I wonder how many more days I will be in here. I miss my own bed, bathroom, house, and especially my pillow. I miss my family's home-cooked food too. But most of all, I miss my family and friends.

It is already almost one whole week that we have been in this place, and I cannot wait to get outside for some fresh air. It feels as if I have missed an entire week of life. It's as if my life has stopped when in reality, my life is still going on, just not in the place I prefer. I will also have a lot of catching up to do with my schoolwork. It is pretty warm inside, and I have been wearing T-shirts and pajama shorts since arriving.

Mom returns from her conversation in the hallway, and I ask her who she was talking to. She explains to me that right next door, there is a teenage girl who is fourteen years old with CF, and her name is Jenny. I say, "Wow, another person with CF just next door." I ask if she is here a while, and my mom tells me she is here a bit longer than I am, a week and a half.

This is when I start realizing I am not the only person with cystic fibrosis who is sick in the hospital right now. I am sure if there are two of us here, then there must be many others around the world. Just right next door, Jenny is going through what I am dealing with. I hope I can get to her age someday and I hope she gets to leave here soon. Throughout the week, I have seen other kids get to leave, and I have also seen new ones arrive.

A few days go by, and it is almost the weekend again. It is Friday, and I am looking forward to seeing my dad. He says he will be up to visit me on Saturday with Nanie. Francesco is staying with Nana and Grandpa this weekend.

Saturday morning comes, and I am taking a walk with Mommy in the hallway. My morning therapy is already finished, so I have a bit of freedom to do what I want to. We bring the IV pole along, and I ask her if I could stand on it as she pushes the pole. Mom agrees to it, and it feels like I am on a ride. We go up and down the hall, to the elevators, and back to my room. I have a smile from ear to ear, and we go up and down the hall. We are learning to make our own fun during this not-so-fun time. My mother heads into the bathroom to take a shower, and 2:00 p.m. is approaching, which is the time that my dad says he is going to arrive.

I peak my head outside of my door, and the hallway is pretty quiet at the moment. I am hooked up to my IV pole, and usually, I am not excited about having to wheel around this heavy pole, but I remember the fun Mom and I had a few hours prior. I unplug my IV pole from the wall, and when no one is looking, I hop onto the base of it as if it were one of those scooters. Into the hallway, I go and I use one foot to hop on and the other foot to push off of the floor occasionally. I head toward the elevator, and to my surprise, it opens, and who is at the door? My dad.

"Jillian, what are you doing? Be careful, you are going to crash."

I laugh and speed up and scoot back to my room before Dad reaches the door first. As we go into my room, I tell Daddy that I was doing that earlier, and he laughs and tells me not to do that by myself. He tells me that the nurses are going to yell at me. I am happy to see my dad after a long week, and it is nice to enjoy the weekend together. It is quiet here at the hospital over the weekend. Of course, there are doctors and nurses, but there is less staff on weekends than during the week.

*****

The weekend flew by, and it is Monday, January 8, already. I wake up, and I cannot believe my eyes. The amount of snow that is on the ground is incredible, and I have never seen anything like this before. My mother has the news on our TV, and they are calling this the blizzard of 1996. The snowfall in New York City is supposed to be over two feet, and we already have almost one foot on the ground. I had spoken to my brother over the weekend, and he was preparing to go sledding with our cousins, if we got a lot of snow. I guess you can say I am a little jealous that I wouldn't be joining them, but I know everyone is meant to be where they are.

I enjoyed looking at the snow. It was a different scenery and was the most snow I had ever seen in my life. The hospital was extra quiet with the blizzard. It was quiet inside the way Seventh Avenue was on the outside. The next morning came quickly, and there's a lot of commotion on the floor. We hear the staff talking about how they ran out of food to serve the patients and that there is a shortage. Today, the food trays have the bare minimum on them.

The day goes by slowly, and it is almost dinnertime. Luckily, my cousin called my mother a few minutes ago and asked us if we needed anything. He had been in Manhattan after work, and the trains were somehow still running. My mother's response was, "Yes, food, please. Thank you, Chris!"

Without hesitation, he found a Chinese takeout place open, and he visited us, and we all had dinner together. Wonton soup is one of my favorite foods, and I am so happy and thankful that Chris helped us tonight. After we eat, my cousin sits on the edge of my bed and hands me a small gift bag. He tells me it is from his mom, my Great-Aunt Kay. I open it, and it is a beautiful pink and gold angel pen. This is the pen she was telling me about when she visited last week. I will cherish this forever. It is beautiful, and I can't wait to write with it.

Aunt Kay knows that I love angels and that I am a spiritual person. As I mentioned earlier, she always tells me that God loves me and that I have a guardian angel protecting me. I tell Chris to thank her for me.

It is Wednesday, and my dad is planning on coming to the hospital to visit us and bring the things that we need. Thank God my parents own a truck with four-wheel drive because the roads are still a mess. I look outside and wonder where they will put all of this snow when they clear the streets. The phone rings, and it is my dad calling to tell us he is leaving soon and wants to know what we need. We ask him to please bring food because there is still a shortage at the hospital. All of the restaurants are still closed around here. There is a room here called the pantry, and you can put your name on your bag of food and put it in the refrigerator.

In a couple of hours, my dad arrives, and we are so happy to see him. Mom asks him how the ride was, and my dad says, "There was barely anyone on the roads, and it was a bit rough. Thank God for the truck. It was great in the snow." Dad tells us how much fun Francesco had sledding, and I wish I could have been sledding too.

The rest of the week went by smoothly, and I continued to do my IVs, blood draws, along with three chest PTs per day. I also caught up on some much-needed rest. My nurse walks into my room and says, "Jillian, it's time to take your IV out for good." Taking it out is so much easier than putting one in. The nurse takes it out at my bedside, and she places a small bandage where the IV was to stop it from bleeding. It is time to go home.

The door opens, and that New York City smell fills my nostrils once again. You know the smell of bus fumes combined with pretzels and roasted chestnuts cooking at the corner? My mom and I wait at the entrance as my dad goes to the garage to get our truck. Our black truck now looks like it has been painted gray and white from the salt that is caked on the sides and back of it.

I try my best to not lean against the truck. I don't want my coat to get dirty. We put all of our bags in the truck, and I buckle up in the back seat. The ride home goes smoothly, and I take in the beautiful Manhattan skyline that sits a bit behind the Verrazano Narrows Bridge. The Manhattan skyline is twinkling with its bright lights. It looks so magical, but I am ready to be home.

We pull into our garage, and I cannot wait to go inside. Our Christmas tree is still up. Mommy didn't have time to take it down before being admitted, but seeing it makes me happy. My brother is sitting on the couch with my grandparents, and I run over to hug and kiss them all hello. I also run to grab my pillow. I hug it and smell it for a few minutes. I have an obsession with my pillow for as long as I can remember. The scent of my pillow is always comforting, and I missed that at the hospital. I know I am home again.

My parents didn't allow me to bring my pillow due to all of the germs. If I would have brought my pillow, they would have made me throw it out before returning home. I don't think I could have permanently parted with it. We are home for a few hours, and I ask

Francesco if he remembers the promise that my parents made me while I was in the hospital. When Francesco came to visit me the first time, I asked my parents if I did what I am supposed to do and get better, would we be able to get a bird? I love birds, and my grandparents always had birds as pets. I love going to their house and playing with their bird, Chippa.

My parents agreed at the hospital and told me if I did what I was told, then they would get me a bird. For the next couple of hours, I hound my parents about wanting my own bird, and my parents look at each other and say, "We promised her."

A few days pass, and Francesco and Dad go to the pet shop near our house, and they bring home an adorable cockatiel. He is gray and white with orange cheeks. Francesco and I name him Spike because his hair sticks up like a spike on top of his head. This is our first real pet besides having fish.

After the weekend, I return to school and normal life again. It is nice to be back with my family and to see my friends every day. All of the kids at school are happy to see me.

*****

A few months passed, and it was time to see my CF doctor for a checkup. My lung function has dropped again, but this time, my doctor didn't think it was due to a lung infection where I would need to go into the hospital for treatment. Unfortunately, I was allergic to the dandruff coming from Spike's feathers. This was so upsetting for Francesco and I. Spike was getting used to us, and we were able to let him out of his cage a lot and interact with him. He sat on our shoulders, and he would sing and dance outside of his cage. He would even yell my brother's name. He was mimicking Mom in the same way she would call Francesco for dinner each night. He would even walk up my back and then onto my parents' shoulders and stay there as we did my chest PT. I even used to put him in my doll carriages with my dolls as well as my Barbie doll cars and push him around. He became part of our family quickly.

After the doctor's appointment that night, Nanie called to see how my checkup went, and she asked me why I was crying. I told her about how I wasn't able to keep Spike because he was affecting my lung function. She told me not to cry and that she would take Spike to live with her and that I can visit him whenever I wanted. Knowing that Spike wouldn't be with a stranger made my brother and I happier, but we missed our new family member. We are happy that we will be able to visit him often since I always visit Chippa, and he hasn't affected my lung function. My doctor says being around the birds is fine and even sleeping over my grandparents is okay, but living with the bird all of the time isn't.

It was springtime, and that meant there were some fun activities coming up. Soccer season was starting soon, and it was my second season playing this sport. The outside scent of the flowers and fresh cut grass is a sign of spring. The warmer weather was coming too.

The month of May is cystic fibrosis awareness month, and it is also my birthday month. The cystic fibrosis Great Strides Walk was approaching, and this was my family's fourth walk. It was a time where our family and friends came together to raise funds to find a cure for this monster that is living inside of my lungs and intestines. I had my first hospitalization, and I was more aware of what CF does. I was excited to invite my new friends from school as well as my teammates to walk with us.

My parents have a letter campaign, and each year, they send letters to family and friends asking them to join us as well as sponsor my team, Jillian's Team, at the walk. My father would also ask the businesses to sponsor us that he does business with regularly, which would help us become the top fundraising team at our local walk. At our walk, we have something called mile markers, and we ask the businesses to donate, and their names will be displayed on the mile marker signs. I also enjoyed celebrating my birthday. My parents gave me dinner and a birthday cake with my family, and then I also had a separate birthday party with my friends. It was time to blow out the candles with my family gathered around, and I didn't have to think hard about this one.

My wish was simple yet complex. It wasn't to get something material or to go Disney World like most little girls my age, but my wish was to be cured and for everyone with CF to be cured. I wanted a cure for CF patients. The walk was the next weekend, and I had a great time with everyone. It meant so much to me that my family and friends were there to support me and contribute toward a future cure.

The weeks had gone by, and I was enjoying being age six. The warmer weather was approaching us, and the school year had come to an end. It was kindergarten graduation day. I could hear my mother's alarm clock going off down the hall, and I knew it was almost time for me to get up. My mother was showering first, and then I heard the blow dryer running. I knew any minute she would come to get me out of bed.

It's almost 6:00 a.m., and graduation is at 9:00 a.m. It is time to begin my normal routine consisting of a nebulizer followed by chest PT and next breakfast. After breakfast, my mother dresses me in a pretty blue dress and brushes my hair and curls it with the curling iron. She then pins it back and pins my blue graduation cap to my head. It is pretty hot outside, and I hate having my hair down in this type of weather.

Downstairs, my father and Francesco are waiting in the kitchen. Mom and I come down dressed with our hair done, and it is time to head to my school. I never explained this, but I am in a private catholic school close to my house. My parents felt that with all the challenges I would face in life from a health standpoint that being in a smaller school where I would be known on a first name basis would be best for me. Most importantly, they also knew that in order for me to get through life's challenges, I would need a strong faith and foundation in Jesus Christ to get me through my struggles. They believed a catholic school offered that type of daily support.

It is time to put on my graduation gown and join my classmates for our ceremony. There are over eighty of us graduating, and I am excited to find out that most of us will be going to first grade together in September. All I can think about at graduation is going home and cooling off in our pool. After my graduation ceremony, I go out for lunch with my parents, brother, and grandparents. Francesco also finishes third grade a week after I am done. We were both looking forward to the summer and having a break from the long school year.

Francesco has summer reading, but I don't, and we are looking forward to going on vacation in August to our family's time-share at the Villa Roma Resort. It is one of our favorite places to go in the summer. We enjoy spending time with our family, and we also have friends that we see each year. A couple of weeks after graduation, my parents take us down to the Jersey Shore. My mother's parents have owned a waterfront summer home for quite a few years now. I love going there and spending summer days with my grandparents and crabbing from their backyard, which is just what we wind up doing. Although we go away for a few days, CF doesn't get to go on vacation. It comes with us.

As we arrive and bring our bags inside, my parents carry my medication bag which consists of all oral pills and nebulized medications along with my nebulizer compressor. As soon as I see my grandparents, I kiss and hug them, and then I head to the back sliding door to the yard. As I race to the water, the rocks go everywhere, and they are kicking up from the bottom of my shoes.

The water is beautiful with the sun beaming and bouncing off of it. The water looks sparkly, and I start pulling up Grandpa's crab nets. A bunch of boats go by, and there is a calming breeze coming from the water. It is high tide, so I wind up catching a bunch of crabs. Grandpa tells me, "Jill, if they are babies, you have to throw them back so they can get bigger for next year. If they are big, then we can keep them."

I smile at Grandpa and ask him to come and check out the ones that I have caught. Whether big or small, I am so happy to have crabs in Grandpa's nets, and he is happy too. As he inspects them, he tells me to put back two of them and allows me to keep the other two. I lift the nets over the fence and onto the ground. The two crabs come running out, and I chase them with a pair of tongs since I am afraid to grab them with my hands. I am already having so much fun and tell Francesco to come and crab with me. It is fun to catch the crabs and then cook them on Sunday evenings for dinner with marinara sauce and spaghetti. Eating the crabs is fun, but the best part is spending time together around the dinner table.

The next day, my parents take Francesco and I to the beach, and Grandpa does the not-so-fun part of cleaning the crabs so we could have them for dinner together. The water is rough at the beach, and the waves are pretty strong. My parents tell me to not go in the water unless I am with one of them. The water is always rough at Long Beach Island, but it is a huge and beautiful clean beach. I love when the water sprays my face when I get close to it.

My father and I go in the water to cool off, and I bring my pail to fill up with water so I can build a sandcastle. As I bend over to fill up my pail, the waves rip the pail right out of my hand, and within seconds, my pail is out to sea. My dad tries to get it, but it goes too far, and he tells me he will get me a new one. I freeze for a few seconds and think how strong this ocean water really is. I would have been swept away pretty quickly. I now know just how strong this water is, and I only let the water hit my toes.

My brother and I use the rest of our beach toys to do our best to build something that somewhat looks like a sandcastle. We arrive back home from the beach, and as I walk into the house, I can smell the marinara sauce cooking with the crabs. My mouth begins to water, but I have to shower to get all of this sand off of me, and then my second chest PT must get done along with my nebulizers before dinner. My therapy finishes just in time to eat with everyone, and we sit and enjoy the sunset from the dining room table. I must admit my grandparents have one of the best views of the sunset, but Grandpa and I are left not only seeing the night sky together but also eating crabs until you can see almost every star in the sky.

Grandpa and I are always the last ones to leave the table and clean up when we have crabs. I also think Nana was happy that I was still eating because that meant that I wasn't getting into trouble. Often at the beach house, Nana would be asking, "Does anyone see Jillian?"

Most of the time, I was doing something that I shouldn't have been doing, such as going through Nana's desk. The second time down the shore this summer, my brother, cousins, and I didn't feel like going on the boat ride, so Nana had an idea on how she would keep us busy. She decided to give us all a section of the playroom wall to paint on. I took my paintbrush and decided I was going to paint a blue sky with the sun and then grass and maybe possibly a rainbow. I was so excited to paint on a wall because my parents would never let me paint on their walls. Everyone else was excited to paint also.

Within a few minutes, I started blending all of the colors together. Nana came in to see what we were all painting, and she told everyone what a nice job they were doing. At first, Nana told me it was very nice, and then less than two minutes later, she said, "Jill, what happened?"

"Well, I don't know either, but I am having so much fun painting on the wall that I forgot it is supposed to be a picture." Let's just say my entire section of the wall became gray lines with streaks of many different colors throughout it, and I was very proud of my "art."

Everyone has returned from the boat ride, and I am excited to show them my painting. My parents come in the room and say to Francesco and my cousins, "Nice job." Now they are looking at mine, and they both say, "Wow," and they start laughing!

Francesco gets up from his area and stands behind me and says, "Jillian, what's that supposed to be?"

I really didn't have a response for him. I said, "Well, it's supposed to be a sky with the sun and grass like hers" as I point to my cousin's painting. My cousin is no artist, but hers looks way better than mine, and you can see the sky and sun.

Francesco starts laughing and says, "Nana, did you see Jillian's painting?"

Nana tells him, "Yes, your sister is very artistic and smiles."

It was bedtime, and I was thinking about how much fun it was to paint on the wall, and I wondered, *What will I be doing tomorrow?*

*****

The next day is fun and relaxing. Grandpa has a different type of net in the water, and he shows us that he caught an eel. He also shows us how it catches the small guppy fish. I really like the guppy fish, and I wish I could keep them all. My grandparents let us keep the ones we catch in a big bucket, but they tell us when it is time to throw them back. I think back to a couple of years ago. It was a very hot and humid day and our parents decided to go out. Nana set up a kiddie pool for me, my brother, and cousins as well as a Mickey Mouse sprinkler.

As I was in the pool, splashing around with my cousin, the boys decided to try and scare us by pouring the bucket of guppy fish into the pool. My cousin jumped out of the pool, yelling. However, I didn't even realize they were swimming with me. I stayed in the pool with them until Nana pulled me out of the pool as she yelled at the boys as they continued laughing at me. I heard them say, "Jillian was just sitting there with all the guppies!"

As the weekend comes to an end, I ask my parents if I could take two guppies home, and they said sure, but that we would need salt water to keep them alive and that the water would have to be changed a couple of times each week. Grandpa walks over to the lagoon in the yard and fills up a couple of gallons of salt water so that I would have clean salt water for my new fish friends. Each time Nana and Grandpa go back and forth from the shore, they tell me they will bring us deliveries of salt water for the guppies.

With the summer coming to an end, I am getting ready to take on first grade, and Francesco is getting ready to start fourth in a few days. My mom heads upstairs to our bedrooms and has us try on our school uniforms to make sure they still fit us. I try on my uniform which consists of a plaid jumper skirt with a button-up light-blue shirt and knee-high socks. Everything fits but my shoes. They are a little snug, and my brother's as well. We drive over to Tyrone's Shoe store in Port Richmond, which is the only store on Staten Island that sells catholic school shoes. The girls' shoes are ugly; they are blue with gray laces and gray soles, but if I want to go to the same school, I must get the ugly shoes which match my ugly uniform.

My brother's shoes aren't bad; they just look like plain casual black shoes. The uniform is by far the least of my worries for one living with a disease like CF, but my regular clothes are much more stylish than my school attire which I will be wearing for about thirty-five hours per week. We order our shoes, and now I have school on my mind. I start thinking about the bright and early wake ups, bringing my pills and applesauce with me every day and having to take them in front of some new faces. There is also no snack time in first grade, and I am told by my doctor that I will have to have my own snack time, like I do at home to maintain my body weight. My weight is much better than it used to be, and if you look at me, you won't say, "She is underweight." But CF-wise, I still need to maintain and gain some weight. I wonder what the new kids coming into our school will think when they see I am the only one snacking as we are in the middle of a lesson. I know my friends won't think anything because they already understand my situation.

The last week of summer had flown by. I soaked up as much sun as I could while swimming and playing in our yard. My favorite thing to do is to swim and then ride my bike later on in the afternoon when it isn't as hot out. Swimming and riding my bike is great for my lungs, especially while soccer season isn't going on at the moment. It's the first day of first grade, and I am a bit nervous. My mother is bringing Francesco and I to school. As we arrive, we get on the line of cars in the school's parking lot, and one by one, parents drop off their most precious goods. It is our turn, and we kiss Mommy goodbye, and she tells us she will see us at 3:30 p.m.

I think, *Wow, it's only 8:30 a.m. It's going to be a long day.*

She tells me, "If you need me and you don't feel well, make sure you have the school call me."

I nod my head and say, "Okay, love you." We walk inside to the busy and extremely loud gymnasium where the entire school is waiting for their names to be called as we are divided into classes. I look around and find my friends. There is Ashley, Kristen, Corrine, and Nicki. They are my preschool and kindergarten friends, and we sit off to the side of the gymnasium. We all hope that we are in each other's class. There are two classes per grade and a lot of new faces. I am always willing to make new friends, and once I sit down beside my friends, my nerves begin to calm down.

The kindergarten classes get called, and now it is our turn. Kristen's name gets called, and then Corrine's name, and then I am up next. Luckily, we all wind up in the same class, and Ashley and Nicki are last. Our names get called in alphabetical order going by last name. Ashley and Nicki are also in our class. I have the biggest smile on my face because I get to be with my friends for another entire year. We all keep looking at each other, smiling. I have a bunch of other friends from kindergarten that wound up in the other class that I will still see every day at recess, but I am happy that my closest friends will be with me all day. This is a great start to first grade, and our teacher is very sweet.

The first week goes by pretty fast, and it isn't too challenging. We are still getting settled into our new surroundings. My mother is happy that I am with my friends, but she also told me to not be afraid to make new friends, which I am already doing in the first week. There is a new girl named Colleen that sits next to me, and we have already hit it off and became friends instantly.

As the weeks pass, we begin to learn English, Math, Science, History, as well as the Catholic Religion. I enjoyed mostly every subject, but History was my least favorite. Religion was one of my favorite subjects, especially when the priests and nun would come in and tell us a story from the Bible. My favorite stories from the Bible are Noah's Ark and the Christmas story. The nun and priest would come in once per week, and they don't come in at a set time. They show up at a random time on a random day whenever they are free. Each week was different.

I cannot believe it is already November, and the holiday season is approaching soon. We are in the middle of a science lesson, and we hear a knock on our classroom door. The student who sits closest to the door is in charge of getting the door. My classmate gets up and opens the door, and it is the nun. My teacher asks us all to please clear our desks and to put everything away. We all do so, and my teacher leaves the room, leaving us with just Sister as she tells us a story from the Bible. It is very relaxing to listen to her speak, and I enjoy learning about my faith. While she tells us a story for about forty-five minutes, she does not allow for anyone to have even a pencil on the desk, and she does not allow anyone to leave the room, even if they have to use the restroom. They are told to wait and that they will live.

I am in shock and taken back by her response for one wanting to use the restroom, and I don't think that is very "Christian like." I keep checking the clock on the wall, and it is just about 2:00 p.m., which is when my snack time is. My mother packed me four Oreo cookies to help give me some extra calories for the day as per my doctor's orders. The school has a doctor's note on file, which allows for me to have a snack while in class; however, my teacher did not inform Sister of my situation, and I know she is going to give me a hard time if she sees me eating. As I listen and pay attention and participate in the lesson, I quietly take out my cookies from my backpack and keep them underneath the desk. I quietly take a bite of one of them and chew slowly, trying to not make any noise. My mouth is getting dry, and I won't even attempt to try and take a sip of water.

Well, you guessed it, Sister stands up and tells me I have to throw them in the garbage. I guess I didn't do such a great job hiding them, and I then explain to her that I have a doctor's note, and due to my illness, I have to eat a snack at this time every day. She tells me that I will survive if I don't have them and that I must put them on the teacher's desk and to not interrupt her story time again. I had already taken my two enzymes, and if I don't eat fat, I will have some GI issues and constipation. Instead of fighting with her, I do as I am told, and when my teacher returns, I explain to her what has happened.

My teacher is upset and tells me it is her fault for not speaking with Sister and that she is very sorry this happened. She tells me she will speak with Sister and that it will not happen again. My teacher gives me my cookies back, and I finish eating them right before dismissal.

After each school day, my mother asks me if I ate all of my food that she packed me, and so I explained to her what had happened. My mother is enraged and says when she drops me off tomorrow, she is going to speak to the principal. My mother says, "That is why you have a doctor's note. It's not just because you feel like eating in school. You have a medical condition."

I tell her that my teacher knows and that she told me it won't happen again, but my mother still wants to ensure that it won't, and I don't blame her. My mother says, "Your teacher is right. It won't happen again."

I really think Sister thought I was trying to take advantage of her just to have a snack, but that was far from the truth. Sister also didn't allow anyone to have a pencil on their desk, and if they did, she would walk over to their desk, and without warning, break it in half and throw it in the garbage. She was tough, and I didn't stand any chance that day without the help of my teacher. I probably should have just picked up my things and gone to the principal's office, but I was taught to always respect your elders, which is just what I did, even if it meant not making the best health decision for myself.

After seeing how mad my mother was and explaining the situation to my doctor and seeing how mad he was, I was more afraid of my mother and my doctor's reaction than Sister's reaction. They both told me, "It happened once, but don't ever let someone intimidate you, no matter how old they are." And that I must advocate for myself. Knowing I have their support was important, and I am not afraid to stand up for myself.

This wouldn't be the first time at such a young age that CF would cause me trouble in the first grade. Lunchtime had also become a problem for me almost every day. Every day, I sat with my friends, but we also sat across from people that were new to us this year. Our lunchroom wasn't large enough to move our seats, and we were assigned lunch table seats. Halfway through lunch, I take out my Beech-Nut baby food applesauce and digestive enzyme pills and swallow them. I take eight of them with meals, and so it takes me a couple of minutes to get them down. My friends are cool with me taking them, and they know it is part of lunchtime for me. They always make me feel comfortable, but there are a few new girls that find it funny and laugh at me. They point and say, "Ew, look, she's eating baby food."

I tell them that it is medication and the baby food makes it easier. That way, the pills don't get stuck in my throat. This goes on almost every day, and Ashley always sticks up for me and tells me to just ignore them and that they are stupid. A part of me also feels it is jealousy because the girl who makes fun of me the most doesn't have any friends. She makes fun of me and then is nice to Ashley, but Ashley wants no part of her. I am lucky to have Ashley. She has become my best friend and is a true friend.

Ashley and I hang out a lot outside of school too, and this past summer, we had a lot of fun going swimming and having barbeques. I was always taught that two wrongs don't make a right, but it is really difficult to hold my tongue since this is every day. As soon as I say something insulting back to the head bully, she runs to the office to her grandmother who is in charge of the front desk at our school. She is also the school pet. Her mother is one of the head people in our parish for many years, and so everyone believes she can do no wrong. I realize the adults at the school are on her side and do my best to stay away from her, but somehow, she always finds a way to get close to me. She is also triple my size and the tallest first-grader there is out of both boys and girls.

The bell rings, and I throw out my garbage from lunchtime. Ashley and I head for the large double doors that lead to the schoolyard. We don't have a normal schoolyard. It is the parking lot to our school and church. Although it is cold out, it is my favorite time of the school day, and I could use some fresh air.

Ashley and I go toward our favorite part of the parking lot where the tree was that was just beyond our kindergarten classroom. The bark of the tree is starting to peel, and there is sap dripping down parts of the brown fading bark. It is truly a beautiful pine tree, but it is getting bear with the winter approaching. Ashley says, "Jill, come here, I have a good idea."

As I head over to the tree, Ashley takes out a paper clip from her pocket and bends it so that one end of the pointy part is facing away from her like the point of a pen. She begins to carve an A and then a J into the part of the tree where the bark has faded, and then she carves BFF. I smile at her I say that is so cool. We will be best friends forever. She smiles back and tosses the paper clip to the ground. We both then run off to play freeze-tag with the rest of our friends with only ten minutes remaining to recess.

I love playing freeze-tag, and I have not been caught once this year by any of my classmates; well, maybe one or twice by the boys but definitely not by any of the girls. I am the third shortest in my class and probably the fastest. When we play Steal the Bacon in gym class, I always win, and I am always the only girl left playing with the boys. I guess you can say I am a bit of a tomboy.

It is funny because Ashley is a girly girl and not really into sports, but I am beginning to love sports, and we are best friends. I am also close with my friend, Nicki, who is also into sports. Nicki is a very good soccer player, and we always challenge each other in gym class as well as at recess. The bully is also athletic, and if you ask me, she is a bit of a sore loser.

Later this week, it is recess time again, and we have both been playing freeze-tag with everyone. I stand frozen toward the back of the parking lot, and after a few minutes, I am out for good along with the bully. As I am approaching the beginning of the parking lot, I lean down to pick up my Twizzler pack that I had dropped on the ground. The bully sees me knelt down and comes over and stomps on my hand. I yell, "Ouch!" and I pick up my head, and she is standing there, laughing at me

And then she says, "Oops, I am sorry."

I know it isn't an accident, and I tell her, "I know you did it on purpose, I'm not an idiot, and I will get even with you."

At this point, my hand was bleeding and all cut up. The black asphalt had gotten inside of my cut, and all I wanted to do was get it cleaned out. That way, I don't get an infection. I really prefer to beat the crap out of her, but I know cleaning my hand is more important. I go running over to the teacher that is watching my class, and I say, "I am not sure if you saw, but so and so just purposely stomped on my hand, and I have to go and clean it."

Without hesitation, the teacher escorts me to the bathroom, and she tells me after I clean my hand to see the secretary at the front desk to get a bandage. We don't have a school nurse, so if we get hurt or aren't feeling well, we go to the secretary. The secretary is the bully's grandmother. She is in charge of giving out the bandages. I can't wait to tell the secretary what happened.

As I finish drying my cut-up hand, I approach the desk. The secretary looks at my hand and says, "Sweety, what happened to your hand?"

I then respond with, "Barb stepped on it as I went to pick up my Twizzlers off the ground, and she did it on purpose."

She looks at me in shock and says, "Not my Barbara?"

I say, "Oh, yes, your Barbara."

She looks back up at me very confused as she helps put the bandage on my hand. I thank her for the bandage and return to the schoolyard. I think to myself maybe this incident will prove that her granddaughter isn't the angel that she thinks she is, but then again, if I know the bully, she will lie through her teeth and do anything to cover up the truth. She will totally make it like it was an accident to everyone.

Within minutes, the bell rings, recess is over, and it is time to get in line to head back to our classrooms. I am third in line, and the bully is last, so I don't have to make eye contact with her, but my friends ask me where I went because they had been looking for me. I explain to them what had happened while playing tag. I apologize for disappearing on them, but I didn't have time to tell them what was happening as my hand was bleeding. My friends are angered by this and tell me to try and not be upset, and Ashley says that the bully is such a witch, and I totally agree with her. I have never done anything to her, and for whatever reason, I have become her target. Talking to my friends cheers me up, and I am thankful to have friends that have the same qualities as I and that treat everyone with respect.

It is Saturday, and I am with my parents at Francesco's first basketball game. I don't really understand basketball too well, but what I do know is that Francesco's team needs to score in the basket at the other end, and when they do, I clap and cheer as if I am watching a professional game. Francesco is a lefty, and I notice the rest of his team is right-handed. Francesco is better at dribbling the ball with his left hand which gives him an advantage when he is on the left side of the basket. Francesco is not great at dribbling the ball, but he is a pretty good shooter.

My father yells, "Francesco, shoot the ball!"

A few minutes go by, and the ball is passed to Francesco. He is open and takes a jump shot right below the arc.

My father claps and says, "Attaboy, Francesco!"

Francesco scores two points, and I begin smiling and clapping also along with my mom and the rest of our family. Basketball is becoming my new favorite sport to watch, and it looks like so much fun to play. There is a lot of running which would be good for my lungs but not as much running as soccer. The buzzer goes off, and it is halftime. I run over to the concession stand to get a snack and drink. They are selling my favorite snack: soft pretzels with salt stuck to them. Now I am really enjoying these games. I get to watch a game, be with my family, and eat one of my favorite snacks. What can be better than this? My grandparents are there along with my aunts and uncle too.

I head back to my seat on the bleachers and tell everyone, "They have snacks over there and drinks!"

My family smiles at me and says, "That looks yummy," and from the looks on their faces, I realize they knew what the concession stand carried. I eat my pretzel as the second half of the game goes on.

The game comes to an end, and Francesco comes off of the court, and I tell him he played a good game. He looks at me with an upset face and says, "Not really. We lost."

I try and think back to what it felt like a couple of months ago losing my soccer game, but I couldn't really remember. All I remember is how challenging and fun it was. I had fun watching, and I assume Francesco had fun playing. My brother was a little different from me. He didn't enjoy losing like most kids.

On the drive home, I ask my parents if I can play basketball just like Francesco, and they say that they will look into it and see if they have a team for my age group, but it most likely wouldn't be until next year.

Spring was approaching again, and soccer season would be starting back up. My parents did look into basketball for me, and they found out that my school offered intramural basketball for my age group. I was too young to play CYO this year. They signed me up, and my first game is scheduled for March of this year, 1997.

MOMENTS OF IMPACT

It is a brisk sunny Saturday morning, and my parents' alarm goes off. It is time to do my morning therapy. The sound of my nebulizer compressor rattles our end table in the family room. As I do my best to keep my eyes open, I take a deep breath, and the smoke from my nebulizer fills the room. My father does my chest PT by clapping on my chest, back, and sides. I cough my brains out, and a lot of nasty yellow thick mucus starts coming out of my mouth. I hate spitting the mucus out and I hate to see it. I am not like most CF people. I prefer to swallow that nasty mucus.

It is breakfast time, and the excitement starts coming over me. I have butterflies in my stomach, but I can't wait to arrive at the gym to meet my coaches and teammates and try playing a new sport. We arrive, and my game doesn't start until another half hour. My coaches introduce themselves and tell me to change into my red-team T-shirt which reads number seven on the back. I ask my parents if I can pick a lucky number like I did for my soccer jersey, but they explain that we can't order a jersey for this league and that I must wear what is available. So I picked the closest number to my lucky number four, and that happened to be seven.

I love picking number four because it is my birthday. I put on my oversize red-team T-shirt which is down to my knees. My mother tells me to go over by her so she can help me tuck it into my sweatpants. I lace up my Nike sneakers nice and tight, and I am ready to go. It is now my team's turn to step onto the court, and we are shooting around and warming up together. My team consists of both boys and girls, and I don't mind this at all. Truthfully, I enjoy playing gym class with the boys in school, so I am looking forward to being challenged. A few of my friends from school are the boys on my team. The referee blows the whistle, and it is time for my first basketball game to start. The rims are lower than they were at Francesco's game, but Francesco's team is much taller than mine.

I could hear my parents clapping and cheering for my team. My coach is giving us instructions, and I am doing my best to do what I am told. I am having such a great time running up and down the court while chasing the ball and trying to get it out of the other team's hands. I am faster than most of the boys, and the time is going by so quickly.

Before we know it, it is half time, and my parents make sure I have enough water to drink and Gatorade. I am sweating up a storm, and my skin is pretty salty, so I must replace the salt I lost by drinking Gatorade. When we arrived at the gym, it was cold, and there wasn't any heat on, but the cool air is starting to feel good. I was also told by my doctor to make sure I did my albuterol inhaler right before playing sports, so that is just what I did. Besides cystic fibrosis, I also have asthma which can make it difficult to breath mostly while exercising.

After half time, the rest of the game flies by, and before you know it, it's over. My first basketball game is complete. I wish the game didn't come to an end, and I cannot wait until next weekend's game. I didn't score at all; however, I did steal the ball a few times from the other team. I think I am starting to get the hang of how basketball is played, and I think I will do better next week and better in the future games.

After my game, we are hungry and decide to go to the diner to have lunch. My father always works on Saturday at his house building business, so after lunch, he comes home to get his pickup truck and then heads to the job for the rest of the afternoon into the evening. My father is very handy, and so he does whatever work he can himself at the houses.

My dad owns the business with my grandfather and their two partners who are like family to us. Dad also meets with potential buyers to show them the houses and to discuss pricing. Often, my mother will take my brother and I over to the job to visit Dad and Grandpa. I love looking at the new houses and always want to help, but my dad doesn't want me touching anything because new construction is very dusty, and that is not good for my lungs. Soccer season has also started, and things are getting pretty busy for us between my sports schedule and Francesco's.

This spring is an exciting time for our family. My Aunt D is getting married to her high school sweetheart, my Uncle Steve. I am the flower girl, and this will be the first time I am in a wedding. Francesco was in our cousin's wedding when he was little. We had picked out my dress during the fall, and it is time to go and pick it up from the dress store in Bayonne, New Jersey. It is a big beautiful white dress, and everyone keeps saying I will look like my Aunt D's twin. I think they may be right. I resemble her quite a bit. She is also wearing a beautiful white gown, and my hair is just like hers, very thick and curly.

It is the morning of the wedding, and my mother is making sure that she has everything ready to bring with us. Nebulizer: check. Enzymes: check. Inhaler: check. Snacks: check. Applesauce: check. And then the regular things that you need for a wedding—hairspray, lipstick, extra bobby pins, purse, and a change of clothes for later.

My morning chest PT is complete along with breakfast, and it is time to get our hair done. My mother and I head to the salon, and we both get an updo, and Mom gets her makeup done. I am squinting my eyes closed as the hairspray is hitting my face, and the smell makes me want to cough. I am not a big fan of getting dressed up, but after my hair is curled and pinned up, I love how pretty it looks, and Mom's hair looks gorgeous too.

We return home and quickly change into our dresses. Daddy and Francesco are waiting for us to leave and go to my grandparents for pictures. They have already gone to Uncle Steve's and took some pictures over there with the groomsmen. As we pull up, there are a lot of people and a few faces I have never seen before. I know most of my aunt's close friends and our family, of course, but there are a couple of faces I am not familiar with. When we enter the house, everyone says, "Jillian, you look so beautiful, and, wow, you are D's little twin."

I smile and say, "Thank you," and I can't wait to see my aunt. I head over to kiss and hug my grandparents, Aunt T, and cousins. The photographer is snapping a lot of pictures of my aunt in the bedroom. The huge spiral staircase is decorated with white lace draped coming down. Within a few minutes, Aunt D is standing on the staircase, getting her photo taken, and then the photographer begins taking family photos and bridesmaid pictures. All of the bridesmaids are dressed in emerald green color gowns with matching heels, and Nanie is wearing a silvery beige color gown. My dad, Grandpa, and brother are in sharp black tuxedos in the living room as they wait their turn to take pictures with my aunt.

About an hour and a half goes by, and it is time for the church. We all head outside to where the limousines are waiting for us, and off to the church we go. Outside of the church, you can hear the music playing, and the bells ringing, and my brother and I are a bit nervous, but I am happy to be walking into the ceremony with him. The bridesmaids and groomsmen go in front of us, and we are the last ones to walk in before my aunt comes down the aisle. We walk in slow and look straight toward the altar, and as we approach it, we branch off and go in opposite directions.

I sit next to my mom with the rest of the bridesmaids, and Francesco sits with Dad and the groomsmen. It is my aunt's time to walk in, escorted by Grandpa, and all I could think about is how this truly looks like a scene from a movie as the father walks his daughter down the aisle. The music is playing, and it is real. The ceremony passed by quickly, and within an hour I officially gained an uncle. So this is how people who are total strangers become family, literally overnight.

We take a ton of pictures outside, and it's time to get back in the limousines again. It is a pretty cool day outside, and I can't wait to get back indoors. After the ceremony, we go to Moravian to take some outdoor photos near the water as well as to the indoor studio. I could feel the cold air pass right through my bones and could not wait to be inside for good tonight.

My mom covers my shoulders with a sweater in between pictures which helps warm me up a bit. Although it is springtime, it is not exactly spring temperatures just yet. We have a two-hour drive to the hall from Staten Island to Queens, and my parents tell me to rest in the limo. The reception is at Russo's on The Bay, and it is one of the prettiest halls I have ever seen. I want to socialize with everyone, but it is time for my second chest PT. As everyone relaxes, talks, and eats, my parents do my chest PT. We finish in time, and I put my dress back on and join everyone for the cocktail hour.

I can't believe my eyes: the choices of food are never-ending. Every kind of food you could imagine is here to eat. I am in my glory and love that I could taste everything without having to choose just one thing. I also love going to the bar and getting unlimited soda. One time, I would get a Sprite, and then the next a Coke, and then an orange soda. The cocktail hour has come to an end. and little did I know the party was just getting started. My parents come to get Francesco and I to tell us that we have to be with the bridal party because we have to walk in with everyone. I am confused. We are already in the doors.

We go upstairs, and a lady from the hall is lining everyone up, and now I see that we are actually going to walk in the room where there are about four hundred guests waiting to see the bride and groom. When the DJ introduces the bridal party, all of the guests stand up and begin to clap, and the music is playing loudly. It is our turn. Francesco and I lock arms and walk in together. Our entrance isn't as exciting as the older people, but we both keep smiling and walk toward the rest of the bridal party that has already entered. Everyone clapped and cheered, and I had the same feeling as if I had scored at one of my sports games.

The time has come that everyone has been waiting for. My aunt and uncle finally make their appearance as husband and wife. It isn't your typical way of entering a room. They come down from an elevator that is see-through, but you can only see their shadows as they come down from the second floor. I turn to Francesco and say, "Wow, that is so cool," but I don't think Francesco hears me with the music and the loud crowd. When they reach the first floor, they are kissing, and the screen in front of them is lifted. They make their way to the dance floor to have their first dance. This is like a fairy tale, something out of Disney.

After the first dance, the DJ starts playing faster music, and we all join them on the dance floor. I am not too much of a dancer, but I enjoy dancing with my family members, so I stay on the floor until it is time to eat again. I cannot believe the amount of food there is throughout the night, and as I look across the table, I see Grandpa with a lobster on his plate. I have never seen a full-size lobster served at a party before, although this is the first wedding I have attended. I would imagine a wedding is one of the most expensive parties one will have in their lifetime. My Grandpa Francesco loves shellfish, and as I see him enjoying the lobster, I knew that my main course was going to be just as delicious.

During dinner, I look around and take in the whole atmosphere. Weddings are becoming my new favorite party to attend. Of course, I enjoy my friend's and cousin's birthday parties, but this is a different type of party. It is elegant, and I guess you can say I like elegant affairs. Halfway through the night, Francesco puts a few chairs together and falls asleep across them, but I am wide awake. I don't want to miss a beat tonight. The cake is rolled out, and it is time for dessert. I am hoping for a couple of desserts, but I get much more than I bargained for.

The DJ announces, "Help yourselves to the Venetian tables."

And I am guessing Venetian is another name for dessert. In the middle of the floor, there are about ten long tables filled with all kinds of desserts, ranging from a chocolate fondue fountain to pastries and every kind of cookie you could imagine along with fruit and chocolate. It is a true sugar rush for me, and my eyes light up as if I have walked into my favorite candy shop. I have a real sweet tooth, and my plate has all of my favorite goodies on it. I have never seen anything like this in my life, and as I sit down with my plate, I wonder just how expensive this all had to be. The thought of how much it costs doesn't linger for too long.

I finish my goodies and dance the rest of the night away with my family. The limousine pulls up outside of the hall to pick up my family, and I can't wait to get inside of it so I can sit and relax. It is a long day and night for a six-and nine-year-old. As soon as we start driving, I fall asleep, and Francesco falls back to sleep too.

*****

The weekend is over, and we spend Sunday recuperating. It is Monday morning and time to go back to school. As I sit in class, I cannot stop thinking about how much fun I had on Saturday. My teacher begins the day with an English lesson, and she asks us to write about something that we did this weekend. This couldn't have been a better week for her to ask us to write a paragraph on what we did this weekend. Normally, I would be writing that I had a sports game or that Francesco had one, and then we went to my grandparents' house for dinner on Sunday. This weekend was different, and I am excited to share my experience with my teacher and classmates.

Another student also had their family member's wedding this past weekend, and it was nice to hear about their experience. My teacher goes around the room and asks for us to read our paragraphs out loud. Some of the students had exciting weekends, and some were pretty boring, but everyone's weekends were different. We all have different lives, and it is interesting to see what each of us do when we aren't in school. At lunch, my friends ask me how the wedding was and what it was like to be in it. I explain it in a more detailed way than the paragraph I read out loud. They tell me that it sounded like a really nice party, and I agree.

At dinner, I tell my parents about what we had to write about in English class, and my mother tells me she is going to print a picture for me to show my teacher and friends. Each night at dinner, my parents, Francesco, and I talk about how our days went and what we did. It is always nice to hear what everyone did, which is what makes me feel close to my family.

Later in the week, I brought in a picture of my aunt and I from her wedding, and everyone cannot believe that was me in the photo. My friends are not used to seeing me with my hair curled and up like that, and they keep telling me how pretty I look. To be honest, I like the way I looked that day, but I explain to my friends that I don't have enough time to curl my hair like that, especially before school. I know my friends don't understand how time-consuming my medical regimen is, but with school and sports, I am not left with any time for my hair. My hair is naturally curly, and after I brush it, I throw it up in a ponytail mostly every day.

It is almost my seventh birthday, and the weather is getting warmer. The month of May has just begun. I am excited about my seventh birthday party, which is going to be at a place called Fun Station. Fun Station has a bunch of arcade games as well as laser tag. They even have sports games and rides. I invited my friends from school, and we had a great time celebrating together. My cousins also attended as well as some close family friends.

It is midweek at school, and we don't have air-conditioning, so for someone with CF, it can sometimes be difficult to breathe during the warmer months. Things at school have been going smoothly, and I can't believe in less than two months, I will be heading to the second grade. Recess has just finished, and our teacher has taken us to the bathroom for our daily afternoon bathroom break. The boys are lined up in front of the boys' room, and the girls are lined up in front of the girls' room. There has been some chaos in the boys' room, and my teacher is by the boys' room for a while. The girls stay in line, behaving ourselves.

As I wait in line, talking to my friends, the bully is making her way toward me. I can't understand why she is walking toward me when she belongs at the end of the line. She is the last person in line due to her height, and I am the third person out of twenty girls. Within seconds, she comes up to me and says, "You are different and always will be."

At this point, I am enraged and have a few choice words for her. I can also hear my mom telling me that two wrongs don't make a right. I can't keep quiet, so I say, "Yes, I am, and we all know you are different too. You're the only student in our class that can't read."

She begins crying and tells me I am a meanie. I walk away from her, and although I am not proud of pointing out her disability, I felt this was the only way she may understand how she is treating me. Our school teaches us to do unto other as we want done to us. When the teacher goes around the room to read and it is her turn, she has a hard time reading, and it takes her about two to three minutes to read just one sentence. When she takes exams, the aide has to read to her in the back of the room. In our class, there is no such thing as taking a test quietly because the aide is reading to her where we can all hear. She also receives double the time for exams where the rest of the class only has a certain amount of time.

There are other students that were in our class last year that were told they had to leave the school because they had learning disabilities and the school could not accommodate them. I find it interesting how she is able to remain in the school and receive special treatment when no other students have been allowed to. When you go to a private catholic school like I do, if you are not mentally on the same level as everyone else, you are asked to leave. They have zero tolerance for teaching different levels for each student's needs. There wouldn't even be enough teachers at our school to teach each person individually that has a learning disability.

We return to class, and I am having a hard time concentrating. I am still annoyed at what happened this afternoon. I wish none of this had to happen. I never have issues in school with anyone besides dealing with her this year. I go home this afternoon, and my mom notices that I am annoyed. Mom is pretty good at reading my mood, and she knows when I am upset about something.

After some time passes, I tell her what happened and I tell her what I said back. My mother is very angry at Barb's comment. She tells me she is going to speak to Mrs. S. She tells me exactly what I knew she would, "Jillian, two wrongs don't make a right." I am taught to defend myself using my words and to not use my hands, but if someone hits me first, then I am to defend myself and hit back. Dad always tells me to let them hit first and then give them no mercy. His advice is a bit more aggressive than Mom's advice.

I didn't lift my hands at all, but making fun of someone else's disability because they made fun of yours doesn't fix the issue. I feel like it's only a matter of time before she lifts her hands to me, but only time will tell.

The next day, my mom speaks to my teacher, explaining what happened because she knew if she spoke to the office, she wouldn't get anywhere because the bully's family runs the school. My teacher is enraged, and when she calls the bully out of class to talk to her, she has her in tears in less than a minute. The bully also lied to the teacher and said she didn't say that to me as the tears came down her face. This isn't the first time the teacher caught her in a lie this year, and I'm sure it won't be the last. The teacher isn't buying her story this time.

Later today, before dismissal, the bully passes my desk with her eyes still teary and says to me, "You got me in trouble today."

As I smile and stare her straight in the eyes, my response is simple: "No, you got yourself in trouble, so thank yourself." I am hoping the issues with her are over with, but it almost sounds too good to be true.

The summer cannot come fast enough. I need a break from this compulsive lying girl, and I am looking forward to soaking up the sun with my friends and family. My teacher is very nice and sweet, but not all of the faculty is like her. Majority of the staff are a bit mean, and most of them have an attitude. I enjoy being with my friends at lunch, and we joke around and say we have to all suffer together as the school days go on.

My parents tell Francesco and I that they will be putting a basketball hoop in the yard over the summer, and we can't wait.

*****

It is time for a CF clinic checkup again. The past few months have been going well. I have also been treated by a few other CF specialists in the same office as my doctor, due to him being sick himself. I am sad when I hear my doctor is sick, but it makes me happy when I see him return to the office and see that he is okay. Thankfully, he is back today after being out for quite a while. It is an adjustment for me to get to know the other doctors, but after a few visits, I warm up to all of them and feel comfortable being in all of their care. The reason my doctor is so special is because he knows what to do before I even explain to him every detail. I guess when you live it and have hands-on experience, you just know what your patients need.

I have heard my mom explain to my doctor a handful of times how I experience certain side effects from the antibiotics and that the pharmacist tells us those aren't side effects from the antibiotic. My doctor smiles and tells Mom that on paper it isn't, but it is, and I may feel those side effects. He tells us that the pharmacists aren't always aware of all of the side effects, but he knows how I feel because he has felt the same way on those medications. My doctor's knowledge is priceless and like no other.

As I begin playing more sports and become more active, I am told to make sure I take in enough calories for the day. The nutritionist at the CF center meets with my parents since the summer is soon approaching. She speaks to us about calorie intake as well as salt intake. She goes over what my normal meals and snacks should consist of each day and how I can add more calories to each meal. She also gives us ideas as to how to add more salt to my diet for the days I will be exercising. She explains that people with CF have to be aware of dehydration.

Although I am a picky eater, my appetite is getting better, and things are coming full circle for me. I had just turned seven years old, and we still do not have many medications to treat cystic fibrosis. As far as antibiotics go, we have oral, and the only inhaled one we currently have is Coly-mycin (Colistin). We have the IV antibiotics as our last resort.

When I turned five years old, I started an inhaled medication called Pulmozyme which helps thin out the mucus in my lungs. I have been told that a new inhaled antibiotic called TOBI is being studied and it should be approved by the end of the year. TOBI is being used to help fight off Pseudomonas Aeruginosa, which is a bacteria growing in my lungs. We hope this new medication will stop permanent lung damage from happening and help slow down the loss of lung function.

Dad and Francesco pull into the far driveway closest to the backyard. They took a ride to Modell's, the sporting goods store. I see a huge box in the back of my dad's pickup truck. It is a warm June sunny day. The pool is open, and I cannot wait to go swimming later on. I slip my shoes on and run outside. I ask, "What is in that huge box? What did you guys get?"

Francesco answers, "It's a basketball hoop, but we still have to put it together."

I have a smile on my face and I ask, "When will it be ready to shoot around?"

My dad says, "After I put it together."

I stand there for a minute and think to myself that still doesn't tell me when, but I better not push my luck. I guess in a nice way, he was telling me he wasn't sure when he would get it all set up. It is hot and humid, and I should probably go back inside and finish eating my breakfast. I don't want to get in the way. I head back into the house and I am laughing at Dad's response. I peek through the back window, looking at the pavers where the hoop is going to be set up. I notice one issue: the large tree is going to be in the way, but this is the only place we are able to put it.

As I daydream out the window, I begin to think that the tree can be my opponent when no one wants to play ball with me. I hear Dad make his way to the yard with the heavy box as he slices it open and begins assembling the hoop. After an hour and a half, the hoop is almost ready to be used. Dad is just adding water to the base of the hoop to hold it down so it doesn't tip over or get pulled by the wind. Once the base is filled, Francesco and I take shots, and our dad joins in.

Mom smiles at us and watches from the screenhouse. I am wearing my bathing suit, so when it gets too warm for me, I can jump right into the pool. After playing basketball for almost a half hour, I jump into the pool from the pool ladder. I am a pretty skinny girl, and our pool isn't heated, so I only last a couple of minutes before I am shivering and my lips have a slight blue color to them. Dad asks me, "Jill, why are you out so fast?"

"I cannot stay in there, it is too cold for me." As I wrap myself in my towel, the shivering is better.

Mom can't believe my lips are blue, and she tells me to not go in the pool anymore until my parents figure out what they want to do about the cold-water situation. My parents threw around the idea of adding a heater. Dad comes out of our house, and as he looks up at the huge trees in our yard, he points at the four trees surrounding our pool that block the sun from hitting the water. He points to them and says, "This is the problem." There wasn't any sun in the pool area of our yard, come to think of it.

Dad has a good idea, and he tells us that after the weekend, he is going to call a guy who cuts down trees to see if the tops of the trees can be trimmed. This way, the sun can reach our pool. A couple of weeks go by, and the trees wind up getting cut while Francesco and I are at school. The trees sure did get a haircut, and the sun is now beating down on our pool from morning to dusk. I am looking forward to going in the pool and being able to enjoy it. The cold water in the pool didn't bother my brother at all. He could literally go in there for hours and swim like a fish. He would always say the water was cold, but he also said he didn't mind it. I am not sure how he handled such cold temperatures, but I am utterly impressed by it.

Having the trees cut is such a game-changer, and now I can invite my friends to go swimming without having to warn them first. Throughout the summer, I invite my friends over a bunch of times and also go by their houses to hang out and swim in their pools. It is a great summer. We also go to visit my grandparents at their shore house, and I am very interested in the hermit crabs.

I talk my parents into getting me two of them to take home with us from Long Beach Island. I am excited to pick out their little cage. I pick out a cage with a pink cover and pink gravel for the bottom. I also pick out a shell dish to put their food in as well as a sponge for water for them to drink. I am an animal lover, and there are no animals that scare me to have as pets. Francesco also picks out a hermit crab, but he chose a blue cage for his with blue gravel.

While we are down the shore, my cousins happen to come to visit also. As we are getting ready for dinner and waiting for everyone to get ready, he asks me if I could help him with something. Of course, I say, "Yes." I have no idea what helping him entails, but I am sure he knows I am the only person in the house that would agree to help him since he chose the youngest person.

I follow him into the toy room. As we approach the room, I see a huge cage set up with lights, and in the corner of it is his five-foot-long corn snake. I realize he is going to ask me for some type of help with Pinky. I am a little bit interested in it, but I am also a little creeped out by Pinky. I ask him if it bites, and he says, "No, he is friendly." He then opens up the cage and tells me to put out both hands and places it in them.

I dare not to move. I remain as still as I can be, and I am hoping it doesn't move closer. The cool part about the snake is its skin. It feels so smooth and like nothing else I have felt before. A few seconds later, my cousin opens a box, which he had just brought back from the pet shop. What is inside grosses me out a bit as if the snake wasn't enough.

Inside of the box are three white baby mice. My cousin picks one of them up by the tail and feeds it to the snake as I am holding him still. Not even a second goes by, and the mouse is gone. I am in shock and can't stop thinking about the poor little mouse that has just been swallowed whole. Nana is looking for us, and she comes inside and asks my cousin, "What are you making her do? That is gross, Jill! Don't touch that anymore."

He says, "Nothing, I just asked her to help me, and she said yes."

I tell Nana that he asked for help but never told me what we were doing. She yells at him to feed the snake himself and to put the snake back in its cage.

I ran out of the room and into the kitchen to wash my hands. I cannot wait to go and have dinner. I am not mad at my cousin, but I will never agree to help him again without knowing what he needs help with first.

We go out to dinner with everyone and then take a ride to Fantasy Island, which is a kiddie amusement park that has an arcade and rides. There is also a bunch of ice-cream shops, candy shops, and shops that sell gadgets and clothing, which we take a look in as well. My favorite ride is the Ferris wheel. As we go on the Ferris wheel, I love to look around, and it is so cool how you can see all of Long Beach Island from up here. When we reach the highest point, it is breezy, and I wrap my sweatshirt around me. One thing that is visible at night on the Ferris wheel are the stars. You can see all of them, and they are bright and twinkling.

The Ferris wheel only goes around for a few minutes, and it is time to get off. We head over to the mini golf. I love mini golf, but I am not very good at it. I am not very patient and prefer fast-paced things. It takes me ten tries before I get the ball in the first hole, and I can tell it's going to be a long game for me. Francesco and my parents are hysterical, laughing at me as I hit the ball six times back and forth, going over the second hole. There is a huge line behind me, and my mother says, "Okay, drop it in using your hands, and let's go to the next one."

I use my feet instead and guide the ball into hole number two. Onto the next one we go. I keep telling my family that I give up, and I imagine by the time I get all of them in, this place will close with me standing inside of it. My parents decided going forward that I would get four tries for each hole, and once my tries are used up, then it is onto the next one. I always thought bocce ball was a slow-moving game, but mini golf is the slowest for me.

It is almost time to go upstate to the Villa Roma again, which is an Italian style resort. Bocce ball is a big thing up there, and there are tournaments all week long. I never played in the tournaments, but I always play with my family and friends. Bocce is also a game in which you have to have patience, but I enjoy playing that much more than mini golf. In the Italian language, the word *bocce* means kisses, so the point of the game is to try and get your ball to kiss the white ball. Whoever's ball gets closest to the white ball wins or rather whoever's ball kisses the white ball wins. Besides playing bocce ball at the Villa Roma, there are many other activities that we enjoy, but our favorite time is relaxing and eating by the pool as we listen to the live band and singers.

Although we have a pool at home, it is a different feeling, especially when you don't have to be the one barbequing your own lunch or skimming the pool of leaves and bugs. One of my favorite parts of our traditional vacation is dinnertime. When it is dinnertime, everyone in the resort is in the dining room. The dining room is huge, and it is located in the main building. Our time-share building is up the huge hill. My brother and I enjoy racing each other up and down the hill throughout the week, but it is exhausting and definitely a workout. I always wind up out of breath and in a coughing fit, but it is a good coughing fit, one that helps me get up a lot of mucus, similar to the way soccer and basketball do.

Right near the main building, there is also a half basketball court, and while everyone is at the pool, I always ask my dad if we can go shoot some hoops while the court is free. The resort holds a free throw shooting contest earlier in the day, but I never make it in time to attend those. I am not a morning person, and my therapy is too time-consuming for me to get out of our room early. While everyone is at the pool, Dad and I shoot around a bit on the half court. It is extremely warm out, especially with the sun beating down, and within minutes, I am sweating. My skin is building up salt like most CF people do when sweating, and I can taste the salt dripping down my face. It gets pretty humid here in the mountains.

We do many other activities throughout the week. We also have a lot of downtime at night, sitting in the lobby and talking to our friends. My parents like to go off of the resort premises from time to time and try a couple of the restaurants in the town of Callicoon. Before you know it, the week is already coming to an end.

The summer was also almost over, and I am dreading the start of school in just one short week. It is still warm out, and I am not looking forward to wearing school uniforms and not having air conditioning. I got used to wearing shorts and tank tops, and soon I will be wearing a collared shirt and a long heavy jumper skirt with knee-high socks again.

*****

I am going into the second grade, and over the summer, I was assigned summer reading to have completed by September. I wasn't happy about it, but I am happy that I will be completing it in time. I hate to read unless it is something that I am interested in such as sports, biographies, or anything to do with animals. Reading is not my strong point. I prefer math, science, and religion classes, but I am told that all subjects are important.

As the school year starts, I do my best in each subject. This year seems more difficult than the previous year, but I know from Francesco that as the years go on, the workload gets heavier. Each year, I see Francesco spending more and more time at our table doing homework, projects, and studying. To my surprise, our school now offers a new uniform consisting of shorts with a collared shirt as part of the summer uniform and, of course, I choose that option over the normal attire. Most of my friends choose that option for a summer uniform too. This uniform is making the warmer days a little more tolerable; however, breathing still isn't the easiest.

The school we are in is one of the most difficult elementary catholic schools on Staten Island from what I hear. Francesco and I both spend at least two hours per night doing homework and at least an additional hour studying each night. This is the year that I will be receiving my First Holy Communion, so religion class is a little different too. I am now understanding what I saw Francesco do a few years ago in our church on his Communion Day. As a couple of months pass, I realize that his communion wasn't just about being able to eat a piece of bread at church and the party that we had afterward that night with our family and friends in a fancy hall. I am learning that communion is much more than all of that.

School has gone by quickly today, and all of my friends couldn't stop talking about tomorrow and how much fun we will have together. It is Friday afternoon. My mother is here to pick us up from school. It is a brisk, partly sunny and cloudy day. On the way home, we pick up some pizza so we could be nice and full before we go trick or treating.

Francesco and I are both dressed as *Power Rangers*. I am dressed as the pink one, of course, and he is the blue one. *Power Rangers* is my favorite show to watch with Francesco after school. Each weekday from 4:30 to 5:00 p.m., we sit in our living room and watch *Power Rangers* together. I'm sure Francesco wishes he could be a Power Ranger in real life, just like I do. Today, our wish comes true, and we get to sort of be Power Rangers. I am a bit shy, so Francesco rings the doorbells of the people in our neighborhood, and we both say, "Trick or treat." Our bags start to fill up with candy and other goodies. We do not last too long before we get tired and ask Mom if we could head back home.

It is starting to get colder out as the night goes on. My cheeks become rosy and my nose is cold. After about three blocks of trick or treating, we started heading back to our house. I notice the wind is really whipping, and I could feel the winter is approaching soon. As we get back home, I ask, "Mommy, can we go show Nanie and Grandpa our costumes?"

My mother says, "Yes, let's get your enzymes, and we will head there."

We always visit Nanie and Grandpa on Halloween after we finish trick or treating. If we aren't too tired, we will usually trick or treat in their development too.

In a few minutes, we are in the car and at my grandparents' house. It is a madhouse by them. There are a lot of parents with their kids trick or treating and crowding the street. You can barely drive though. I hear one lady say to her children, "This is where the rich people live. They give good stuff here. Make sure you go to all of the houses!"

My mother and I look at each other. We are both taken back by this woman's comment as we head into my grandparents' home. We let ourselves in through the garage because my grandparents' front door is bombarded with children and parents. There must be at least thirty people standing in front of the door right now, and when one group leaves, another one comes. My grandparents are not rich; however, they are hard workers, and just because they own a larger home doesn't make them rich. I will admit Nanie and Grandpa hand out small bags of chips to each child trick or treating, so I can see why the kids enjoy coming here.

The development where my grandparents live consists of larger custom-built homes consisting of hardworking families. Most of the people that come to trick or treat here are outsiders, and you can tell because all of the street parking is taken up, and some cars are even double parked. On a normal day, it is quiet, and there is usually plenty of parking, except when people have a lot of company. The trick or treaters come around until about 9:00 p.m.

I am exhausted from school and trick or treating, and I wonder how these kids have all of this energy. Helping Nanie hand out the goodies is also tiring, mostly because we spend half of the time asking the kids to back up so we can open the door.

*****

MOMENTS OF IMPACT

Saturday afternoon is here, and I am so excited. Mom and I are going to a Halloween party with my Girl Scout group. I am dressed in my pink Power Ranger costume again, and my mom is wearing a witch hat. This is our second Girl Scouts Halloween party. Girl Scouts is very different from sports, but it is a lot of fun, and every Friday after school, our group meets up for it. I enjoy the activities that we do weekly together, and it helps break up the monotony of school and sports. The week prior to Halloween, we went pumpkin picking at a local pumpkin patch.

As we arrive and enter the main entrance of the school, there is scary music playing and, of course, Michael Jackson's song, "Thriller," comes on. You cannot have a Halloween party without "Thriller" playing, at least not where I live. I am not a huge fan of the scary things that go along with Halloween, but I won't pass up a fun time with my friends. I enjoyed the pumpkins and candy, but ghosts and scary things are not my thing; however, I had a great time tonight.

Once Halloween is over, I know the holiday season is approaching, which is my favorite time of the year. Christmas is my favorite holiday, and it is only a couple of months away. I love helping Mom decorate and put up the Christmas tree. My favorite part is putting my ornaments on it that I have collected over the years.

My grandparents and parents buy me the hallmark granddaughter and daughter ornaments every year, and I enjoy adding those to our tree. Thanksgiving is first, of course, and so I also love this time of year. I enjoy spending it with my family and love the variety of food. I am not a fan of turkey, but all of the sides are enjoyable, and the sweet potato pie is my favorite. I can't decide if it should be a dessert or side dish, but my family chooses to have it as a side.

This year, Thanksgiving is being spent with Dad's side of the family, and there is always an abundant amount of food and desserts. It is nice to know that on Thanksgiving, everyone in our family is off from work, so it will be nice to see everyone and spend the day and night together. We arrived at Nanie and Grandpa's house for Thanksgiving. The driveway is filled with cars, and I am pretty sure the house is packed inside with just as much love as the driveway is. Nanie has done most of the cooking, but everyone has prepared something and brought it with them. We let ourselves in through the garage, as usual, and the inside door squeaks open as we enter. The inside door always makes a squeaking sound whenever it opens, and that's how we know someone is coming in. I love being inside and hearing that squeaking sound, especially on a holiday because you never know who is coming in next.

As we enter, Grandpa is sitting on the couch, and he is happy to see us. The smell of the food is mouthwatering, and I can't wait to eat. Antipasto is already set up on the table, and I sneak into the dining room and grab a couple of pieces of *sopressata* and pepperoni along with a slice of Italian bread. The antipasto could be the entire meal by itself; that is how much of it we have. The bread and meat taste delicious together. It sure smells like a holiday at the Monitellos.

The fat content is so high in the *sopressata*, and if I don't take my enzymes soon, I will be spending all of Black Friday as well as the entire weekend in the bathroom. When I forget to take my enzymes, I don't have any issues on that day, but the next day or so is complete hell. The stomach pains and cramps are like no other. Once you use the bathroom, you feel relieved, and then bam! Again it happens over and over for at least one to two days.

Within minutes, Mom sees me through the mirrors snacking and tells me to come and take my enzymes now before it's too late. As our family fills the dining room, and everyone starts eating. It makes me smile having all of us together. We are laughing, eating, and enjoying one another's company. Francesco, of course, imitates some of his favorite comedy movie scenes, and we all laugh. He is great at imitating them and does it so perfectly. We are all full just from the antipasto, and we need a break before the next course.

There are still about two additional courses to come, plus dessert that won't be over until around 1:00 a.m. Right now, it is only 4:00 p.m. As we take a break, my mom tells me I should get my chest PT done before it gets late. I agree. I do my nebulizer, and then my dad does my PT by hand. Mom is helping Nanie clean off the table and get the next course prepared along with my aunts.

In our family, the women are always the ones in the kitchen, and the men can usually be found sleeping or watching TV in the living room. It takes about an hour total, and my nebulizers take about twenty additional minutes to complete. I cough a lot and also laugh a lot, which makes me cough even more. I would say it was a productive therapy, and I cleared out a bunch of mucus. Any chance that Francesco and I get, we ask Aunt T, Aunt D, and Uncle Steve to play a game with us, and they usually agree too unless they are helping in the kitchen.

It is time to play hide-and-seek, and there are a lot of spots to hide in this house. I wonder if Grandpa took hide-and-seek into consideration when building this house because you never run out of places to hide. Sometimes there are too many options, and you have to keep in mind if you will even be found. There have been times when we have been left in a hiding spot and had to eventually surrender.

I have also come out of a hiding spot and found my Aunt T sitting at the dining room table having a snack, and it was then I realized that she may not have ever come to find us.

One of my favorite places to hide is in the garage inside of the car. Pretty much, if you could think of the spot, then it is yours. Besides playing games, I enjoy going into the formal living room and playing the piano. I never took lessons to actually play the proper way, but I do play by ear and practice songs over and over again until I learn them. I kind of sound like a broken record as I am playing.

My Aunt T knows how to play the piano the right way. She reads notes and has taught me the little bit that I do know. There is so much more that I don't know, and one day, I hope to take lessons. As I sit and play the few little songs that I have learned after eating the third course of dinner, Great Nanie (my great-grandmother) quietly sneaks into the formal living room and sits on the couch and listens to me play. She must have been sitting here for about ten minutes before I turned around and noticed she was there.

As I stop playing and look behind me, Great Nanie says, "Jillian, that's beautiful. Please keep playing."

Next thing you know, one by one, the room starts filling up, and I have an audience. I quickly start running out of songs to play, and I think of different ways I can add onto them. If only I knew a few more songs, I would have been able to keep everyone entertained a bit longer. The song that I play the best is "Heart and Soul" by Hoagy Carmichael and Frank Loesser. I play the long version of it. I also enjoy playing parts of an Italian song called "Come Prima" by Mario Panzeri, Alessandro Taccani, and Vincenzo Di Paola. My Aunt T always plays it so beautifully. I can't play all of "Come Prima," but I play some of it, and Great Nanie sings along. I am glad I can put a smile on her face. Her vision is not good, but her ears are amazing. She hears everything, even when you whisper. I guess when one of your senses isn't too good, your other senses are sharper. I am glad she is able to experience things through her ears.

It is time to turn the piano over to my Aunt T. She opens up the bench and takes out a bunch of sheet music and starts playing one song after the other, making it look so effortless. I love listening to her play the piano. She plays it beautifully, and it is relaxing to sit and listen. I almost fall asleep sitting on the couch, and you can hear the piano throughout the entire house. She plays "Come Prima," and I listen closely to the sounds that the keys are making so I can hopefully learn more of it and hopefully, one day, play the entire song.

There isn't enough room for all of us on the couch so some of us sit on the rug. Dad is laying on the rug, and it looks like he may have fallen asleep along with Uncle Steve. I also love Christmas music, and during Christmas, I play all of my favorite Christmas songs. I make a lot of mistakes as I try to learn them. "Angels We Have Heard on High" is one of my favorites to play. It is a beautiful song but also fast-paced, which means my fingers have to move quickly across the keys. I enjoy trying to make up my own songs too. When I practice on the piano, hours pass by, and it only feels like a small amount of time to me. I don't keep watch of time the way I don't keep score when playing sports. I feel like I have left the real world, and all of my worries fade away for a bit.

A month goes by, and Christmas morning is here. Last night, we had our family by us, and my dad made the seven-fish dinner along with pasta and antipasto. My favorite part was the baked clams. Today, we will be spending Christmas with my mom's side of the family at my grandparents' home, and before going there, we will stop and see my dad's side for a bit and exchange presents. At Nana and Grandpa's, the holiday is a bit quieter. My grandparents do antipasto and the main meal and dessert. There are less courses, but we are still pretty full. After we eat, we exchange gifts and play with our cousins.

We love playing doctor, and Grandpa is always our patient. He goes by the name Mr. McDoogle. I am the secretary, and my cousin is the doctor. We look for things in Nana's office to use. I saved the respules from my nebulizer medications, and we pretend to give Mr. McDoogle his medicine. We also have a medicine bottle filled with Grandpa's favorite candy, Good and Plenty. Grandpa is such a sport, and he goes along with everything we want and makes us laugh. He even scares us a bit and pretends he has passed out. We always make him shake and then take his temperature. We immediately give him good and plenty candy when he pretends to faint in his chair.

My favorite holiday has come and gone so quickly. I had a great time with my family. On Christmas, we went to church, filled our stomachs with delicious food, and spent time exchanging gifts with one another. I am taught the reason we exchange gifts is because when the three kings came to see Jesus after his birth. They each brought a gift to the Savior of the world. By exchanging gifts, we are showing a representation of what happened the day Jesus was born and not to mention Jesus is the real gift to us.

I wish the past couple of days could have lasted like this forever. It is Monday night, and my brother and I are in his room, listening to the new Chumbawamba CD that he had gotten for his birthday earlier this month. Mom comes in and tells us our aunt will be staying with us for a bit while she runs out. I ask her where she is going, and she responds, "I have to go somewhere, but your aunt is going to stay with you guys for a bit." She tells me she will be back soon. It is unusual for this aunt of ours to stay with us, and I could sense something was different, maybe even abnormal. My aunt arrives, and Francesco and I go into the kitchen and hang out with her downstairs, and we begin showing her all of the cool things that we got for Christmas. Something doesn't feel right to me, but I am not sure what it is.

After about an hour and a half, my dad comes home. My aunt and dad speak briefly and she leaves. An hour or so passes, and I hear the garage door go up, and my mother's truck makes the noise it does as it pulls in. I sit in the kitchen, eagerly waiting for her to open the door. It is late, and I know it is time for me to have my bedtime snack and then go to bed. I am anxious and wired up and maybe a bit nosey too. I want to know where my mother went and why my aunt was watching us. Mom tells me to eat the cookies and milk that she has put on the table as she gets my enzymes out to take.

Within minutes, I have eaten my snack, taken my pills, brushed my teeth, and I am ready for bed. I say goodnight to my dad who is in the family room. Mom brings me up to bed and tucks me in. I lay awake in bed for a couple of hours thinking about what could have happened tonight. I am glad to see both of my parents are home and safe. I thought maybe something happened to my dad at work, God forbid.

I hear my parents talking, and within a few minutes, my parents are arguing downstairs and raising their voices at each other. It doesn't sound too loud from up here, especially that my room is in the front of the house and they are downstairs in the back of it. I quietly climb out of my bed and tiptoe around the hallway and sit on the landing of the steps. I sit on the landing and look into Francesco's room and make sure he is sleeping and that he can't see me. If Francesco were to see me, he would tell me to go into my room and stop being so nosey. I hope I don't start coughing and wake my brother up, but I don't think my parents will be able to tell how close I am. I could always pretend to go into the hall bathroom.

I sit here for a bit and listen. I could make out a little bit of what they are saying, but I still don't understand what has started their argument. I continue to listen, and ten minutes later, I know what they are speaking about. Hearing this upsets me, and to be honest, I am completely shocked. This is not what I want to hear or what I was expecting to hear. I can't hear everything, but the little bit I do hear I piece together. After a few minutes, I begin to block out the rest of what they are saying because truthfully, the tiny details aren't important to me.

As I head back into my room and lay in the dark, tears slowly roll down my face and I can taste my salty tears. My nose also starts running, and I have to go into the bathroom to blow my nose. I also wash my face with cold water and try to get rid of the thoughts I am having. I am not one who likes to show my emotions to everyone, so it is good that I heard some of what is happening. I am able to process this and also give myself tonight to take it all in. My dad always taught me to be strong and to not cry, but this is hurting me, and it isn't always easy to hold in your emotions. I would rather be upset by myself than be upset in front of my family. I tell myself that when I wake up in the morning, I have to think of things that make me happy, so this way, I won't think of the bad things going on.

Dealing with my CF can be challenging, but I am already finding this to be more difficult for me. I am sure my parents will be telling Francesco and I this week sometime what I just heard but a much more modified version. Knowing this already has prepared me emotionally. Truthfully, I can only think of one solution to this scenario, and it is one I hoped would never happen to us. As I lay in the dark, the streetlights pierce through the verticals covering my bedroom windows, and my head starts feeling heavy from crying. I hope when I wake up, this will all go away, but I know this is just the beginning of what feels like the worst nightmare ever. This feels worse than any medical procedure, and I guess emotional pain can be worse than physical pain at times.

I stay up for many hours, thinking about how this could happen to my family. I know my family isn't perfect, but to me, everything seemed okay. I can see how situations can appear as one thing and turn out to be something completely different. Now I will be in the same boat as some of my friends at school. They say you don't understand a situation until you are in it, and this is very true. Now I will be able to relate to many other children and families in this world.

After I heard my parents talking, a couple of days later, my parents tell Francesco and I that they will be separating and that my dad is not going to be living at our house anymore. We are told that we will be living with Mommy and staying in our house. My brother seems to be shocked and a bit upset, but I was prepared for what my parents told us. I think my mom thought I didn't fully understand, but I understood a lot and maybe too much for my age. The biggest fear I have is that I won't get to see Daddy, but Mom tells me that I can see him whenever I want to.

The holidays are over, and school resumes today. We are back to our normal routine again consisting of school, sports, Boy Scouts, and Girl Scouts. This is my first year playing CYO basketball for my school, and I am on the older third grade team. My school didn't have a second-grade team, so I tried out, and they moved me up to the third grade B-level team. I hope to make the A-team next year in my age group. I am enjoying playing basketball at a more competitive level, and it is fun having practices twice per week as well.

*****

It is January, and we are halfway through the season. Our team has won half of our games, and I have made a bunch of new friends too. All of the girls are really nice, except for the bully being on my team. There are three of us in second grade that were put on the older team, and one of them, unfortunately, is the bully. The bully's father happens to be the assistant coach, and truthfully, he seems like a really nice person so far, and as far as she goes, she hasn't done anything mean to me yet at basketball. Maybe she doesn't want her father to think she isn't the angel that they think she is. For whatever reason, she is choosing to be nice to me. I have no idea, but this gives me a break, and I am enjoying being drama-free.

Playing CYO is giving me more experience with basketball, and I am really learning how to use my speed to my ability at a more competitive level. The part about the basketball games that upsets me the most is that my family is now divided, and they are sitting on opposite sides of the gym. It's a bit embarrassing for my brother and I. I can hear my name coming from many different places as my family claps and cheers me on. It is tough for my brother and I when we go to each other's sports games too because we have to choose which family members to sit with, and making that decision is not easy. I try and alternate at each of Francesco's games.

Francesco's team and my team didn't make it far in the playoffs, but we both had a good time and are looking forward to next season. I hope by then, my family will be able to sit together.

The sun is beating, and the windows are cracked open. There is a cool breeze coming in our classroom window. My teacher has chimes hanging in the corner of the room, and you can hear them clinking together as they move back and forth. They are so relaxing to listen to. I feel like I can fall asleep instantly, but I have to keep my eyes open and be alert. I wish I was lying on a lounge chair down the shore at Nana and Grandpa's instead of sitting at this wooden desk. I finish bubbling in the last few multiple choices and finish writing a paragraph on photosynthesis. I cannot wait to enjoy the rest of this beautiful afternoon and be dismissed from class.

Ring, ring, ring!

That is the bell down the hall for the older students, and my teacher tells us to start packing our book bags and to line up for dismissal. She tells us to look over our homework list and make sure we pack the right books needed for the weekend's assignments. I look at my homework list for the weekend and make sure I have everything I need. When it is time for the second grade to leave, I exit with my friends out of the main door which squeaks loudly as it opens. I see Mom with the other mothers waiting for us to come out, and they are all talking. We walk over to the other set of doors that swing open, and out comes Francesco with his friends.

As we walk to the car, my cousins stop us to say hello and tell my mom they are sorry to hear about my parents' separation. I can see my mom is in shock, and so am I a bit. They are my dad's second cousins, and Mom finds it interesting how they know. I guess word travels fast, even to those you aren't close to.

On the drive home, we stop at the store to get something for dinner. "Jill, what do you want for dinner tonight?" I am the picky one, so Mom always asks me first what I want for dinner. I ask her if we can have chicken cutlets, and without hesitation, she says, "Sure." I also ask if I can get a soda and a bag of chips. My favorite is orange soda and BBQ chips. I love the kettle-cooked mesquite BBQ ones. Mom tells me to put them on the counter so the woman can ring it up.

My parents never say no to my brother and I when it comes to food or snacks. Francesco and I don't ask for much, but when it comes to Christmas and birthdays, our parents treat us very well. I start eating my chips, and when we get in the house, I take them, and with Francesco, I run through the kitchen and into the living room to the TV. *Power Rangers* is going on at 4:00 p.m., and we don't want to miss it. I don't watch many shows, but this is one of my favorites. We enjoy this episode, as usual, and after *Power Rangers*, it's time for a chest PT and nebulizers. I ask Mom if we can call Daddy as I do every day after school, and of course, she says, "Yes."

We are tired from the week. We spend the night relaxing and watching our other favorite shows on TGIF. Tomorrow, we will be seeing Dad as we usually do on Saturdays. Spring is in full swing, and it is Saturday morning. It does not feel like the spring today. It is downpouring out and is cool and damp. It also smells like rain outside. You know the wet grass smell and flower smell combined with the fresh cut grass of yesterday. This morning, we are going to try on my Communion dress to see if it needs alterations. In just one month, I will be receiving my First Holy Communion with my class.

We arrive at the dress store, and I try it on. It is beautiful and big, but I am not into dresses too much. I see the other dresses that I had tried on with the itchy lace, and just looking at them makes me want to break out with hives. My mother looks at me and says, "How pretty it looks." I am not very girly and into getting dressed up. Picking out my Communion dress was a family outing a couple of months ago. Francesco and Dad came along that day too.

I look in the mirror and smile a bit. If I have to wear a dress I will, but I prefer to wear comfortable clothes such as a T-shirt and basketball shorts. My mother is smiling as they pin the dress to hem it, and I can tell she loves the dress that she has picked for me to wear on my special day. I know she is going to be taking me for pictures to the photographer soon like she did for Francesco. I am not so sure I am looking forward to that. I don't mind the pictures. I just don't enjoy being in dresses for a long period of time. If I had to choose what to wear for a photoshoot, it would be my basketball and soccer uniforms for sure. I am starting to turn into a bit of a tomboy, and

Mom makes jokes by telling me that the next time I will be wearing a dress like this will be on my wedding day. I am starting to think she may be right.

After the dress alterations, we head to another store to try on headpieces, and finally, we find one that matches perfect with my dress. The lady at the store has made the back of my head a bit sore from digging the comb part of the headpieces into my hair, and I am wondering how am I going to withstand this the entire day.

A month passes of school, soccer practices, games, and almost every day of communion practice. Things between my parents also seem okay. I talk to my dad every day after school, and on Saturdays, he takes me and Francesco out and over my grandparents' house. My parents are still separated, but my mom now allows my dad to come over every night to see my brother and I at the house.

When my dad comes over, my mom will either go into another room or sometimes she will go out. I am glad they don't argue in front of us, and that is comforting and much less stressful. I wish that my family could all be together in one house and live together the way we used to, but I understand that it isn't meant to be right now and may never be possible again. Thinking of the times when we were all together makes me happy, and maybe I am living in the past, but the reality also feels so real.

We are just a couple of weeks away from receiving our First Holy Communion, and our class is doing an activity in school where we answer questions. One of the questions is about our godparents, and for me, this has become a touchy subject in my household. I was supposed to see my godparents during the Christmas break, but with everything that happened with my parents, those plans had gotten cancelled. I keep asking my mom when we will be getting together with them and their children again. I am told that we won't ever be seeing them again. This was not what I was hoping to hear, but I had a feeling that would be the outcome.

Back in January, I had been home from school sick, and my godfather rang our doorbell. I had peeked through the window and saw it was him, but I was told to not answer the door. I miss not seeing my godparents and their kids. They are like an aunt and uncle to us, and their kids are like cousins to my brother and I. I have an idea as to why we aren't seeing them any longer and am pretty sure it goes hand in hand with why my parents are separated. It isn't fair to my brother and I along with their kids. I wonder if they ask their parents to see us, but I will never know. Knowing them as well as I do, I am pretty sure they want to see us too. I wonder if their parents are still together.

As we get ready to celebrate my communion in a few days, I only wish that they would be attending the way they attended our other family occasions. My mother told me that we wouldn't be seeing them any longer and that my godmother did something that wasn't very nice. My mom goes on to say that she can no longer trust her.

It is our final communion practice, and communion is tomorrow morning. My class is lined up to practice how we will enter the church and come down the aisle. I am the third shortest in the class out of twenty girls. I am nervous to be in the front of the line; however, I am glad to not be the first one, at least. A friend of mine is right before me, so that helps us both feel less nervous. My closest friends are much taller than I am, and they are toward the middle and back of the line. I concentrate as I slowly take one step at a time down the aisle with my hands in a praying position.

When I reach the altar, my partner and I bow our heads at the same time. I go to the left, and he goes to the right. My partner is actually one of my best friend's cousins. It is a long ceremony, and when it is time to receive communion, I go up and take both the bread and wine. This is the only time my mother tells me I will be allowed to take the wine. She has asked the school that when the cup is being rotated for me that I will be the only one to put my mouth on that section of the cup. There are a lot of germs that can be passed around from that one cup, so I have to be careful.

The mass is over, and we exit the church. It is a gorgeous spring day outside. It's sunny with beautiful blue skies, and the flowers have bloomed. Everyone is taking pictures inside and outside of the church with their friends and family. After taking pictures, we head home to have lunch and relax before my big party tonight at the

Historic Old Bermuda Inn. It is nice to be out of my dress for a bit. After eating, it is time to get my therapy done. I put on my vest and do my nebulizers. We are all dressed again. My parents put the favors in the car, and within a few minutes, we are on our way.

The room is decorated beautifully. It has an old historic feel, just like its name, but it is restored, and the tables are decorated with beautiful linens and centerpieces that my family had made up at a local party shop. Our guests start to arrive, and I am feeling excited as everyone makes their way through the entrance doors. My parents hired a DJ, and he asks me to tell him some of my favorite songs so he can play them throughout the night. I am excited to see my cousins whom I haven't seen in some time, maybe even a couple of years. The party begins, and my parents make a toast and thank everyone for celebrating with us. My father and I have a father-daughter dance, and then everyone starts to join us on the dance floor afterward for some faster paced music.

We dance in between food courses. The night is flying by, and it is time to cut the cake, but before we do so, my cousins and I decide we want to take the microphone and sing a song together from the *Lion King*. We are not great singers at all, but it is so much fun, and everyone listens and claps for us. We were a bit nervous, and my dad even videoed it. I guess we sounded okay together. I am surprised by a few of my guests that are attending, but I am so happy that they came. My parents invited two of my doctors, my new CF doctor with her family, and my chiropractor with his wife. My CF doctor that has CF himself has been pretty sick for about a year now, and so I started seeing one of the other doctors in the same office who happens to be the center's director. My parents chose to invite her today. I love her and I have gotten very comfortable with her in such a short amount of time. She happens to also be from Staten Island, but she no longer lives here.

As the night comes to an end, there is one last surprise from Nanie and Grandpa. Nanie tells me to walk with her to the corner of the room where there is something large covered with a white tablecloth. As she takes the cloth off, my eyes light up. They may have even lit up a little more than on Christmas morning. It is a huge candy cart filled with all kinds of candy, chocolate, candy apples, cotton candy, etc. I look at my grandmother in disbelief and then hug and kiss her and thank her and Grandpa as I race to fill up a bag with my favorite goodies. The other kids as well as the big kids head over to the candy cart and begin indulging in the sweets.

As I am filling up my bag, my CF doctor, Dr. G., is next to me, filling up a bag with her son. I think to myself maybe she will say, "That's too much candy for you," but she doesn't. She smiles and says, "Wow! Jillian. This is so cool, isn't it?"

I smile and say, "Yes, I love candy." She tells me that she knows I do and that she does as well. She also tells me how her son can't get over the candy cart and how much fun it is. I am exhausted from a long day and night, but it is one of the best days I have had in my life. I really enjoy big parties like the one we had tonight. I am looking forward to sleeping in tomorrow.

*****

It is late Sunday morning by the time I wake up. It is time for me to start my morning nebulizers and chest PT. Without hesitation, I head down the steps and get started. My parents are already awake and drinking coffee and eating bagels in the kitchen. The smell of coffee and everything bagels makes the entire house smell so good. My mother tells me we will be going to church today, and I will be able to receive communion like everyone else. I am excited that I can partake in receiving communion rather than just waiting in my seat until my family returns from receiving the Body of Christ.

After doing my albuterol nebulizer, I do my chest PT using a machine called "the vest." I recently started using The Vest Airway Clearance System this year. It is a new machine which consists of a nylon vest with tubing attached to a big compressor that shakes my chest to help loosen the mucus in my lungs. It has a few different knobs that allow me to change the settings and increase and decrease the frequency and pressure. It also has a timer that dings when the time is up. While it shakes me, it also makes my voice sound funny when I talk and that makes me laugh as well as everyone else too.

When my friends see me using the vest for the first time and speaking as it runs, they get the biggest kick out of it. I am not crazy about doing the vest too much. I find manual chest PT to be more effective. When I am talking about manual therapy, I am referring to when someone uses their hands and claps on my chest, shoulders, and back. Since getting the vest, I have only used it a handful of times. It is supposed to give the CF patients more freedom and allow us to be more independent, but I see it more as giving my parents more freedom. I am still attached to the wall for one hour per day, and when I am sick, it becomes one and a half to two hours per day. My nebulizer also has to be plugged in, and that takes me another hour per day if not a little longer.

While I do the vest, Mom is able to cook dinner, and I could get my therapy done at the same time which allows us to eat earlier. I miss spending that time with my parents, and I feel like I am doing my therapies pretty much alone now. I am glad my parents don't have to hold my hand, but I guess doing my therapy with my parents is something I got used to and this vest thing is all new to me. I'm sure, in time, I will learn to appreciate the freedom that this machine is capable of giving me. After I do my vest therapy, it is time to do Pulmozyme. I also do an inhaled antibiotic called Coly at times that is through my nebulizer.

Coly is done last after my chest PT, but it is only used when I have a lung infection. It has a funny taste to it and smells a bit strange. It also sticks to my nose and chin, and I hate having to clean it off after each time I use it. I do feel better after inhaling it, and it is usually used for twenty-eight days at a time. Coly, along with oral antibiotics, mostly does the trick along with extra chest PT when I am sick. My chest PT is finished and it's time for a bagel. I love when we have bagels since I don't eat them every day. I love adding a ton of butter, and even eating the butter right off the knife by itself. Mom tells me to stop eating it by itself and that I am going to get a stomachache. I laugh and continue eating it as I look over at my enzyme bottle. I better take them now.

My pills are down, and I hope they do their job in time. I do not want a stomachache and going to school the day after forgetting to take enzymes is just awful. In the past I tried to hide my digestive issues from my parents, but Mom would know when I didn't take my enzymes or when I forgot to. After all, Mom is the one who cleans the bathrooms, and forgetting to take enzymes will for sure leave behind evidence no matter what you do. It is time for church, and as we arrive, the parking lot is packed. It is much more crowded than on a typical Sunday.

As we go inside, finding a seat is much more difficult too, but we find a few in the back. Forty-five minutes go by, and it is time for communion again, and this time, I don't just have to sit until my family returns. I get to go up with them to the altar. After church, we are all pretty exhausted from yesterday, so we head home to relax and get ready for the week. There's about a month and a half left of school, and the year is coming to an end soon, which means we will be studying hard for finals.

As the weeks pass, we are back to those scorching hot June days, and we are back in our summer uniforms. It is great that our school added in shorts as part of the uniform because my friends and I are really taking advantage of it. Everything health-wise has been calm for the most part. Of course, throughout the school year, I am on and off oral and inhaled antibiotics to fight off lung infections, but thank God, no recent hospitalizations. As for my lungs, I am told I am doing well, but lately, I notice that when I get hungry, I have a burning pain in my stomach as well as in my throat. It almost feels as if my food is coming up into my throat but it isn't food.

I am not sure how to explain this to my parents or my doctor. When this burning happens, I also feel like I am going to throw up. The only thing that helps is when I eat pretzels or bread. I am happy this school year is coming to an end because at least at home when I get this burning feeling, I am able to just go and get some pretzels and feel much better. I hope I feel better by September. This way, I won't be feeling like this in class.

So far, this summer is a lot of fun. Our pool is open, and we are going on a family vacation, which I didn't think would ever happen again. My parents are in the process of working things out, and they are sort of back together. It is so nice to have my family all together again and planning a vacation together. I am no longer getting nervous stomach pains and spending time in the bathroom and having to blame it on CF problems like I have in the past eight months.

Let's rewind back to the springtime when my grandpa was watching me. We were sitting at the table, and we just finished having a snack. I started working on my homework, and out of nowhere, I had a nervous pain that felt like butterflies in my stomach and I had to run to the bathroom. I remember Grandpa knocking on the bathroom door to make sure I was okay. I told him that I was okay and that I just had to use the bathroom. This would happen to me whenever I was left with a family member at home and my parents weren't around.

Being home with family members brought back flashbacks to when we were left with my aunt that night this past December; you know, the night I sensed something was wrong. I never know when that night will repeat itself. As the weeks went on, Dad pretty much moved back home, and things felt a bit back to normal again, but I will always have these memories in my head and not know if this will happen again, God forbid.

This summer, we aren't going upstate to the Villa Roma on vacation. Instead, we are headed to the Hershey Hotel in Hershey, Pennsylvania, for the week. It is August, and it is pretty warm out. The forecast is projecting to be between 85 and 90 degrees all week. I am looking forward to all of the candy that the chocolate factory has to offer. I have recently become a fan of the Hershey bar with almonds. I am excited to see where Hershey bars are made, and I hear the factory has so much more! As we load the car, I have the most luggage out of the four of us as usual.

Whether I go away for two days to my grandparents' shore house or an entire week somewhere, I require mostly the same number of things. I still have to bring my medical equipment which takes up a lot of space in our van. I have my two machines as well as a lot of pills and inhaled medication. I also require a cooler when traveling to keep my refrigerated medications such as the Pulmozyme cold. We always have to make special accommodations with the hotel to get a private refrigerator in our room.

Going away is a lot of work, which is why we usually prefer our family's time-share unit. Time-shares are similar to a full apartment. Our time-share unit has two bedrooms, a family room, full kitchen with dining table, two full bathrooms, and a balcony overlooking the resort.

Packing for Hershey took a lot of preparation, but after many hours, we are ready to leave. My parents have everything in the car, and the directions are in hand, printed from the latest best place you can get directions from the one and only MapQuest. Our family is known for getting lost when we travel, so Mom asks Francesco and I to keep our voices down and to not distract Dad. I have my headphones on with my Walkman, listening to some of my favorite songs by Elton John who is also one of my parents' favorite singers. I hope to see him in concert one day in Madison Square Garden like my parents have in the past. Maybe one day, they will take me with them. I would love to see him play the piano live.

Francesco also has his Walkman in his ears, but I am not sure who he is listening to. I have also brought with me the Backstreet Boys, NSYNC, and the Spice Girls CDs. They are some of my other favorite groups to listen to. I enjoy listening to many diverse genres of music and singers. We are driving for about an hour and a half, and my dad puts his flashers on and pulls over. I take my headphones off and ask, "What happened?"

My mom says, "Nothing, we are lost, as usual." And she chuckles a bit as they try to figure out where they went wrong. I think we may have made a wrong turn or something, but I hear my parents say to each other that we aren't too far out of the way, which is pretty good for us. It takes us an extra twenty minutes to get there, totaling three hours, but we reach the hotel in one piece. We park the car and check in. I jump out of the car and walk into the Hershey Hotel.

As the door opens, we are greeted by a person dressed in a Reese's costume, and they hand me a mini Hershey bar and Reese's cup. I thank the Reese's person, and I ask my mother if I can eat it. She says, "Yes, but you have to take your enzymes."

Here we go again with the enzymes, but Mom is right. She tells me, "I am sure a lot of people will be handing you chocolate, and it has fat in it, so that means you will need enzymes each time you eat chocolate."

I look at her and agree, even though deep down I am dying to not take them, but I don't want the stomach pain. A couple of minutes could save me a whole lot of discomfort. I eat the chocolate and take a couple of enzymes, of course.

I am enjoying my time here already. Every door we have entered, we have been greeted with some type of Hershey chocolate. I am hungry for lunch, and the chocolate helps my hunger for a bit while we check in and put our things in our room. My mom puts the medications in the refrigerator, and we don't waste any time. Back downstairs we go.

It is a beautiful hotel, and the lobby is decorated tastefully. Everyone is very friendly, and you know you are not in New York City any longer. We ask the receptionist where we can get some lunch, and she tells us, "Right down the steps here, we have our own restaurant."

We decided to try her recommendation and eat on the premises. As we head to the restaurant, I see there is a small arcade room. My eyes light up, and I show Francesco. He looks inside as well and says, "Maybe later on we can go." He doesn't seem too impressed by it, and if you compare it to the arcade at the Villa Roma, this one has nothing on that one.

I ask my parents if I can play the games and they say later on and that we have to eat first. My dad asks us if we really want to play in the tiny hotel arcade. He then explains that Hershey offers so much to do and that the arcade is something to do later on when we are bored and back at the hotel.

As we sit down and order lunch, my parents take out a few brochures that they were given when checking in. They are reading off things to do and what there is to do in this area. My dad is interested in going on a train ride. He says that it is a train that also has a food place on it so we can go for a ride and have lunch one day. My brother and I aren't too excited about this train ride, but my mother explains to us that Daddy always does things that we want, and it is our turn to do something that he wants to do. It looks like we won't have much of a choice, but I am happy to see different scenery. Where we live is always very busy with tons of traffic, and it is very peaceful and calm here.

After lunch, we put on our bathing suits and decide to go swimming for a bit since it's getting late already. The food from the restaurant was pretty good, and I am looking forward to eating there again throughout the week.

*****

It is the next day, and it is also a warm sunny day, so we decide to go to Hershey Park. Hershey Park is an amusement park with lots of rides. I am not a big ride person, but I enjoy walking around and going on a few of them. I get nauseous easily, and so the slower rides are better for me. It is our third day in Hershey, and today, it's raining, so what better day to spend it at the Hershey Chocolate Factory. So far, this is my favorite part of our trip. As we walk in there is a huge store full of candy and chocolate, every type of candy made by Hershey in every size imaginable. I want to buy and eat everything, but my parents tell me after we go on the factory ride, which is a tour of the factory, then I can pick out a few things.

As we get on the ride, I sit with my dad, and my brother sits with my mom. The ride is so cool, and it moves slowly throughout the factory. They show us how the chocolate is made, and as we ride around, we can smell the chocolate, and it smells heavenly. It makes me want to buy everything that I saw before and even more so now. As we exit the ride, we enter the opposite side of the store. I get a mixed bag consisting of Reese's cups and Hershey chocolate bars, and my parents find these delicious soft chewy caramels filled with a drop of chocolate syrup in the middle. We have never seen a caramel made like this before by the Hershey company, and my mom and I love anything caramel. Daddy and Francesco are also enjoying them as well.

By the next day, the caramels are gone, and before the week is over, my parents say they are going to get a few bags to bring home with us since we aren't sure if they will be available at our local stores.

The caramels by far are my favorite candy that I have eaten while being here. We are having a great time together, but our week is coming to an end. We will be heading home tomorrow, and it is another rainy day.

My father's dream is finally coming true. We are at the Strasburg train station with our tickets, waiting to board the train as it approaches in a few minutes. As we stand under the underpass, my dad takes out his video camera for about the tenth time this week and says, "Say hi, Jill."

I smile and wave and say hello as the train is passing us, and it comes to a stop. It is loud on the tracks, and you can hear the horn and see the steam. My father says, "Diane, Jill, and Francesco, let's go so we can get a seat." We all smile and get in line and, one by one, step foot on the train. It does not look the way I thought it would look. It is very old-fashioned, and it has comfortable chairs and booths that look like you're in a restaurant. My dad was right when he told me it's not a regular NYC subway train or SI railway train. Actually, it is pretty cool.

I am loving this ride so far, and I can't wait to eat my lunch and take in the scenic surroundings of the trees and summer greenery. It feels a bit country to me. I raise my eyebrows and laugh as my mother is using her camera to take pictures of all of us. I still cannot believe there is a kitchen on this train.

When my dad first mentioned it, I didn't think many other people would be on it with us, but all the tickets were sold out from what I understand. I thought we would be the only ones riding it. Two hours pass, and we are having a great time enjoying the train ride. I have only been on a train one other time in my life. I think Francesco may have even dosed off to sleep for a bit in his chair after eating.

We got back to the train station and headed to our car. Tonight will be our last night here.

*****

Our vacation is over, and I am sad to be returning home so quickly. This week really flew by much faster than any school week ever has.

My parents have finished packing up the car, and we just finished checking all the furniture and drawers as well as the bathroom to make sure nothing is left behind. It would stink to forget anything behind, especially something medical-related. Everything is empty, and we hit the road. My brother and I aren't getting along too well today, and we keep arguing and fighting. Our parents yell at us to stop so they can concentrate on not getting lost. I think being tired from having to check out so early and being in the car for almost an hour now is getting to the both of us.

Dad pulls the car to the side of the road, and within seconds, my brother is told to sit in the front, and my mother joins me in the back seat. My mother continues to give my dad directions, but somewhere, we make a wrong turn. After about forty-five minutes, Dad looks up and sees a sign that says Scranton in the same direction that we are going. He yells out, "Scranton!"

And my mother says, "Huh? Where are we?"

We pull over again and realize we have been going the opposite way for almost forty minutes. My parents look at the map and figure out how to get us back on track. From here, we are about two hours away from home, which should have only been about one hour away. My brother and I look at one another and remain silent. We realize our arguing is the reason we are so far out of the way.

After returning home from our vacation, it is time to finish up my summer reading, I am a little behind and only have about a week and a half left before school begins. As September approaches, we aren't the only ones getting ready for the school year, but so is my mother. Mommy is getting ready to meet with my new teacher ahead of time. This way, she can explain my medical situation to her. Waiting for the first day to speak with her would be too late.

On this first day of school, I will need to tend to my medical needs, even if there isn't much happening. CF is one of those diseases that doesn't go on vacation but rather goes to a vacation. It comes with me everywhere I go and cannot be neglected. I must always put my medical needs first, and everything else comes second. My mom always makes sure my teachers understand my situation, and that is just what she did a few days before this upcoming school year.

A few days before school started, I sat on the bench by the principal's office as my mother went and spoke with my teacher. My brother had this same teacher a couple of years ago, and to be honest, she is not a warm person. She is known to be the nastiest teacher in our school, so I know what I am in for and am not looking forward to it. If I can handle CF, then I can sure handle her and the way she speaks to her students.

My uniforms still fit from a few months ago, and I did not grow much over the summer. I have only gained a couple of pounds. It is difficult for me to gain weight, but the main thing is that I am maintaining it the past few months, and my new doctor is happy with that. Of course, she wants me to gain weight, but not losing weight is also a plus right now. I have gotten used to my new doctor, and to be honest, I love her. She is fun and sweet, but she is also tough when she has to be, and there is no cutting corners with her. She is on the same page as my parents, just like my previous doctor was.

My previous doctor, as I explained, has CF himself, and he has been sick for the past year. He hasn't been healthy enough to care for me and his other patients. I miss him very much and hope he gets better soon so that he can take care of me again. It's been a while since I have seen him, and I am told he is very sick. I think about him often, and every time I go for an appointment into the CF center, I wish that I would be walking all the way to the right-hand corner at the end of the hall into his office and that I would see his face and hear his voice. I can hear him saying, "Jillian, please take a deep breath" while he moves around the cold stethoscope and closely listens to my lungs. His hands were always cold too, and I would jump, but it was also a comforting feeling for me and became a normal part of my CF checkups. This is what I am thinking about as I am doing my nighttime chest PT.

My vest machine shakes my chest and sounds like it's going to take off and head for space. My mind continues to wander off to many different thoughts pertaining to my health. I start to think how one can always take all of their medications and do their therapies just like I do and my doctor does and still wind up so sick. Sick to the point where he can no longer see his patients has me wondering how sick he really is. Each day, I feel like I am challenging myself to see if I can just stay alive and make it to the next birthday. I challenge myself every three months to try and beat my highest lung function each time and set a new record for myself. It feels like I am competing with myself and competing with time. I think about my daily regimen and how life really is short, but even with all my troubles, I still love living life to the fullest.

As I finish trying to put this all into perspective, I realize it is better not to think of this all. In the end, I can't control time and I can't control my situation, but I can choose to be happy and make the best of it. I know God is in control of everything and it will all go his way. Everyone tells me that God loves me and is watching over me, so I think I will be okay.

My therapy is complete, and the vest is deflated. I sit here for a minute, taking in a deep breath as I hear my mother in the kitchen say, "Jill, it's time to eat." I unhook myself from my vest and I fix all of the tubing and join my family in the kitchen for dinner. We are having hamburgers with peas and salad. I smelled them coming from the BBQ outside, and I am excited for dinner tonight.

I cut it close, but my summer reading is all finished. I decided to take notes as I read all three books, this way, I can review them before taking any exams. I am lucky if I can even remember the titles of them, let alone the details in all three books.

Today, I begin third grade. My mother is driving Francesco and I to school. We do not take the bus, but we also don't qualify for bus service because we live too close to our school. I am always cutting it close, but I manage to arrive just on time. The bell rings in the gymnasium, and the classes are divided up. I already know that I will be getting the "mean teacher" out of the two third-grade teachers. My class isn't too excited about our teacher. You could hear everyone saying how mean she is. A lot of us have older siblings that had her already, and so we know what to expect.

The first day is a half day, and she is already catching an attitude with most of us. She starts doing multiplication tables with us today and sends us home with homework already. We are the only class in the school to be given homework on the first day. Before I can even start the homework assignment, I have to go to the store and buy what the teacher wants us to have for class. I think this is going to be the most challenging year for me.

The first week has gone by, which was a short week, and by the second week of school, she decides to give us a pop quiz on multiplication. The majority of the class is struggling, especially me and a few others. There is a lot to memorize and not enough time to focus on math because we have been bombarded with the other subjects as well.

The quizzes are graded by the next day, and I have red ink all over my test to the point where I can barely see what I had written in. She didn't just circle and cross out and put X's on things; she also wrote "You need to memorize your times tables" all over the page. I got a fifty-five, which is better than I expected, but it is the worst grade I have ever gotten and possibly one of the worst grades in my class.

I bring home my test and am embarrassed to show my mother. She tells me that I did not do well and that I have to study more and memorize my times tables. I agree with her. My teacher tells us we will have a repeat exam soon. It was very soon. It was less than two days later, and I didn't do much better. The next week, I only got a sixty-five. At this point, my mother is angry because she told me all I had to do was memorize them, but I got a bit confused during the exam, and there wasn't much time given to us to take it. If we counted on our hands or drew boxes or anything else on the side of the paper, our teacher would automatically fail us. I am the type of person that likes to understand things rather than rush through things and memorize them. I guess she is right; there isn't time to understand when it comes to multiplication. As the weeks go on, I finally memorize all of my multiplication tables.

*****

It is October, and I am excited that CYO basketball is starting. I am now old enough to try out for the team in my age group. Tryouts are on Saturday mornings, and my dad is going to take me. Tryouts are a lot of fun, and I enjoyed doing the drills and shooting the ball. I enjoy activities that are a challenge. The next day, the phone rings. It is the coach asking to talk to my parents. My mother gets on the phone, and I hear her say, "Great, thank you so much. She will be very happy."

"Ma, did I make it?"

My mother replies with, "Jillian, you made the team as well as the A-team."

I am so happy and have a huge smile on my face! I feel like I am on top of the world right now! This motivates me even more to complete all of my homework. I ask my dad if we could go and buy new sneakers that match my new blue uniform, and he says, "Yes, we can go after I am home from work."

The next week, we go to Model's to get a nice pair of Nike high-tops with a navy-blue shiny Nike logo on the side. At first, they weren't comfortable to run in, but it takes time to break them in. I walk into the gym and start warming up with my team, and then we begin a layup drill. The coach approaches my mom and tells her that in order for me to go forward, they are requiring a doctor's note. My mom is confused and asks him, "For what? I have never heard of such a thing."

The coach says that the school wants clearance due to me having CF.

My mom says, "I have never needed this in the past for either soccer or basketball. Jillian has been playing soccer here for the past four years." My mom tells the coach that I am healthy enough to be on the court and that my doctor wants me to play. She then tells him that if I wasn't healthy enough, I wouldn't be playing and that Dr. G wouldn't be encouraging me to play sports.

The coach tells my mom, "She cannot practice until we have a note from her doctor."

Mom tells the coach that she hopes everyone has to hand in a note to prove they are healthy enough to play.

My coach says, "We are worried for Jill and we don't want her to collapse and have to perform CPR on her in the middle of the court."

My mother is beyond infuriated, and I am just completely confused as to why they are treating me in such a way. I am allowed to play gym class and run around at recess without clearance, but I am not allowed to practice with my mom watching without clearance. Mom tells me to grab my things and that we are going home and she is putting a call in to my doctor. When Dad hears of this, he is infuriated as well, and my parents say that this is discrimination against me. Although Francesco is healthy, they never had to sign any waivers for him. I also have friends with asthma on my team, and they aren't required to hand in a doctor's note giving them clearance. They use their inhalers more than I do at practice.

I have to agree with my parents and so does my doctor when we tell her. She sends in a note so that I can play and get exercise. She tells us that it is discrimination, but the main thing is she wants me exercising, so we hand them in the note. My parents even think of suing the school, and I don't mind if they do. I have no problem transferring to a new school, but because of Francesco being happy here, we decide not to go that route.

I hope to switch schools one day because things here seem to get more evil each day. I enjoy basketball and I love my team, but the school staff overall are not very "Christian" by any means. They teach us to act as Christians but don't portray those teachings themselves. My parents speak with the athletic director whom we are fond of, and she explains that it didn't come from her but that it came from someone higher-up in the parish. Hmm, what a coincidence. The bully's mom happens to be the higher-up in the parish. I cannot wait to get away from here someday. I am not opposed to attending another catholic school because I know of other friends who are happy going to the other catholic schools on the island.

My parents set up a meeting with the coach, athletic director, and the parish management and speak their minds on this situation. They even admitted in a roundabout way that it was wrong of them to do this to me. As much as I would have loved to see my parents bring them to court, I know the man upstairs is watching their actions. I guess some things aren't people's place to handle.

At school the next day, my friends ask why I left practice, and I have to explain to them what happened. They all say that they didn't have to get any medical clearance. My coach's daughter has asthma worse than mine, and she didn't need a note to play. This all is just completely unfair. I still decided to play out the season for the exercise and my love for the game, but you can feel the tension in the gym between my family and the bully's family.

One of my coaches is the bully's dad, and he has remained friendly to us and, of course, we do the same. We know he wasn't a part of this ordeal. You really can tell who is who by their actions. The Bible speaks about knowing them by their fruits, and their fruits are being produced in a rotten way.

As the weeks went on, we all got past this, and I was just happy to be playing without any further issues. Last night was our first game, and we won that as well as our first few scrimmages. Francesco also started CYO basketball again, and his first game is beginning in a few minutes. His team has a few new players on it, and they have a better team this year than last year. We walk up to the two-story gymnasium. Francesco is playing upstairs in the little gym, and downstairs are the older kids.

It is a very old gym called the CYO Center. This is my first time here, and it is pretty warm upstairs. I am happy I am not the one playing tonight. There are a few windows open, but the air is still and isn't circulating. As more people walk in and look for seats, it gets even warmer. Parking was tough over here too, but my dad dropped us off first, and then he parked the car around the corner.

As my dad walks in, I wave my hands so he could see where we are sitting. He is talking with one of the other dads. My dad tells us to come and sit in another area and that he wants to introduce us to one of the other families that are there. Dad has attended Francesco's practices, so he knows more people on the team than we do. My dad says, "Jillian, this is Joe and his wife."

I smile and say, "Hello." I am also introduced to their son who looks like he is around my age.

Joe pinches my cheeks and says, "Hello, sweetie."

I smile and say hello to Joe and his family. I quietly sit next to Mom as she and Dad talk with their new friends. Their older son is on Francesco's team, and he and Francesco have become friendly.

I am looking forward to the game, but it goes by pretty quickly. My mom and dad are still talking to their new friends, and they ask if we all want to go and have pizza together at Denino's.

Denino's is packed, and so there is a bit of a wait. After waiting, we are seated, and my family sits across from their family. I am quiet and shy as well as their younger son. Francesco and his friend are laughing and very talkative. I am sitting across from their younger son at the end of the table. I hear Joe tell his son, "Michael, talk to Jillian. Make friends. She's only one year younger than you."

As everyone keeps talking and eating, it gets louder and louder. Across from me, I catch Michael looking at me as I drink my soda and take bites of this delicious pizza. I feel like I am being spied on from far away, but as I look up from my plate, he puts his head down and is staring under the table. This happens a bunch of times, and I cannot figure out why he is staring at me and then turning away. I start looking behind me to see if something interesting is happening at the bar or on the television, but there isn't much going on.

It is getting late, and there are less customers here than earlier. I am pretty sure now that he is staring at me. What is he so fascinated with? To be honest, he isn't bad-looking, but I am just eight years old.

We are all done eating, and Joe invites us back to their house to have coffee, and my parents accept their invitation. They only live about five minutes from our house and one block from my aunt and uncle's house. I figured they had to live close because they go to the same church as us. Our parents hang out in the kitchen, talking and having coffee. We all hang out playing video games and computer games and watch some TV.

Francesco is playing a game and listening to music on the computer with his friend. Michael and I are with them too. Michael and I start talking and begin getting to know each other a bit. Michael tells me he is a little shy around new people as well as our parents and brothers. He says to me, "If you want, we can hang out upstairs."

I say, "Sure, I don't mind as long as your parents are okay with us going upstairs."

He tells me to follow him. The upstairs of the house is perfectly in order, and it looks like it is never used. On the table right up the steps, there are photos of him and his brother, and he points to show me which one is him. I can already tell who was who, and I smile and say, "So cute." I then ask him if they use the upstairs part of their house. I go on to tell him that I know most Italian families like using the basement. I tell him that my family uses the basement too but mostly to hang out and for larger birthday parties. We still use our upstairs every day. I explain to him that my mom likes to keep the formal living room and formal dining room for holidays and special occasions and that those rooms are off-limits on regular days.

He says, "We only use the basement most of the time, and the upstairs is used for sleeping mostly, and we also use the bathroom up here."

I look at him and think that is different, but every family has their own way of doing things. He laughs and tells me the upstairs kitchen is pretty much for show as well as the living room. He also says, "The dining room is used for holidays." I think this is pretty interesting.

He shows me the upstairs of their home, and then he tells me he wants to show me his snapper turtles in his bedroom. I tell him that I have a turtle also, but mine is a Southern painter. We head down the hall into his bedroom. He has some cool posters on the walls, and on his dresser, he has a small cage similar to my hermit crabs cage with two turtles in it. I say, "Those are the cutest things ever, and they are so tiny. Mine is much larger. She is in a regular-sized fish tank."

He smiles at me and says, "They are snapper turtles and they will bite your fingers off."

I am shocked at how quickly they open their mouths to bite, and I definitely won't be putting my hands anywhere near them. He then grabs their food and shows me how he feeds them and asks if I want to feed them. I am a bit afraid, so I say, "No thanks, I'll just watch you do it."

My turtle you can feed right from your hand, but his turtles? Absolutely no way. He asks me how long I have my turtle for, and I tell him only about six months. It was a gift from my grandparents, and I picked it out right after my communion. I also tell him my other grandparents bought me tadpoles since I wanted to try and grow them into frogs, but they didn't live too long. He thinks that is cool. It is pretty cool how we both have turtles and both like animals.

We begin talking about school and basketball. He tells me he plays also but that he isn't the best. He is on the B-team, and when he hears I am on the A-team, he is shocked and tells me I must be good. Most of the boys that I am friends with are in shock when they find out I am on the A-team, and so his reaction doesn't surprise me.

He shows me his posters with his favorite basketball players and wrestlers on them. I am only familiar with the basketball players, but I know nothing about wrestling. He tells me about the wrestlers and the WWF. As we both sit on his bed, we talk for a couple of hours, and the time flies by. We cannot believe it is almost 12:00 a.m. already. I have never sat with a boy talking for that long before but have with friends of mine that are girls. We both made each other smile and laugh a lot and had a good time tonight. From upstairs, we can hear our parents calling our names, and I hear my parents say, "Come on, Jill. It's late. Time to go."

Michael asks me, "When am I going to see you again?" I tell him I will be attending my brother's next game, and he says, "Me too. I'll see you then."

We also spoke tonight a little bit about CF since he asked me why I was eating baby food during dinner. I didn't get into all of the details. I just explained a little bit about how I use the baby food to take my pills and what I do each day. I explained how CF affects my lungs and stomach, and I also explained that I have to do therapies each day. He seemed interested in learning more. He was in shock when I told him my parents have to clap on my back and sides with their hands and asked if he can see my therapy being done one day. I told him that if he was over one day, he can see how my therapies are done. All my friends have mostly seen me do therapies when they are over, and having CF has not been a secret kept from them. If someone wants to be my friend, then they will unfortunately be exposed to the details of CF at some point.

I could see as I spoke to Michael earlier he was trying to understand it, and maybe this wasn't the time to have told him, but he asked about the baby food, and one thing led to the next.

*****

We are back home, and as I get ready for bed, I am excited to have made a new friend tonight. For the last few hours tonight, I didn't feel like an eight-year-old, I felt a bit older. Not sure why, but things just felt different. A few weeks go by, and I go about my normal life consisting of school, basketball, Girl Scouts, hanging out with friends and, of course, taking care of my health.

Halloween is here again, and it is the morning of. Francesco has a CYO basketball game, and I am attending. Truthfully, I don't have much of a choice, even if I didn't want to attend, but I enjoy watching my brother play. I am really loving basketball and can sit all day in the gym and watch any team play. As we walk in the gym, we join our new friends and sit higher in the bleachers. I take a seat next to Michael, and our parents are sitting above us. I bring my basketball with me because in between time-outs, the referees let the kids who are watching run on the court and shoot around during the thirty-second timeouts. In order to do so, you must bring your own ball. It's challenging to see how many baskets I can get in within a tiny amount of time.

Michael asks if he can join me in between the time-outs, and of course, I smile and say, "Sure." I now have someone to rebound and pass the ball to me as I do the same for him. As the game goes on, he takes out a Duncan Brain Yo-yo and shows me some of the tricks he can do. I have never seen those types of yo-yos before, and he lets me try it. He shows me "Walk the dog" and "Rock the cradle." I need a lot of practice, but I am getting the hang of it early on.

I ask my parents if I can buy a Duncan yo-yo after the game, and they give in and take us to the store. We all go to the store and pick out a red one for me. I am excited to learn some new tricks, and Michael tells me he will teach me. Francesco gets the same one as me but in blue. It is fun to learn something new. I always want to do what the boys are doing, and for once, I don't feel out of place. My brother sometimes makes me feel like I should be doing girly things, but my new friend accepts me for who I am. I'm not saying Francesco doesn't accept me. I just don't think he wants me copying him. It is cool to have a friend that has the same interests as me. I have a lot of common interests with my female friends, but not many of them are into sports.

After the store, the four of us change into our Halloween costumes, and we go trick or treating in their neighborhood. I am dressed as a professional basketball player wearing a New York Liberty Jersey, and the boys all have different masks on with black sweatsuits. Michael is also carrying a fake plastic knife. He has fake blood on his mask.

The boys find it fun to try and scare me. I am not a huge fan of Halloween, but I still take part in the festivities. I love the fall season. It isn't cold enough to need a heavy jacket, but it's cool enough to not sweat. I find Halloween to be a bit depressing, especially when you see the fake tombstones and skeletons. Within a couple of hours, our bags are filled with so much candy, and we can't wait to get home and relax and eat some. Before eating it, we all sit on the floor and empty our bags. We check to make sure none of it is opened and that it looks safe to eat. We even trade with each other to get our favorite candy. After we sort out our candy, Francesco decides to stay by their house.

Michael comes over by mine, and we have pizza. Michael and I also trick or treat on my block and get to see my neighbors. The houses by my house are more spread out, and so we don't get too much candy, but we already have a ton. As we are on our way back to my house, we stop at a couple houses more that we missed when starting out. We ring the bell to the red house, and the dog behind the fence starts barking and growling. He isn't too friendly at all.

The owner opens the door. She is Asian, and we can barely understand her. She hands us this homemade candy wrapped in a wax paper bag. Michael and I say, "Thank you."

Michael looks at me and whispers, "What is this?"

I say, "I don't know. Probably some type of Asian candy, but it isn't sealed properly. We should throw it out when we get home."

When we get back in the house, Dad is home from the building job. We show him the candy, and he laughs. He tells us he will try it. I think he is crazy, but he takes a small bite of it. He says, "It's not bad, but I just don't know what it is. Some type of fruit candy." He tells us, "I wouldn't eat it since we aren't sure. If something happens to me, you know it was that candy."

We laugh.

It's nice not having to deal with our brothers right now. Our brothers don't always want us around. I get it that they are a bit older and into different things than we are. We always hear them ask, "When are Jill and Michael going to leave?" They tell us, "Can't you guys go and play a game or watch TV somewhere else?" They even throw us out of the video game room from time to time and lock the door. We learned early on it is best to do our own thing. We don't need their company to be entertained.

After having pizza, we talk about how much fun we had today. Michael asks me if I want to play Truth or Dare, and I never played before but agree to play. We are asking each other funny questions and daring each other to do stupid things. He dares me to jump on one foot and rub my belly and tap my head at the same time. I laugh and am able to do that. I have done this before with my friends, but not during Truth or Dare. During Truth or Dare, Michael dares me to write on a page in my diary. I am a bit hesitant as I don't know what he wants me write. He says, "I dare you to write 'Jill loves Mike.'"

I look at him and say, "I know it's a dare, but I am not doing that."

Michael laughs and tells me I am going to lose, but I don't care. He grabs the key to my diary off of my desk and unlocks my diary himself and goes to one of the pages toward the back and writes it in himself.

I ask him, "Why did you go all the way to August?"

He says, "I wrote it on my birthday so you know when my birthday is." He closes the diary and locks it and hands me the key and says, "Here, put it where you want."

MOMENTS OF IMPACT

I am glad there is a lock on my diary. That way, only I can see what is written in it. I am thinking about ripping the page out. What if something happens to me and someone finds it? I don't want anyone to think I wrote that. I really don't even use that diary. Before this, every page was blank. I am not one to write in a diary. Nanie bought it for me, and I had it sitting in my treasure chest.

I take the locked diary and lock it in my treasure chest. Every memory I have is in my brain, and there isn't much of anything I forget. Life's situations seem to impact me on a daily basis.

*****

Halloween was a lot of fun, and the weekend is over. It is already November, and the school week has begun. It is Wednesday, and I am not feeling too well, so I stay home from school. "Jillian, what do you want for dinner tonight?"

I answer, "Can we have chicken soup, please?"

My mom gives me the dinner choice since I have a sore throat and a cold. I feel like I am drowning in mucus. My appetite isn't well right now, and earlier, we went to my pediatrician. He checked me out and called my CF doctor. I am put on an oral antibiotic to try and avoid the cold from going into a lung infection, but I think it's already in my lungs. My pediatrician heard the mucus crackling, and he tells us he hears some plugs also. My doctor has also put me on three chest PTs per day, which will most likely be for the next couple of weeks. It is important to get the mucus out of my lungs so that it doesn't settle and cause a bigger lung infection which could lead to permanent damage. Currently, my lung function is in the high seventies, which is my baseline, and my doctor is happy with that. I still must work hard every day to maintain that function.

Keeping this function is a daily challenge, especially when I have a cold, but playing sports has helped it a lot and has even increased my overall function. I see other people my age getting sick with CF that aren't as healthy as I am. One of the young boys named Clay, whose family we are friends with from the CF walk hasn't been attending the walk. I know he has unfortunately lost his battle to

CF. The thought of knowing Clay is no longer with us scares me and shows me just how important it is to find a cure. The thought of him passing replays in my head each time I am sick, and I can only imagine how he must have felt. I imagine that all this thick mucus must clog your lungs to the point where you can no longer breathe. I can only imagine how that felt for him and how his family feels, but I do know that Jesus loves children, and he must be comforting him right now. Clay was younger than I am. My parents have no idea that I am aware that he has passed.

One afternoon, while Mom was showering, I was home sick from school; and I was looking in Mom's Bible. I found a memorial card in between the pages. As I looked at the name on the card, my heart sank into my stomach. This was Clay's memorial card. I held it in my hands, stared at it for a couple minutes, and could not believe it. My parents and doctor tell me that if I don't do my therapies, I can become very sick, which I know, in a nice way, means that I could die. CF is feeling very real to me at the moment. Knowing CF is terminal is one thing, but to know I have lost friends to CF hits much different. It's moments like these that shape us into who we are.

A week passes by, and a couple of days after being home from school, sick, I return. Francesco has been bringing home my homework and classwork each day, so I am able to keep up with it. Especially with the "Gestapo" teacher I have this year, falling behind isn't an option. I hope I can stay out of the hospital or this will be a miserable school year for me. My friends have warned me that the workload is way too much.

After doing a week and a half of extra therapies, I am exhausted and just need a rest and relaxation day. My doctor advised me to stay home from school to catch up on some rest and to return after the weekend. Mom sees how exhausted I am, and she let me stay home today to sleep in and rest an extra day. On Monday, I will be going to school, so I have some time to catch up and get all of my assignments done.

*****

MOMENTS OF IMPACT

It is Monday night, and I am finishing my second therapy nice and early. I shut the nebulizer off and I go back to pretending to be a teacher and write on my little chalkboard in our living room. I enjoy my favorite sucking candy, a starlight mint before dinner. My mother bought me the five hundred count of mints from the Price Club, and I am eating them like they are going out of style, but Mom does limit me. Mom is cooking one of my favorite dinners tonight: roast beef and mashed potatoes.

Ring, ring, ring. I ask my mom who it is. She says, "The caller ID is reading Saint Vincent's Medical Center." It must be about one of my appointments or something CF related. "Hello!" My mother is on the phone no more than a few minutes, and within seconds, she is tearing up and pretty sad. She thanks whoever she is talking to for calling and hangs up. I am behind the half wall in the living room and just stare at her for a few seconds from far away. I then walk quietly into the kitchen. I hope it is not what I think it is, but I am prepared for the worst.

My mother looks at me with tears in her eyes and says, "That was Dr. G." And she said, "Dr. Jay has passed away."

I hesitate moving closer and respond, "What happened?"

She says, "Issues with his liver and kidneys from CF."

I nod my head. I had no idea that CF also can affect the liver and kidneys. *Wow, this disease impacts so many organs.* I quietly make my way back into the living room and hide my tears behind the half wall that divides the kitchen from the living room. I now feel like the rainy weather outside and my tear ducts are raining like the November clouds right outside our window. I am sure so many are mourning his loss. He was one of a kind and so special. This is a feeling I will never forget. It's not just a bad memory but an entire feeling.

Dinner is ready, but I don't have much of an appetite. My parents are upset, of course, even though it was sort of expected. It still doesn't make things any easier. After dinner tonight, I lay in my bed, praying like I do every night and talking to God as I listen to the rain hit the windows. I can't believe my "angel doctor" is gone. I'm still trying to figure out what being gone means. I hope he believed in Jesus. I will never see him again and never get to thank him for the care he has given me. We always thanked him after each appointment. Another person with CF has lost their battle, and he was the closest person with CF to me. He is also the oldest one I personally knew. To think he was a doctor that studied this and he couldn't even save himself from CF, this shows me that we aren't in control of our lives. And when it is our time, we have to go. I can't believe that we can do everything right and still not live.

I lie in bed and think to myself, *When we are gone, where do we go?* I am taught that Christian people go to heaven but is it a real place? *How do we know our loved ones made it there okay?* I am taught our spirits go to heaven, but what is a spirit? *Is it our hearts and what's inside of us?* This is a lot to try and understand, and I get exhausted trying to figure it out. I guess one day, it will all make sense.

I know God is real. I talk to him each and every night, and he has helped me get through the toughest time in my life when my parents separated. I spoke to him daily. I never heard his voice, but I knew he was hearing me and helping me. As the weeks go by, I think about Dr. Jay often, and his strength gives me the strength to push through every day. He worked so hard and became a doctor, and I am inspired by him. I remember what he said about not taking shortcuts when it comes to my therapies. I know if I take his advice, then I have somewhat of a chance to live until the age of forty like he did. Forty is pretty old. I could hear his voice saying, "Jillian, the most important thing is your therapies. Do not skip them, even when you are tired. You must do them."

A few days later, my parents leave Francesco and I with my grandparents as they go to Manhattan for the wake. When they return home, they don't look too great, and you can tell this sucked the energy out of them.

*****

It is Saturday morning, and I have a basketball game tonight at our school. It is nice to play on our home court. I like playing where I practice as most teams do. I am used to this court, even though running on the tile isn't as comfortable as running on hardwood, especially when falling on the floor or diving for the ball.

My father's new friend, Joe, has stopped by Nanie and Grandpa's house. I am sitting at the table, having pancakes with Nanie and Dad. Joe has joined us for coffee, and the adults are talking. I am eating and drawing in my notepad. I enjoy drawing in my spare time, but I am by no means an artist. I try to draw the body and feet of one cartoon and attach it to the head of another. I laugh because my drawings look so funny. I am not very artistic, but I find it relaxing.

Nanie's pancakes are my favorite, covered in a lot of butter and syrup. After eating, I head into the living room to watch some TV and continue drawing. In the kitchen, I hear Joe say, "Jim, my son likes your daughter." He laughs and he says, "Michael says Jill's cute."

Dad looks at Joe and lets out a tiny chuckle, but I could tell my dad doesn't take what he says too seriously. I am a bit shocked that Joe just said that to my dad, but I am not too shocked at what he said. I am in more shock that Michael told his dad this. Michael is supposed to come to my game tonight, and we normally hang out after games, so I am wondering if he is going to say anything to me.

As I head into the kitchen to say goodbye to Joe, to my surprise, he tells me, "Sweety, my son likes you. He thinks you are cute."

I am even more taken back now he has said this to me, and I don't know how to respond. I just give a tiny smile and think to myself, *Why in the world did he just say that?* Nanie sits there and smiles because, truthfully, I don't think she thinks anything of it either. Nanie starts cleaning up the kitchen table. This is all new and a bit awkward for me. I am not sure how to act in this kind of situation. Do I smile or just show no expression? I decide to just go with the flow and not say anything and pretend I have no idea.

It is game time, and my team hits the court at 1:00 p.m. today. All of my family is in the bleachers, and Joe's family is there sitting next to them. Michael is right in front with his black and red sweat suit and matching Jordan sneakers. I was never a fan of Jordan sneakers, but they are starting to grow on me a bit. I wave to Michael and hear him say, "Go, Jill!"

My teammates look at me and ask, "Who is that boy, Jill?"

"He is a friend. His brother and my brother are friends."

One of the girls happens to know Joe but not Michael. She says, "His dad is very nice."

I say, "I agree. They are very nice people. We have hung out with them a bunch of times."

The girl on my team that starts as the other guard with me says, "I think he likes you, plus he's cute."

I smile at her and say, "We will talk later." The whistle blows, and the ball is up in the air. Our tallest girl tips the ball to me, and I pass the ball down near our basket to the other guard, and within seconds, she goes for a layup, and we score. We are up by two points and then four and then six. We keep this momentum up the entire game. Our team plays well together. So far, we are undefeated, but we will be playing the better teams in December and into the new year. I finished the game with eight points.

After shaking hands with the other team, Michael comes over to me. He says, "You are pretty good and probably better than me and most of the boys on my team. We should play one-on-one soon and see if I can beat you."

I say, "Yes, that would be fun." I am always up for a challenge, especially against the boys. They are always bigger and stronger than I am. Deep down, I think I can beat him, but he doesn't think I can. I hate to burst his bubble. If I can play against the boys, then I can definitely keep up with the girls. I am looking forward to the one-on-one challenge with him, but that probably won't happen until the nicer weather gets closer so we can play outside. It is tough to get gym time indoors. Our gym is always being used for something.

After the game, everyone comes back to our house to have some pizza. The adults hang out and have coffee upstairs, and we go into the basement and hang out there. We play Nintendo 64 and then hide-and-seek in the dark. We don't play your typical hide-and-seek. We set up traps and make it difficult for our brothers to find us. Our brothers fall quite a few times and get hurt. When it is our turn to seek, let's just say payback is not fun. I trip a few times and hit the basement carpet. I end the night with a few bruises on my knees, but

I guess that is what I get for wanting to keep up with the boys. I am thinking about what will be a good trap for the next time we play.

Every time I go to my CF specialist, if she notices a bruise, she will ask me how I got it. I always respond that basketball or soccer caused it because that is where they are from. This situation is a bit different because they are caused by the traps we set up during hide-and-seek. I have a checkup this week, and I hope she doesn't notice the ones on both knees and my elbows. My doctor will probably laugh and tell me I am a crazy girl but mean it in a fun way. I don't think my parents would be too happy knowing we were pretty much injuring one another in their house. I am not good at lying and don't like to lie, so I will have to spill the beans. Hide-and-seek was kind of dangerous, but we all couldn't stop laughing at each other when someone would fall. After all, Michael and I were the ones that started the trap idea. I don't know why, but watching people fall makes me laugh, even though in reality, it isn't all that funny.

*****

A few days go by. We park the car and head up to the office for my CF checkup. I am excited to see what my lung function will show. I love the challenge of doing the Pulmonary Function Test and seeing how long I can blow air out of my lungs for. I believe the longer you blow out air for, the better your function is. Besides having the cold a few weeks ago, I am feeling pretty well. I am still having that burning pain in my stomach, and lately, when I eat something, it doesn't go away.

When I was at Nanie's, I saw her taking a liquid medication out of the refrigerator, and I asked her what it was. She told me it is called Gaviscon, and it helps with acid reflux. She tells me the acid reflux gives her burning in her throat and in her stomach underneath her rib cage. I told her I think I have been having the same type of burning pain and that sometimes, pretzels help me feel better. Later on, she explained to my parents what I said I was feeling, and we are going to mention it to my doctor today.

We enter the waiting area, and as we sit, I look at the toys that are in the office from a distance. My parents tell me to not even think about touching them. I tell them I know, and then I think to myself that I am a bit too old for them anyway. Within minutes, I am called in. First, my nurse takes my height, weight, and oxygen, and then it is pulmonary function time. The respiratory therapist hooks the mouthpiece to the large tubing. I take a seat on the bench with the wheels. I scoot myself close to the machine, giving myself enough room to move the tubing around. The mouthpiece tastes like the plastic bag it just came out of, similar to when I open up a new nebulizer cup. I don't like using the nose clips that most of the other patients use. I like holding my nose during the PFTs.

I squeeze my nose tight with my left hand; that way, there is no air flow coming in and out of my nostrils. In my right hand is the mouthpiece, and my lips are sealed tightly around it so that no air is lost. After inhaling deep, I exhale as fast and as strong as I can into the mouthpiece. I blow air out until my lungs are completely empty and my face turns beet red. "Keep going, keep going, keep going," says the respiratory therapist. I inhale for a few seconds and then release my nose and take the mouthpiece out of my mouth. "Very good, Jillian, you are doing great!"

I look at my parents who are standing in the doorway and watching me give it my best effort. They are smiling also. I know they are quietly cheering me on, but sometimes it can feel strange when everyone is watching you. I have two more to go, and each time, I try and exhale a little bit longer. I try to see if I can increase the amount of air I blow out each time. As I finish my second attempt, my doctor walks in and is smiling at me. I didn't notice at first she was standing there too, but when I did, I smiled. She tells me to not pay any mind to her and that she is just seeing the numbers. She says, "Pretty good so far."

My parents had stepped outside when she came in, and I heard them ask her, "How is she doing?"

She says, "Very good. We will discuss them in a bit."

The next time I exhale for 0.3 seconds longer, and I am happy, and the third time I plateau at seven seconds of exhaling. I ask my doctor, "The longer I exhale, then that means I did better, right?"

She says, "Not necessarily. We don't look at that number too much. We look at the FEV1 which tells us your overall lung function, and we also look at the lower airways."

My lung function isn't measured by how long I exhale. It is actually measured by the first second of exhaling, which is called the FEV1. This is a challenge against myself each time and also me against CF. Today is my first day actually understanding how my lung function is measured. The PFT results are printed, and I am asked to take them into my room. I look at them quickly as I go into the room and don't understand a thing. This is like a whole new language.

Dr. G comes in and starts talking to me about school and basketball. She tells me my numbers are up and look great and to keep playing basketball. She tells me to make sure I eat a lot of calories as always and to have salty foods and drink Gatorade. She tells me that I lose a lot of salt when sweating and that it must be replaced afterward and during. I am becoming more involved in the details of my disease. I nod my head yes and smile.

Before examining me, she and the nurse sit and talk about my health and a lot of other things. As I sit there, listening to Dr. G and my parents, I get hungry and take out some snacks. One of my favorite sweets is Swedish fish. I offer my doctor and nurse some, and they accept and thank us. A part of my CF doctor appointments includes eating snacks and sharing with the staff at the office. My parents always bring enough for everyone. We also always bring them goodies around Christmas time. It's sort of become a tradition.

She examines my belly after listening to my lungs, and my parents and I tell her about the burning feeling I am having. Right away, she says, "You have acid reflux. A lot of CF patients have it. It isn't uncommon, and we will figure it out." She asks me how long I have been feeling like this, and I say quite a while. She asks, "Why haven't you told me?"

"I didn't know how to explain it. I thought I was just hungry and that the burning was from not eating soon enough."

She prescribes Prevacid and says, "I want to send you to a gastro doctor here who can go in there with a camera and see what is going on. He is one floor up in this same building."

We agree to see him, and Mom puts the new prescription paper in her bag as she writes all of this down in her marble notebook along with the gastro doctor's info. My doctor tells us that my lungs sound great and that I am doing very well. The one thing I struggle with is gaining weight, and the nutritionist meets with us to try and give us ideas on how to gain weight and what to eat to add extra calories to each day.

I am happy to go home with good news today. I am always tired after doctor appointments, and the car ride home puts me to sleep before we even leave Long Island. I now get my care in Long Island since my doctor has switched CF centers. She was the director in Manhattan and has chosen to now work closer to her home.

*****

It is the middle of November, and that means Thanksgiving is very soon. I am looking forward to relaxing and seeing my family, especially since we are going to New Jersey to my cousin's house. We have music class once per week in our school, and our music teacher is scheduled to come in today. I am pretty sure we will be practicing the usual Thanksgiving songs for the Thanksgiving service that we have in a few weeks. Every student is asked to bring in nonperishable food for the food drive, and we usually sing songs together. The songs are about how God will provide for the less fortunate through our offerings.

Our music class is our last class for the day. Our music teacher enters the room and hands out the words to the music. It has been a year since we have sung these songs. He tells us that he needs two people from each class to get up in front of the school to sing the verses that are on the sheet. He explains that together, the whole school will sing the chorus. I don't remember my teacher asking for people to individually try out singing the verses, but most likely, I may have been out sick. I am not one of those students with perfect attendance, and the fall and winter months are when I am sick the most. I enjoy singing, but I am not good at it. Only five people volunteer to try out, and my music teacher says, "Is that all? Anyone else want to give it a shot? It doesn't hurt to try, even if you have never sung before."

A few seconds go by, and then I decide to give it a try. I know I am not a singer, but I enjoy music and playing the piano, even though I have never taken lessons. I am the last one to sing the words, "When I was hungry, you gave me to eat. When I was thirsty, you gave me to drink. Now enter into the home of my people."

After class, my music teacher informs me that I did okay but that I am not one of the best and that I can try again next year. I say, "Okay, thank you." I don't take it very seriously. Singing and the arts isn't my thing. Sports are more my thing and where my heart truly is.

The weeks of November fly by quickly, and so does Thanksgiving. It was a lot of fun, and we spent it with all of my dad's family at my cousin's house. Our cousins decorated the house for Christmas already, so it was nice to see everything looking so magical. They put up two trees, and they also had the woodburning fireplace, which was really beautiful. We used to have a woodburning one, but my parents converted it to gas a few years ago. My cousin also added purple and blue coloring to the fire by putting in these scented sticks. It smelled like the holidays in their house.

I didn't want to leave, and not to mention, it started snowing too that day. As we were leaving, there we saw a few deer. The way they run is beautiful, especially with the snow flurries coming down. It felt like I was watching a Christmas movie scene.

Christmas will be coming soon, and I am excited. Christmas is my favorite holiday, and I love the entire holiday season that comes along with it. I love helping my family decorate and I love shopping and buying gifts for everyone. Each year, I start my Christmas shopping at the end of October and finish in November. That way, I can avoid the crowded stores. This time of year, there are too many germs floating around the stores, especially with it being flu season. My mom always makes sure we all get flu shots in September, but I know you can still catch the flu, so taking precautions is necessary.

This time of year is also a lot of fun in school for the third-grade classes. Every year, the third grade puts on a Christmas show, and this year, it is my class's turn. We will begin rehearsing next week, and before rehearsing, we are picking out which parts we want to play. After trying out for the Thanksgiving assembly singing part a few weeks ago and getting cut, I don't think I want a speaking part. Believe it or not, when we have the Thanksgiving food drive, no one really pays attention to the people singing anyway. When a play is taking place, everyone is silent in their seats and directs their attention to the stage. I am building up a bit of anxiety with speaking in front of such a large crowd. I prefer to take a part that doesn't involve speaking.

As the roles are being written on the chalkboard, I see a few parts that come to mind. We are going in alphabetical order to pick our parts, which I guess is fair, and that would leave me in the middle of the class to pick my part. The teacher gets to me, and I get my second choice. I am going to be a reindeer. There are a bunch of reindeer spots, and those fill up pretty quickly. Most of my classmates don't want a talking spot either, so the nontalking spots fill up quickly. Our job is to do a little dance and run across the stage. I think I can handle this.

I am told I will be the third reindeer named Prancer. I am glad I am not Rudolph or else I would have to have a big red nose that lights up, which I already get on my own about three to four times per year due to colds.

The next couple of weeks, my class practices for our play, and my mom brings me to the store to buy a brown sweatsuit and a pair of antlers. It is the day before the play, and unfortunately, I am running a fever, so I won't be participating in the play or going to school for the rest of the week. This is such a bummer. I was really looking forward to this.

Christmas and New Year's pass, and I am feeling much better and myself again. It takes me a bit of time to recover when I am sick. I am glad I am feeling better at the start of the new year. School has resumed again. It was nice to have a week and a half off. Since I was sick for Christmas, we stayed home, and our family came over for both Christmas and Christmas Eve.

February couldn't have come any faster. The month of January is gone already. During the month of February, my team is scheduled to play the top two teams in our league. Tonight, my team is playing against the first-place team. We played them earlier in the season and had lost. This will be the second time playing them, and we are determined to win or at least give them a fight. I always try to use my speed to my advantage, but their point guard is just as fast as I am. They also have pretty good shooters like we do, and they have a couple of tall girls, just like our team does. We met our match, but they are a bit more polished than us and more athletic.

Tonight, we are going back and forth with them and taking turns being in the lead by just a couple of points at most. It is the fourth quarter, and we are down by four points. My team decides to turn up our game in the final minute and give it our all. The ball is passed down low to one of our forwards, and she gets it in. That's two more points for us! We are now down by just one point! It is now their ball. We are in a man-to-man defense, and I am covering their best three-point shooter. My heart is beating out of my chest as I keep up and feel the adrenaline rush. I stay close to my girl, not letting her get the ball. My team keeps on them, and we stay close to our opponents, not allowing them to get open.

We manage to steal the ball back with just ten seconds remaining. They are still up by two, and this is probably the longest ten seconds in any of my games. Now my heart is really pounding. I quickly fix my sweatband and reposition it on my head. The ball is inbounded to the other guard, and I fly halfway up the court as the ball is passed to me. There is five seconds left as the ball is in my hands, and I dribble to the corner of the court, almost out of bounds, on the side line next to our basket. I am at the three-point line, and there isn't much time left. If I drive to the hoop, their forward will be waiting to stuff me.

Here it goes. I square up my body as best as I can and take a three-point jumper right behind the line. I hope my feet aren't touching out of bounds or go over the three-point line. Swish! The buzzer sounds, and the scoreboard lights up red. It goes in. I am in shock, and I hug my teammates in excitement for beating the best team in our age group. Everyone is cheering and clapping, and I can hear my family yelling. They are sitting at the bleachers in the corner right where I took my final shot for the night. I cannot believe it as I clap and jump up in the air and into my teammates' arms.

We line up to shake the other team's hands. They are in tears as we shake their hands, and we say, "Good game" to each other, but they barely mumble back to us as their heads are down. I happen to know some of them, and I cannot believe they are crying and acting like such sore losers. After all, it is just a game, and my team is usually the ones losing. I can tell you we don't act like that when we lose. I guess when you are expecting to win, it could be upsetting or possibly shocking. Who would know better in life than I that nothing is guaranteed and that expectations are disappointing at times? Maybe I just have different priorities than others my age.

I hope after today's match-up they learn to never underestimate the underdogs. Anyone can win at any time if you play hard enough, and we just happened to play a little bit harder tonight. It felt great to beat them, but whether we won or not, I had fun, and it was a great competitive game. I walk over to my family, and they hug and kiss me and tell me I played well. Nana and Grandpa have the biggest smiles on their faces. Nana says, "I wish Nanie was here today. She would have loved to see this."

I nod in agreement and say, "It's okay."

*****

It is Sunday, and I am still on a high from the night before from hitting the winning shot, but I am busy all day doing schoolwork and studying. As I strap on my black nylon therapy vest and click all of the buckles closed and tighten them around my chest, I grab all of my schoolbooks that I will need to study. It is annoying to have to start and then stop and disconnect my vest machine, so I like to get everything I need ahead of time. It is a great time to study while

I do my therapy since I can't do much. When the vest is going, it's difficult to hear the TV without disrupting the entire house. I can listen to music, but it's best to use my Walkman. NBA games are doable with my vest since I don't need to hear what the broadcasters are saying.

I have a lot of studying to catch up on, and so my nighttime therapy finished quickly. This month, I am inhaling a newer medication called TOBI, which is an inhaled antibiotic that was recently FDA approved. This is done after my chest PT, and it takes fifteen to twenty minutes to complete through the nebulizer. It is done twice per day after each therapy session. It helps keep the bacteria in my lungs controlled. My doctor believes I won't need as many oral antibiotic courses, and hopefully, I won't need to go back to the hospital anytime soon for IV antibiotics. After my medical regimen and dinner, it is time to shower and get ready for bed again.

*****

The school week is already here, and I cannot wait for next weekend again. Monday and Wednesday evenings, my team has practice for one and a half hours, and I am looking forward to that. Basketball helps break up the school week monotony, and I have made some new friends this year on my team that I really enjoy being with. It is Friday night, and Francesco's team has a home game which is nice. It is cold out, and I am tired from the school week, so it is nice to be close to home tonight. I am glad we don't have to travel across the island. It's Francesco's last regular season game, and their next game will be a playoff game. Our playoff games will be starting next week also, and I am pumped up to see how far we go.

After Francesco's game, we are hungry and so we decide to go to our favorite diner, which is only a few minutes away. My parents decided to invite Michael's family. We arrive at the diner, and they are pretty busy, but they have a few tables left. One of the larger booths can squeeze six people, but four fit comfortably. There is another tiny booth right next to the larger booth that will only fit two. "Jillian and

Michael can sit there," says our brothers as they point to the small booth and laugh.

Within seconds, our brothers are the first to be sitting in the big booth, and of course, our parents weren't going to fit in the small one. Michael and I sit in the tiny booth across from each other. I look at our brothers and say, "Are you sure you guys don't want to sit here?"

They say, "No, we will look like we are on a date with each other."

Michael and I laugh, but that is just what Michael and I look like. The waitress comes over to our table and asks what we would like to drink. She then asks us, "Are you guys by yourselves?"

I look up, and it is one of the waitresses I know. My family knows all of them. I smile at our waitress and say, "Hello, Iris."

She laughs and says, "Hi, hun." She points and says, "You kids are with them?"

I nod and say, "Yup."

Iris returns with our drinks.

Michael laughs and says to me, "She thought we were on a date."

I say, "Yup, but then she realized we were with them. I've known her for quite a while now."

A little while later, our burgers come out. I have a turkey burger with a Greek salad, and he has the typical cheeseburger with fries. I am starving and take a bite into my burger. It is delicious and juicy, and it goes perfect on the pita bread with ketchup. As we eat our food and hang out, we talk about life. Michael tells me to take some of his fries because he isn't going to eat them all, so I steal a couple. They are delicious. We both agree that they have the best diner fries around.

I laugh and say, "They are pretty much covered in lard. My dad says the same thing about the fries when we come here."

We both finish eating, and it is pouring outside. As I traced the raindrops with my eyes falling down the windows, our parents are enjoying some dessert and coffee. The diner was almost empty, and there was only one other table with people sitting at it. Michael asks me to go sit by the other booth closer to the entrance. The waitress gives us permission to sit at the window seats. Michael tells me the reason he wants to switch seats is so he can ask me something in private. I am not sure what he has to ask me, but I am interested to know. He says, "Valentine's Day is next week. So I was wondering if you have a valentine."

I say, "No, but are you serious?"

He laughs and says, "Yes, I'm serious."

I say, "What about you?"

He says, "No, that's why I am asking you. I would like for you to be mine."

I say, "Sure. Who else did you think would be?"

He says, "I know, but I just wanted to know."

I slightly nod my head and give a small laugh. I tell him, "I'm surprised you asked me this."

And he says, "Who else would you think would be my valentine?"

As we talk, I keep looking over to the other table. Everyone over there is having their own conversations, and they are laughing and not paying any mind to us. I am happy they aren't listening to us, but I did already know he liked me, and his parents know also. I'm not sure if mine really know anything.

As time passes, I am starting to have an interest in him too. I always have a great time when we are together, and all we do is have fun. We literally are always laughing and joking around. It is different from when I am with my other male friends. I sit at the table in a daze for a few seconds, just zoning out. I am pretty tired since it's almost 12:00 a.m. He sees I am zoning out and says, "Jill, we could forget about the whole Valentine's Day thing."

I say, "No, I am fine."

Michael says, "What I really mean is will you be my girlfriend?"

And I say, "Yes." I think to myself, *Why me out of all girls?* Then I ask, "Why me out of all the girls? I am a tomboy, and you are cute. I am not a girly girl at all. I never have my hair down or dress up if it isn't an occasion. Wouldn't you want to be with a girl that's like a cheerleader or a dancer?"

He says, "No, that's what I like about you. You are cute and sporty, and I have a lot of fun with you. You are different in a good way. You aren't like the other girls." He then imitates the girly girls and says, "I don't want a girl that says, 'Oh my gosh, my nail broke!'"

I nod my head up and down and say, "I get it," and I start laughing about the nail thing.

He says, "You can play sports with me and ride scooters and bikes. When I get a motorized bike with gas, you won't be afraid to ride on the back of it with me like most girls would be."

I see what he is saying and I would love riding on a motorized bike, but that won't be for a while. I am not old enough. I think you have to be eighteen to ride a moped. I may be into sports, but I do like boys, and I like him. I agree to be his "girlfriend," whatever that means for an almost nine-year-old and an almost ten-year-old. I am shocked to hear that there are boys that like girls that play sports. At my school, the boys like the cheerleaders and the girls that do dance, not the athletes.

Basketball season has come to an end, and my team finished in third place this year. We made it to the second round of the playoffs, but we unfortunately didn't make it to the championship game. My coach has informed me of a league called Amateur Athletic Union (AAU), which is travel basketball for those looking to play on a much more competitive level. I am excited to try out for one of the teams this year. I am told there are a couple of AAU teams on Staten Island, but I guess we will decide where I will be trying out in about a month and a half.

This year is also a big school year for me. It is the state English and math exams, and my health has not been the best toward the end of this winter into the spring. I am having a lot of digestion issues this week. The medications I take to help me go to the bathroom aren't working. I have not had a bowel movement in five days, which is a long time for someone with CF. Every day, I take laxative pills and liquids to help me use the bathroom, and nothing is working. I am worried and in excruciating pain that is wrapping into my back, not to mention I am extremely nauseous with no appetite.

My doctor has prescribed other liquid laxatives, and none of them are doing the trick, so I have an appointment tomorrow with radiology to get a barium enigma. The GI doctor that I go to is going to do the procedure, and I am not looking forward to it, but I am looking forward to not being in this type of pain any longer. Each day, the pain has gotten worse and worse.

It is bright and early, and right after my chest PT and nebulizers, which is almost impossible to even complete, we are on the road and out to Long Island. I hope we don't hit traffic, but the chances of no traffic are pretty much impossible. I am getting used to coming to Long Island. I miss the staff at my old center. It felt like my second home, but I am getting used to coming here now. I'm sure soon this office will feel like a second home to me. I also miss the tall buildings and the busy streets. Switching centers feels like I have closed a chapter of my life. I left the sadness of losing my doctor, but I will never forget him. I always wonder what he would think of my lung function and how I am doing overall.

It is a new beginning for me. I know it won't always be filled with happiness as I am getting older, and CF is a progressive illness, but I will do my best to stay as healthy as I can. Of course, we hit traffic almost the entire way, and sitting in the car is making the abdominal pain worse. I am in the most pain sitting down, let alone sitting for a couple of hours straight in the same position. I feel better walking or lying down, but still, I only get minimal relief.

As we arrive, we ask the receptionist where to go. We are directed to take the elevator to the second floor of the children's hospital. I am trying to not make a peep and remain quiet, but my face says it all. I just look and feel defeated at this point, and let's face it, I am actually full of poop! My mother tells me to take a seat, and I give her a look. Is she crazy? I can't sit any longer than I have been.

I decide to stay right outside of the waiting room. The waiting area is full of small children and babies. The TV is playing *Blues Clues* on it, and I am pacing in the hallway as I wait for them to call my name. Dad is in the hallway with me, and I can see he doesn't know what to say. Nothing can help right now. The sun is shining in the center of the building in the courtyard, which is right where I am staring into. Dad waits with me and sits on the windowsill while Mom waits for my name to be called in the middle of that chaotic waiting area.

We only wait about fifteen minutes, and I am called in. As I laugh, I think to myself maybe I will get scared and poop my pants before they call me, which would be beneficial at the moment. I never want to poop my pants, but this time would possibly be a good time to do so.

I am told to change into the hospital gown and then lie on my stomach with the gown opened to the back. I do not want my butt sticking out, but it seems I have no choice at the moment. My doctor is holding a huge plastic tube attached to a big bag of saline. It looks like the IV saline bags in the hospital, just ten times the size. As I lay down and watch them get a few supplies ready, I am trying to figure out exactly what is going to happen. My doctor begins explaining to me that he will be inserting the plastic tube into my butt, and then he is going to watch the fluid go into my intestines on the screen. He says, "Once it is all in your intestines and the bag is empty, then I can remove the tubing, and you will be able to poop in a little while. You should be able to use the bathroom normal afterward."

He tells me I will feel better, but I cannot imagine how having a tube put in my butt will make me feel better. As he tells me this information, my eyes widen, and it sounds like it is going to hurt a lot rather than make me feel better. All I could think about right now is climbing off of this table and running out of the office. The table is being raised, and I cannot even look at the oversize bag of fluid hanging from the pole. How is that entire bag going inside of me? I already feel overly full.

I am lying on my stomach, and within minutes, the doctor inserts the hard plastic tubing into my butt. I am yelling and want to turn around and rip out the tubing. I tell the doctor I am in a lot of pain, and next comes the medical tape. My butt cheeks are now taped together, holding the tubing in place. I want to laugh at the fact that my cheeks are taped—because let's be real, it's funny—but I can't. I'm in too much pain. I am hoping this goes quickly, but all of that fluid still has to go into my intestines.

I still can't figure out where it's all going. There is no room. There has to be a better way than this. My doctor tells me I am doing well and that the rest of the procedure isn't too bad. I am enraged and

I cannot help myself and say to my doctor, "It's not bad? Well, why don't you stick it up your butt?"

He looks at me and starts laughing. My parents aren't too happy with my response, and they yell at me saying, "Jillian, that's not nice!" They understand that I am in pain, and I see them chuckle a bit too along with the doctor.

My CF doctor also stops in during the procedure, and she is smiling and tells me how wonderful I am doing. She happened to walk in at just the right time to hear my "stick it up your butt" comment. She is hysterical, laughing and laughing harder than anyone else in the room. I am not happy to see everyone smiling while I am so uncomfortable, but if I was in their position, I would have laughed too.

I overhear my parents apologizing to the GI doctor, but he is still laughing and says, "Don't worry about it."

I am a little embarrassed. I am embarrassed about having to sit in this gown with my butt sticking out and the fact that I just said what I did to my doctor. It is extremely painful to be lying on my bloated abdomen, and I just couldn't hold my tongue. I know I was wrong, but it just came out.

The fluid takes about thirty minutes to go into my intestines, and then it is time to wait to use the bathroom, but things are moving very, very slowly. Nothing has happened yet. It is Friday afternoon, so it is quiet at the hospital. I have the room and bathroom to myself in the outpatient hospital area. My dad went to the gift shop earlier and got me a busy board, which is pretty much a dry-erase board with games on it. My mom is sitting in the bathroom with me and keeping me busy by playing games while we wait for the fluid to do the job. I really feel like my abdomen is going to explode, and I didn't even know it was possible for my abdomen to extend this much. It looks like a pregnant woman's belly.

Three hours pass by, and nothing is moving. My doctor and parents are in shock that I haven't been able to use the bathroom yet. With rush hour traffic, we have a two and a half to three-hour drive home from Long Island. How long am I supposed to sit on the toilet bowl? My legs and butt are numb, and I can barely feel them. We decide to take our chances and get in the car, especially that I don't have any urge to go to the bathroom. To be honest, I am very good at holding in stool, which may be the reason I am in this situation to begin with. I hate using public bathrooms and refuse to use them. I never use the bathroom at school. I prefer to sit in pain all day while in class and suffer until I am in my own house. Even after this experience, I am still against public restrooms. I guess I will never change.

We get on the road, and the traffic is horrendous, bumper-to-bumper the entire way. Everyone is impatient, honking their horns, and it looks like a big parking lot. This is resembling my intestines, completely stagnant with no movement. Sitting in the car again is tough for me and even more painful than before. I am now overly bloated and probably double the size I was prior. I am feeling even more nauseous too. It is difficult to stay in a seated position for this long.

Three long hours go by, and we arrive safe and sound in our driveway. Thank God we are home. I dozed off a bit on the way home which helped me ignore the pain for a few minutes. We are all happy to be home. It has been a very long day, and I am pretty tired. I have that exhausting feeling after you fall asleep in the car for a small catnap and wake up confused, not knowing where you are and what is happening. It is chest PT time, and luckily, after being home for a bit, the fluids kick in, and my intestines start working again. Thank you, God, for allowing things to work. I don't know how I would have gotten through tonight without using the bathroom.

I spend most of my night on the toilet bowl and am no longer full of poop. I run back and forth about twelve times between the bathroom and the family room. While I sit in the family room, my parents ask me what I would like my new bathroom to look like. It is a perfect night to discuss bathroom designs after spending all day and night in the bathroom. If I don't know what I like in a bathroom by now, then I never will.

I tell them I want it to have lavender purple in it. I am not sure about the tile design, but after Mom shows me a few ideas, I decide on the pastel coloring and tulip flower tile border for the shower. I tell them that I want white ceramic tile for the floor and a white vanity if possible. As I mentioned earlier, my dad and grandfather are builders, and my parents are building a new home for us too. We plan to move into it by next year.

I am excited to move into a bigger house where my brother and I will have our own bathrooms connected to our bedrooms. We will no longer have to argue over the hallway bathroom. I like to call our hallway bathroom my bathroom, and I always lock Francesco out of it. I tell him to use my parents' bathroom in their room.

My parents show me a few tile samples, and I love the white glossy ones to match the tulip design. I am more excited about picking out towels and other accessories, but my parents explain to me that first we need to finalize the tiles and bathtub color as well as the cabinetry before we could do anything else. Originally, I wasn't going to be able to have my own bathroom, but my parent's new walk-in closet is so large that they are able to cut a part of it out to make me a full bathroom. My parents are always creative, and they do their best to use all of the space properly when building a house. They told me that they don't need a closet the size of a bedroom and that making a bathroom for me is possible.

I am excited and cannot wait to see how our new home comes out. My dad and grandpa build houses pretty quick, and they don't waste time, so I could see how moving in a year or even earlier is possible. Dad is also very handy and does a lot of the work himself if he can. He usually works at the job after he finishes at his other job and on the weekends.

A couple of weeks have gone by. It is the second week in March, and that means it is time for AAU tryouts. My parents look into the two teams on Staten Island, and I have decided to try out for the PAL Diamonds. Tryouts are being held in a school gymnasium about a half hour from my house. They are tonight from 6:00 to 8:00 p.m. Wow, two hours straight of tryouts.

I can tell this is going to be challenging and most likely involve a lot of running. My normal practices are about an hour and a half. As I get my gym bag ready with everything I need, I must not forget my inhaler and plenty of water and Gatorade. Without my inhaler, I will be doomed. If I don't do my inhaler twenty minutes before the tryouts begin, then it will be clear that I cannot keep up with the others. I have always been able to outrun most people my age, and I hope I can keep up tonight. My parents will be there just in case I don't feel well, but I am determined to make this team.

My dad gets home from work just in time, and Mom and I are ready to leave. It is too early for dinner, but I just finished having a sandwich, so I am fueled up. We arrive, and the gym is packed with about forty to fifty girls. They are running around, warming up, and getting in as many practice shots as they can before it officially starts. The gym lights are sort of dull, giving off an orange tint. It is pretty stuffy in here too, so the doors are open to try and give us some air. The air is stagnant, and the open doors aren't doing much.

The coaches blow the whistle and ask all of us to sit down at center court. They introduce themselves, and so far, they seem like nice people. The parents all get very quiet and are watching center court closely. We are split up into two groups, and we start off doing a few drills to warm up. First, we start with layups, and then a three-person weave. Then comes some dribbling drills, and last, we do the Mikan Drill before scrimmaging. The coaches then ask us which positions we play on our CYO teams, and they divide us into a bunch of smaller teams. I am the second smallest here, but height means nothing.

I see a lot of familiar faces, mostly people from the teams I have played against this past season. Now I know why the older girls from my school know the girls on the other CYO teams in their age group. They must play AAU with them during the off-season. It is pretty cool that all of the teams come together to represent their hometowns in this league.

A couple of people are here from my team, and I hang out with them. The bully is also here, but I do my best and keep my distance. The most we say to one another is hello. I hope she is not on my scrimmage team and that she doesn't wind up on the same AAU team as I. I guess only time will tell who plays for which team.

Time is an important aspect in life. It plays a part in everything. From the basketball shot clock to the amount of time in a day as well as the times for medical care and also times for fun. Having fun times are my favorite. I am also learning that time may be against me and not in my favor. As the time passes, we get older, and CF also gets older and progresses, but I am not going to let it stop me from achieving my goals. So, today, I am here to play ball and hopefully get a spot on the Diamonds.

We are divided into teams, and I am teamed with four other girls that I have never met before. It is nice to play with different people for once. I hold my own and am able to keep up with the others. I play the point guard position and am able to run the ball up the court and get it to the open girl to score. I also take a few shots and get some in as well and make it to the foul line for some free throws. It takes some time getting used to the way the others play, and after a little while, we are all getting to know how one another plays. Two strenuous hours have passed, and I come off of the court, drenched. I am dripping in sweat, and my skin is pretty salty too. I can taste the salt in my mouth as it drips down my face.

The coaches tell us that we all played hard and that they will be calling our houses to let us know if we made the team or not. If I made the team, the season would begin in the middle of April.

*****

A few days later, the phone rings. "Hello, this is the coach from the Diamonds. Can we speak to Jillian please?"

I get on the phone and say, "Hello."

"Hi, Jillian, it is Coach calling to let you know you have made the AAU Diamonds team."

"Wow, really? Thank you so much!"

"Great job! Congratulations! Can we speak to one of your parents, please?"

I pass the phone to my mother, and I hear her talking with my coach, and after a few minutes, she is off the phone and informs me that practice will start in about a month. I am excited and cannot believe I made the team. There were a lot of girls, and it was competitive. We sit down for dinner after Dad gets home from work, and we are all excited about me making the team.

I finish the school week with a big smile on my face, and I am motivated to do even better in school; however, I am struggling a bit in English class, and reading comprehension isn't my strong point. I am not interested in reading about subjects I have no interest in. I don't understand why they don't choose something more interesting to read about. Halfway through reading these passages, I feel like I have to go back and reread what I already read. I know there are a handful of my classmates also struggling with the same things as me. I am not sure if I am having issues reading and comprehending or if I just don't want to comprehend something I have no interest in. There are so many other important things happening outside of our classroom windows.

For instance, I must have heard two to three sirens today. I am sure someone not too far was having an emergency. When I hear a siren, I always stop what I am doing and pray to God and ask him to watch and protect those involved. It doesn't matter to me if I am in the middle of a math problem or a reading passage. I will stop what I am doing for a couple of seconds to pray. This makes my attention focus on what is really important in life. I don't think the square root of a number is the most important thing to learn in life, but in our classroom, it's pretty important. We are taught to pray for others, and so I do.

Praying is also the reason why I believe I am still here today and doing fairly well. I have so many family members and friends that have been praying for me since the day I was diagnosed with CF, and I am very thankful for that. I wonder how many people actually take time out of their day to pray for what is really important. I do take the classroom as important, but my mind seems to always wander a bit, and at times, I run out of time on exams. I always seem to be able to rush through math and do well, but reading takes me a bit longer, and when I am not interested or become distracted, the time runs out pretty fast.

I know when I take the state exams, this will become a problem for me, but I will deal with it when the problem arises in a couple of months. Life is too short, and anything can happen before then, so I don't want to worry about the state tests now. I am currently receiving extra help along with about a dozen of my classmates for reading comprehension, and I am not noticing a difference. Not to mention I hate to read books. I am also paired up with a fifth-grade student twice per week who sits and has me read with her instead of going out to play at recess. We don't really read too much. I happen to know her from basketball, and we sit in the hallway and eat candy and talk about basketball, and she explains how playing AAU is and how much fun she has on the sleepover tournaments. When one of the teachers passes by, she tells me to start reading again.

I enjoy hanging out with the older basketball girls and have become friends with a lot of them. This year, the fifth-grade team and my team practiced together a lot since we had the same coach. It was good to practice against the older girls who are much better than we are. My coach's daughter is on my team, and his older daughter is on the older team. The fifth-grader has picked out a basketball book for me to read with her, and I really enjoy reading it. I am also comprehending it. It is the second weekend in March, and I am bored on this Saturday afternoon. Last week, I saw the pet store open near our house.

I am an animal lover. Unfortunately, things didn't work out due to my health with Spike, my bird, but I have had my turtle, Murdle, for about a year now. I also have a few hermit crabs too. From being around my aunt's dog, China, I love dogs and would love to have my own dog. My parents always tell me I am not getting a dog, but I think I can change their minds, even though it will be a difficult task. A friend of Dad's got a Jack Russell terrier, and after hearing about him, I am now interested in getting that type of dog, but I have to find out if they shed. I cannot have a dog that sheds or else I will have to wind up getting rid of it like I did with Spike.

I don't think my grandparents want any more animals at their house. I beg my mother all morning, and finally, she tells me we can go look at the pet store. "Thank you, Mommy for taking me. I am so excited to go and look!"

"Yes, Jillian, we are only going to look."

We pull into the parking lot and park the car. I head for the door, and as soon as it opens, I hear a lot of barking, and it is loud inside. There are a lot of people in front of the dog cages pointing and saying, "Look! How cute!"

I feel like I may have competition to get one, but then I remember my mom saying we are only looking. The workers are busy putting the dogs in and out of the cages. People are walking over to the playpen area and sitting down to play with the puppies that they have asked to see. A woman approaches us and asks, "Can I help you? Are you looking for a certain kind of puppy?"

My mom responds with, "My daughter would like to see a Jack Russell Terrier if you have one?"

The woman walks us over to the other side of the store, and there he is. The sticker says "Male" and includes his date of birth. He is white with a brown spot and has the cutest face, but I notice he is jumping about four feet high in the air, up and down as soon as the woman puts him in the play area. I ask the worker if he sheds, and she says, "Yes, he does."

I explain to her that I can't have a dog that sheds for medical reasons, and within minutes, the Jack Russell is put back in the cage. He was too wired up for me anyway. I want a dog that is a little calmer; however, I remember we are only looking, so that doesn't really matter anyway. This is sort of a tease, but I am thankful that my mom even took me in the first place.

The lady then tells us she has a couple of breeds that don't shed. The first one is a Maltese, and the next is a Yorkie. A couple of my friends have Maltese dogs. I have never seen a Yorkie before. My mother asks, "What is a Yorkie?"

The woman heads over to the cage, all the way in the left corner. It is very calm in that cage, and you can barely tell that there is a puppy in there. The lady says, "In this cage, there are two yorkies." She tells us that there is a boy and a girl, and they are brother and sister. She says that the girl has crooked teeth and that she is going to be sent back to the breeder, but she can be sold at a discount if we are interested. Being we didn't know much about the Yorkies, my mom asks if we can see the boy. I am told to wait in the play area, and within minutes, the woman carries over the cutest little puppy I have ever seen. She places him on my lap, and within seconds, he is kissing my face all over.

I sit on the floor and play with him for about fifteen minutes. After playing, he climbs onto my lap and goes to sleep like a little baby. He is the most cuddly and cutest thing I have ever seen. Mom is smiling and petting him, and I can see she has fallen in love with him too. He is just one and a half pounds of pure love, and I cannot imagine another little girl going home with him today besides myself. "Mommy, can we get him? Please? Please. I promise I will take care of him. Look how cute he is."

I can tell Mommy loves him, and she says, "We will see. I have to call and ask your father." She says, "Puppies are a lot of work."

I hold this little bundle of joy as he sleeps on my lap, and I hope and pray that my dad says yes on the other side of the phone.

The pet store informs us that in order for them to not sell him to anyone else that we would have to leave a deposit for him. My mother agrees to leave a one-hundred-dollar deposit and says, "We will be back later on after dinner."

I hear my dad on the other line say, "Is this the same person I married that said she would never get a dog?"

My mom's response is, "But, Jim, you have to see him. He is so cute." I can tell I may have won my mom over on possibly getting a dog, and I think once Dad sees him, he won't be able to say no to that adorable face.

My mom and I go home, and it is time for me to get my nebulizers and chest PT done. A few hours pass, and we head to the Chinese restaurant for dinner which is next door to the pet store. The second part of the day seems to be dragging, and I am not even hungry. All I can think of at dinner is the puppy, and I am hoping everyone agrees to take him home. The lady also told us that he is one thousand dollars, and I think that is a lot of money for a dog, but I am sure he will bring all of us so much joy.

After dinner, we head next door. Francesco and Dad hold and play with the puppy, and they fall just as in love with him as we did. We agree to purchase him, and within a couple of hours, everything is almost finalized. Francesco and I are in charge of picking out a name for him. We have to choose his name before leaving the store, and after going back and forth between Penny and Zach, we choose to name him Zach. My parents pick out a leash and collar along with a bunch of supplies to help train him. Francesco and I pick out a bunch of toys for him to play with. We are all set.

It is a cold night, and I am the only one who has room in my baggy jacket, so I tuck little Zach into my Orlando Magic jacket. We ride home from the store, and Zach's tiny head is popping out of the zipper part of my coat, right near my neck. Mom has put up a gate to keep Zach in the kitchen. This way, in case he has an accident, the tile floor will be easy to clean.

I unzip my coat and take Zach out of my jacket and place him down on the floor. He stands there for a few seconds and looks around. We all join him and sit on the floor and introduce him to his toys. He seems to like his toys, and Nanie, Grandpa, and Aunt T have come over to meet the little guy. Zach meets his new family members and plays a little bit, chasing his toys around. It isn't long before he is wiped out and lies down on the kitchen floor and falls asleep in the noisy kitchen.

Francesco is downstairs playing video games, and I want to go in the basement, but I don't like going downstairs unless someone else is with me. While Zach is sleeping, I quietly pick him up and hold him for a couple of minutes, and then I take him downstairs with me. I have a car seat for my dolls, and Zach would fit perfectly in it. I grab the doll car seat and empty the dolls from it. I place Zach in it, and he curls up and goes to sleep. I put the car seat on top of my brother's pool table with Zach in it, and I show Francesco. He isn't impressed with my idea and tells me to take the dog out of it and bring him back upstairs. I tell him that I thought Zach would like it.

After seeing how that ticked Francesco off, I quietly carry Zach upstairs in the doll car seat and laugh as I showed my parents. They laugh a bit and then tell me to get him out of there and put him down. Zach is like having a real-life doll, and he is the cutest thing I have ever seen. I cannot wait for my friends to see him. He isn't allowed outside yet since he is too young and hasn't gotten all of his shots.

MOMENTS OF IMPACT

It is late when our family leaves, and I wish I could take Zach up to bed like my aunt can with China, but Mom tells me he may go to the bathroom in my bed. That doesn't sound too nice, so I put him in his crate for the night. I am exhausted and sleep pretty well.

*****

I wake up, and it takes a few minutes for me to realize that Zach is actually mine. I remember that he is downstairs, and I grab my pillow and dart down the steps and into the kitchen. Mommy has already cleaned his crate and fed him his breakfast. He is playing with his toys and running around the kitchen. I am so happy to see him, and I sit on the floor and play too. We have already used almost an entire roll of film since last night. We took so many pictures of him, and I can't wait to have them all developed. I plan on telling my friends about my new puppy tomorrow, but I don't think I can wait till then.

After my therapy and breakfast, I head onto our computer and log onto my America Online (AOL) account, and I open the instant messenger tab. I keep checking to see if my friends come online. I hear the doors open and close every few minutes on the messenger, letting me know who signed off and who signed on. Only two of them log onto their AOL accounts, and I instant message them to tell them about my new puppy. They cannot believe I got a puppy, and they ask me when they can meet him. I tell them maybe next weekend or after school one day. I am also excited to tell my doctor and nurses about Zach. I have an appointment coming up soon.

The school week flies by, and all I could think about while I am in school is coming home to play with Zach. Last night, during dinner, we looked over to where Francesco keeps his school bag, and Zach decided to make a bed out of Francesco's school bag. We cannot believe he is sleeping on top of Francesco's bag, but it is the funniest thing. Having a dog is so much fun.

Tomorrow is my CF Clinic checkup, and I hope everything goes well. I will be doing a Pulmonary Function Test as usual and possibly a chest X-ray. We will also be doing a sputum culture and a physical exam where my doctor listens to my lungs. I may have to also do blood work depending on when it was last done. We also go over my daily medication and therapy routine.

It is early Thursday morning. I will be missing school today since my appointment is at 10:00 a.m., and we most likely won't make it back in time for the second part of the day. It is sunny and cool out, but you can feel that spring is in the air. I am going to my appointment with my mother and father, and the smell of coffee and hot bagels fill the car the entire way there. An hour and fifteen minutes goes by, and we make it in time. My nurse greets me and says, "Jillian, you can head into the PFT room."

I am ready to give it my all and blow down this machine. I always have a difficult time giving a sputum culture which is strange because before arriving, I have a ton of mucus, and then when I arrive, it's like my lungs decide that it's time to stop producing mucus. If my lungs stopped producing mucus, then I would be much healthier. When I tell my doctor that I have a lot of mucus production and then I cannot produce any sputum, it makes me feel like a liar, but I know she understands.

Before picking up the mouthpiece, I sent a little prayer up to God asking for good results today. I am on my sixth PFT attempt and am exhausted and tired. My face is beet red, and my head is pounding. I have had enough, and I don't think I can do anymore or rather any better. My respiratory therapist doesn't look too happy with the results, and he says, "Good effort, Jillian, but I don't think they are going to go any higher."

I have to agree with him. You just know when you have plateaued. Usually, as I do more PFT attempts, my function goes up a little each time, but not today. I can see the number on the screen. I don't understand what they mean exactly, but I can tell they are all the same across the board. I noticed today was a bit more challenging than last time.

My parents are in the doorway, waiting to find out what my lung function is, but when they ask, the therapist says, "The doctor will go over it with you guys."

We all head into the exam room, and my nurse goes over my regimen with me. We are all eager to know how my lung function is, and when my doctor comes in, she lights up the room with her warm and bubbly entrance as usual. For a minute, I forgot about my head pounding and the numbers not budging. It is difficult not to smile and be happy around her. She stands next to the exam table and smiles at me and says, "Hi, Bella. You know, Bella means beautiful in Italian."

I smile and say, "Hello, Dr. G. Yes, I know it means beautiful."

She starts off by talking to me and asks me about basketball and school and life in general. I tell her all about basketball and school and about our new puppy, Zach. We show her and my nurses a couple of pictures of Zach. They tell us how cute he is. She then listens to my lungs and looks at my PFT results, and her face says it all. She is not happy with what she is looking at. However, I have never seen her look at my results in such a way before. The first thing that comes to mind is Zach as I flashback to when we got Spike, but Zach is hypoallergenic and doesn't shed. He has hair like a human. I am not sure what she is thinking. To me, everything seems okay. I didn't get the reaction I usually get or the reaction I was hoping for from her.

My parents are silent and ask her if my function is okay. She says, "Jillian needs IV antibiotics. Her lung function is down. It is lower than we want it to be." She tells us that my lower airways are usually higher. My doctor then goes on to tell us that I am going to need to do a two-week course of IV antibiotics, which is called a "tune-up." She tells me that I am not very sick and to not be worried, but it is something that has to be done, being I have been on and off oral and inhaled antibiotics for some time now. She tells me the IV antibiotics are what are used to bring up lung function as well as helping us maintain my lung function from dropping further.

The last time I had IV antibiotics was when I was five years old in the hospital, and now I am eight years old and just a month shy of turning nine. My doctor explains to me that I will be getting something called a PICC line placed into my arm, which is explained to me as a longer-lasting IV that starts in my arm and runs to my heart. She tells me that it can last up to a year straight if one needs it to. It doesn't have to be changed every three days, and my vein won't blow like it did a few years ago in the hospital.

I am upset about needing an IV course. I feel as if I failed at this, even though I know I did my best. A few tears come pouring out from my eyes, and I usually can control my emotions a bit better. My parents remind me that I am strong and that I can get through this. Dr. G hugs me and says, "It's okay to be upset and to cry. It is nothing you did, but we have to do this." She tells me CF is not easy and that I have been through a lot. My parents tell me to stop crying, and Dr. G says, "It's okay for her to cry." She tells me to let it all out, which is something I don't really know how to do. I am one to keep my feelings hidden and to myself. I nod my head and realize that what I feel is okay.

After a few minutes, I calm down and am ready to take on this PICC line. "Dr. G, when will they put the line in? Will it be next week?"

"No, Jillian, we can't wait that long. It will get done tomorrow. You will be admitted to the hospital to place the line at the bedside. After they put the line in, then we will do the first dose of IVs in the hospital tomorrow. If all goes well, which it should, then you can go home tomorrow evening."

Wow! I think to myself this sounds like a lot, but I have to do it. I then ask, "Do we do the IVs ourselves?"

"A nurse will teach you, Mom, and Dad the first time, and then you guys will do the rest of the doses on your own for the next couple of weeks."

Today's appointment didn't go as well as I had hoped it would, and it has been one of my toughest ones yet. I understand more than I did when I was five years old, but this hit me a bit different than in the past. I am feeling what my mom felt back three years ago when packing my hospital bag. It is definitely upsetting, but I have to do what has to be done. Dr. G also tells me that I will be going from two chest PTs per day to three chest PTs per day again.

Before leaving today, we have to head over to radiology for a chest X-ray, and then I have to go to the lab to have my blood drawn. I am happy that they have a way to do IVs from home now and that

I don't have to stay in the hospital for two weeks. I know my friends are going to ask why I won't be in school for the next two weeks, and it is going to be a little difficult to explain, but when we pick up Francesco from school, maybe I can show them my IV. I think if they see it, it will be easier to understand.

I will also have to explain this to Francesco and don't want him to get upset either. I remember the look on his face when I was five years old, and he is a bit sensitive when it comes to my CF. He gets easily upset and worries about me. It is hard to hide things from people, especially the ones you live with. It's pretty much right in their faces each and every day, and certain things just can't be unseen.

As we drive home, my mom calls our family to tell them about how my appointment went and that I would be having the PICC line procedure done tomorrow morning. I can hear my family members voices, and they sound concerned on the other end. My mom reassures them that my doctor said I am okay, but this is something that has to be done in order to keep me healthy. She explains to them that in CF, it is routine to need IV antibiotics and that most people need them at least once per year. It has been three entire years since my last IV course, and sports are what is keeping me healthy along with being compliant with my nebulizers and therapies. I am exhausted when we arrive home, and I would love to skip my chest PT and nebulizers, but I take a short nap and then get my therapy out of the way.

Right after dinner, I shower and then fall asleep.

*****

Friday morning arrives quickly, and I feel like I am having déjà vu. We are making the same trip as yesterday with the same smell of coffee, but this time no bagels. I had cereal before leaving, and Mom and Dad picked up some muffins along the way.

We are leaving an hour earlier than yesterday. As we pull in the horseshoe driveway and have the car taken by a valet, I feel a bit nervous and get that nervous belly feeling. We enter the main automatic doors and walk to the left into the admittance waiting area. My name is called, and I get up from leaning on my mom's shoulder. I am half asleep and slouched all the way down in the chair. My dad is sitting across from the elevator, waiting for me to check in, and he is smiling and making funny faces as usual. Dad will do anything to make me laugh. He actually is the one who makes everyone laugh even in the most serious situations. I can't help but smile and laugh as I watch him.

The lady at the check in desk asks for me to hold out my arm. "There you go." That dull-looking plastic name bracelet again. The feeling from five years ago comes back, but only this time, it has Dr. G's name on it, not Dr. Jay's. I think of Dr. Jay and only imagine what he went through as he was much older than I am.

The bracelet is tightened on my wrist, and I am handed a folder and told to take the elevator to the second floor. They tell us that once we are on the second floor to make a right through the double doors and to the nurses' station. We follow the directions we are given, and when we reach the desk, I tell the head nurse my name and hand her the folder. Another nurse introduces herself and gets us situated in my room. This room is much smaller than my last admission, but it is also a smaller hospital. She says, "The doctor will be with you shortly to go over the procedure."

As I sit on the bed, my parents tell me to get comfortable and take off my shoes and close my eyes and relax while I can. I am tired, but I am also wired up and want to know what is happening next. It is difficult for me to relax in an environment like this. There are a lot of different sounds outside my door, and I hear all of the doctors and nurses talking. I am interested to see what is going on outside and try and look through the tiny opening of the door as I sit in the bed. My parents close the door and tell me to relax. They tell me that when it's time for the procedure, I will know.

I saw the play room, or rather it looked more like an activity room as we were coming off the elevator. I wouldn't mind going in there to see what they have. It looks like there is more art than any other activity. I enjoy being artistic, but my art never comes out too nice, especially when I try to paint and draw. I sit and think back to the time Nana let my cousins and I paint the wall down the shore and how no one was able to make out what my painting was supposed to be. Maybe I don't want to enter the art room after all. However, drawing sounds much better than getting a tube placed in my arm. I am thinking today could use some color rather than everything feeling so black and white.

As I look down at my name bracelet, even that is black and white. I have a feeling this won't be the last time I see a band like this on my arm. I just hope the next time I see one, it won't be until a long time from now. My parents drink their coffee as I watch the minute hand on the wall clock pass by and listen to the ticking. We are sitting here for about a half hour, and then my nurse comes in. She is very nice and explains to me and says that a special team of nurses will be in shortly to do the PICC line procedure and that they will explain everything to us. She tells me that I will stay in my hospital room and that it will be done at the bedside, and my parents can stay with me.

As I wait, I am dying to go to the gift shop and get some candy, especially Swedish fish and my favorite chocolate bar, a Milky Way. My mom has packed plenty of snacks in case I get hungry. Dad says, "After the procedure, I will get you lunch from downstairs." It is 10:00 a.m., and *knock, knock!*

My parents say, "Come in."

The door opens, and in the doorway stands a young male nurse and young female nurse. "Jillian, we are here to put in your PICC line. Are you ready for us?"

I respond, "I guess so" and give them a small smile. They are accompanied by a cart on wheels which is carrying all of the supplies needed for today's procedures. The supplies are much more than just a regular IV, but I see a few similar supplies such as the dressing cover and parts of the tubing look the same. The scent is almost identical—sterile and a strong rubbing alcohol smell. I also smell something new which the nurse tells me is used to clean my arm.

The alcohol smell has become a comforting smell to me in a weird way. When I smell the alcohol, I know I am sick and associate it with the hospital. I know the alcohol smell is associated with "making me feel better and safe." This procedure seems like nothing I have ever had before. "Jillian, do you know what a PICC line is?"

I say, "Yes, my doctor explained it to me, but I never saw or had one before. I know it is similar to an IV and is used to give me strong antibiotics."

My nurse then tells me, "A PICC line is a central line that is going to be placed into your vein, and it will run right above your heart." She tells me it is like a very thin piece of spaghetti.

That makes me laugh, and it doesn't sound as painful as I thought. The thought of spaghetti in my arm makes me giggle. She tells me that she will be using a tourniquet to get access to my vein and then use a metal sheath to thread the line all the way above my heart. Once the line is in place, then I will be sent down for a chest X-ray to make sure the placement of the line is normal and that it is the right size.

I think to myself, *What does she mean by the right size? What if they hit my heart? Would I have a heart attack?* I keep my thoughts to myself since they are the professionals.

She asks me if I know why I need a PICC line.

I tell her because I have CF and my lung function is down. I need IV antibiotics.

She smiles and says, "Yes, that's right." She hands a paper to my parents for them to sign, giving the nurses permission to go forward with the procedure.

The nurses first put a cream on to numb my skin. As I lay on my back and try not to look, I want to know what is going on. I just can't help myself so, of course, I have to turn my head to the left to see what they are doing. My left arm is cleaned a couple of times to remove the numbing cream. They then cover my arm with this big sterile blue blanket. I am struggling to see past the blanket as it extends to my face and down to my feet, but I am asked not to breathe on my sterile arm. The tourniquet is tightly tied right below my armpit, and it is tied for about ten minutes already.

My arm is starting to go numb. I feel my fingers getting cold, and I can barely move them. My arm is strapped down to a board which is beneath my arm for stability. They take a purple marker and mark the spot where they want the PICC line to go. I am not completely numb and feel some pain where they are poking and pushing. Blood is now running down the sides of my arm and onto my elbow. The nurses tell me they have one last step which is they have to thread the line in. I see the metal sheath in my arm, and truthfully, I can feel it in there. It is painful, and the only numbing I have is the topical cream. My skin is numb, but not my vein or the inside of my arm. The sheath looks like a metal kabob stick but thicker.

As they thread the line through the sheath, I feel a lot of pressure, and it does not feel like spaghetti at all. I am ready for this to be done. My nurses measure from my arm to my chest, and now they are measuring the line and cutting it to the estimated size. I realize how the sizing may not be perfect and why they need to send me for an X-ray afterward. The male nurse says to the female nurse, "Seventeen French."

I wonder what that means? I am sure the seventeen is the size of the line, and I guess the French is something fancy in medical terms, but the only thing that I know with the name French is the language and French dressing. They are definitely not speaking of dressing, even though they still have to put one over the line. Halfway through the threading process, I yell, "I can't hear!" And then I say, "I can't see!"

My eyes black out, and I pretty much feel as if I am in the middle of passing out. Dad says, "What do you mean you can't hear or see?" He thinks it's some sort of joke.

I am rushed into another room, and I vaguely hear them say to me, "Drink this cup of orange juice."

As I drink the juice, I start feeling better, and little by little, I gain my vision and full hearing back. The nurses explain that from the bleeding, more blood was lost than planned, and my blood pressure dropped due to that. I am then quickly brought to the X-ray room, and all goes well, and it's the right size and positioned properly. The site of insertion is covered by a clear dressing, and my nurse puts a board under my arm to keep things in place and wraps a loose bandage around my arm. They tell me to be very careful and to wear the board with the bandage at all times since it is in the bend of my arm, and there is nothing but the dressing holding it in place. It is bleeding a tiny bit and stings at the insertion site, but I am feeling okay and looking forward to going home.

The nurse then takes a syringe with saline and flushes it and asks if I am in pain. All feels fine besides some stinging, but the stinging is coming more from my skin. I tell her that I can taste the saline. I am amazed how they did all of that right at the bedside. When I return from radiology, I ask my parents, "When do we get to leave?"

"Jillian, not for a while. We have to first have the nurses run your antibiotics here and make sure the PICC line is working properly. They also want to make sure you don't have any reaction to the medications before we go home."

My doctor explains to me that if I feel anything strange while the medication goes through to let them know. They tell me to look out for swelling anywhere or if I am having difficulty swallowing or breathing as well as chest pain. If almost passing out wasn't enough, now I am scared if I have an allergic reaction, but I am happy to be at the hospital.

We are back in my room, and my nurse hooks me up to normal saline for a little while before hooking up the first IV antibiotic. I am also warned about hearing issues that can occur from the antibiotics that are used to treat pseudomonas aeruginosa. They tell me that if I have any ringing in my ears to let them know. I am told that over time, it may occur and that it can lead to hearing loss. Anytime I have ever heard of ringing in the ears, it has always been associated with someone speaking about someone else, but I know that is just a joke. I now know that that ringing in the ears is something much more serious. I was never aware that medications could cause allergic reactions like that. I only thought people could be allergic to the outdoors like myself or animals and foods. It is scary to try a new medication and not know if you are allergic or not. I am glad I am trying it out in the hospital and not at home.

Now that things are calmer, Dad goes down to the cafeteria in the basement of the hospital and gets us lunch. I have a hamburger and fries. I am nice and full and ready for these medications. The first antibiotic is running slowly to make sure there are no reactions. I am told when I go home that it will take one hour to run this medication, but here they ran it over two hours.

As my first infusion is running, the child life lady knocks on my door and asks if I would like to join her in the activity room in one hour for an Easter egg art activity she is doing.

I smile and I say, "I would love to, but I am usually not allowed in the activity rooms because I cannot be around other children that are sick." I explain to her that when I am in the hospital, I have to stay in my room usually.

She offers to bring some art stuff into my room as well as movies to keep me busy. I thank her, and then, when the door closes, I ask my parents if I can go into the room. I tell them that earlier, I saw there wasn't even anyone else in there. My parents give me the look that says "Absolutely not," and I know it's a no without them even responding.

After a few minutes of silence, my mother says, "Let me speak with the lady and Dr. G to see if it won't be crowded and if Dr. G thinks it's okay for you." My mom speaks with Dr. G, and they agree that if it's quiet, then it will be okay, but we have to wash down the chair and table first with the hospital wipes. My mom tells me she isn't making me any promises.

Just the thought that I can possibly join the art activity makes me happy. I am sure I am going to miss the Easter activities going on in school for the next two weeks, so it would be nice to do one today. My second antibiotic is about to infuse, and Mom tells me to get out of bed. She has cleaned down the table and chair in the activity room. I put on my sneakers and unplug my IV pump from the wall. I am a bit old to be scooting around on the base of it, so I wheel it alongside of me. My nurse offers to wheel the pump, but I say, "I can do it, thank you." There is only one other kid in the room as well as the child life woman. We are sitting literally across the room from each other at our own tables.

I smile at the other girl. She is probably around the same age as me and is quietly working on her Easter eggs. She smiles back. We don't speak, but I can tell she looks a bit sad, and I think she can sense things aren't going perfect for me either. Sometimes words aren't needed and feelings are felt. I hope whatever she is here for she gets better and can go home soon. Dorothy in *The Wizard of Oz* wouldn't say, "There's no place like home" if it weren't true.

The hospital can be a dreary place, but knowing that people like myself come here to get better gives me a comforting feeling. I smile as I begin decorating a hollow egg with decoupage. This is so cool! They are real eggs that have been blown out and are hollow on the inside. On the outside, we are using colorful and decorative tissue paper and a glue-like liquid. First, we paint the glue-like liquid onto the egg and then place the tissue paper on the gluey area. We then add some more of the gluey liquid on top of it until all of the tissue paper is covered. I use a paint brush to help smooth everything out. The egg is then placed in an empty egg carton and left to sit and dry.

I am here for about two hours while my infusion runs, so I am able to make two eggs. I even have enough time for them to dry. My infusions go well, and I am back in my room. My nurse unhooks me from the IV pump and flushes my PICC with two different syringes. The liquid in both syringes is clear, but one cap is white, and the other cap is yellow. "Oh, that tastes salty," I say, and I can also taste the yellow-capped one too. The yellow-capped one isn't as salty, but it has its own distinct flavor. "What is this one for?" I ask my nurse.

She explains that it is normal to taste the flushes and that this one is called heparin. She then tells me the first one is normal saline. "The heparin is a blood thinner which helps to keep the PICC line from clotting when the medications aren't being infused."

Having the PICC line placed in my arm was tough but the IV antibiotics weren't too bad. I am sure once we get home, things will be a bit more challenging since there are a lot of new things to learn.

We sign a few papers, and off we go to get the car. It is going to be a long night since we still have to do another infusion before bed. A nurse will be coming to our house to teach us how to run the IVs and to teach us how to care for the PICC line properly.

We hit a ton of traffic, especially since it's a Friday afternoon, but a little over two hours later, we are home. I am so happy to see Zach, but I hope he doesn't think my PICC is a toy. I am excited to show Francesco my new IV, but I don't know if he will be excited to see it or more grossed out by it. We walk inside, and Zach greets us. He is so happy we are home, and so are we. My grandparents and my brother will be here a little bit later to join us for dinner. We are going to order pizza for dinner. It has been a long day so far, and I don't think my parents are in the mood to cook.

I relax on the couch for a bit, and it is time for my second chest PT. My arm is throbbing from all of the poking that took place earlier. As I sit and inhale my medications, I am happy that I got through today's procedure. I hear the garage door go up, and Francesco comes in with Nanie and Grandpa. I am so happy to see them, and I show them my PICC line. Francesco looks at it and doesn't say much besides asking if it hurts.

"Well, it doesn't hurt as much now. It is throbbing a bit where the line goes into my vein. It hurt a lot when they put it in my arm."

He kisses me on the cheek and tells me he loves me. Maybe I shouldn't have been so excited as I was to show him. I know he cares, but some people just aren't great with blood and medical things. After a minute or so, my brother asks me if I could please not show him my PICC line again. He tells me he gets a bit queasy when looking at it. I am becoming more interested in medical things as I get older, but I guess that is because I don't have a choice.

Our house phone rings, and it is Michael's dad calling to see how I am doing after today's procedure.

"She is doing okay, thank you, hanging in there. We are waiting for the medication delivery to come, and then the nurse will be here later on tonight. Sure, you guys can come and see her. That is fine with me. Come over for coffee later if you want. Okay, sounds good. I'll see you later."

"Dad, what is going on?" I ask.

"Nothing, it was Joe. He wanted to come with Michael later on to see you."

"Oh, okay," I say. I put on my vest and rattle the mucus up and cough it out of my lungs. I am happy that our family is over, and it's nice that our friends want to come over also. This PICC line is new for me, and this will be the first friend that I will have to explain what a PICC line is to. At least he will also see it for himself rather than just explaining it. Now that I have seen it for myself, it is much easier to understand. I am a bit nervous to show Michael my PICC line. He has seen me do my therapies when he is over, but that is the easy part. During my therapy, all I can think about is how to explain that my lung function is down and that I require IVs and that I am okay and not dying.

I understand how difficult it can be for one to understand CF when they don't live with it. I know that my friends for the past four years from school don't understand what I go through. They think it is similar to having asthma, when in reality, it is much different. I give up trying to explain it after a while.

The doorbell rings, and my mother opens the door. It's a man, and he is putting three decent-sized boxes on our front steps. He asks my mother to sign a few papers and tells her that the medications need to be refrigerated. My dad brings the boxes into the kitchen, and one by one, they open them up. The medications are shaped like a ball, just like my doctor explained to us. There are a lot of them, and they take up the entire refrigerator. Thank God we have an extra refrigerator in the basement in case we run out of room. The third box is packed out with saline and heparin flushes, alcohol pads, dressing kits, and a pack of gloves. There is also a red plastic container that says "Sharps." There are also tubes for blood draws in there with needles, a tourniquet, and a vacutainer.

Wow, this looks like everything you would see in a lab. I guess the nurse will explain everything tonight to us. While waiting for our dinner to arrive, I play Nintendo 64 with Francesco. I love to play the car racing game, especially now that Francesco has the foot pedal and steering wheel connection. I feel like I am driving a real car. I am not a very good driver and keep crashing into the walls and keep coming in last place. Francesco is pretty good at this game, and he always comes in as one of the top three out of ten. Francesco tells me the point of playing the game is to come in as close to first as possible. He is about winning, and I just enjoy pretending I am driving a car and have fun. This is my third round, and it is so much fun! I can't wait until I am old enough to get my driver's license.

We play a few more rounds and rotate taking turns. The doorbell rings. I am starving and looking forward to the pizza that just arrived. I hate being the last one up the steps and am scared to be in the dark downstairs. I feel like something is going to attack me from behind. My parents will yell at us if we don't shut the lights in the basement, and if we leave them on, they will make one of us, if not both, go back downstairs and shut them all. We have another entrance that leads from the yard to the basement outside, and I always think someone is going to be hiding down there.

The pizza tastes so delicious. It is melting in my mouth. I eat three slices and enjoy the cold refreshing Coca-Cola going down my throat. It burns a bit from being so bubbly, but it tastes so good. Our doorbell is ringing a lot tonight, and it is definitely not the last time. I am not sure if it is the nurse or Joe and Michael. My dad gets the door, and I can hear Joe's voice from inside of the kitchen. They come walking in, and I am sitting at the table and talking with Nanie and Mom. Joe comes over and hugs and kisses me and says, "My poor little sweetie. How are you feeling?"

I respond by saying, "I am feeling good, and thank you for visiting."

Michael smiles at me and says, "Hello."

I do the same. He heads over to the rest of my family and says hi to them. I don't know how Michael will react to my PICC line. I can tell he is curious, and obviously, he knows I am not feeling great at the moment. He asks me where Francesco is, and I tell him down stairs playing a game. He asks me if I want to go downstairs with him. I say, "Sure. One minute." I tell my parents I will be downstairs in case the nurse comes soon. They tell me that I can go downstairs, but when the nurse comes, I have to come upstairs.

I thought seeing a friend would take my mind off of things. We both run down the steps to the basement and to the other side where my brother is. Michael and Francesco say hello to one another, and he asks Francesco, "What game is that?"

Francesco says, "Mario on Nintendo 64."

Michael and I go to the other side of the basement where the computer and board games are. We sit on the floor. Michael says, "I heard you have to have an IV in your arm." He tells me he is worried about me and asks if I really need it for two weeks.

As I take the board off and unwrap the cloth from my arm, I say, "It's not a regular IV. It's called a PICC line, and it goes from here to my heart."

He looks at it and says, "Does it hurt? It looks painful, Jill."

"It hurt for sure, but now it is just a little sore with some stinging where the tube enters my arm. The worst part is over." I tell him to not be worried and that I am okay. I explain to him that I do a test that tests my lung function and that my lung function was lower than normal. The IV antibiotics are used to help bring it up.

He is staring at me, and I can see he is trying to take it all in and understand what I am saying. This conversation feels slightly uncomfortable after seeing his reaction. The only way I could have made this conversation less uncomfortable would be if I sugarcoated everything, but I am a pretty honest person. My parents always taught me to not be ashamed of having CF, and the more I share with people, the more awareness it brings to the disease. More awareness means one step closer to finding a cure.

He looks a bit taken back and then asks again, "Do you really have to keep this for an entire two weeks?"

I say, "Yes, that's what the doctor said."

He then leans over and hugs me with his hands wrapped around my shoulders and tells me that I am really strong. I halfway smile and say, "Thanks, but I have to be. This isn't something I want to do."

Michael smiles and reaches into my Barbie Dreamhouse and changes Ken's clothing with Barbie's, and we both start laughing. He tells me he has to tell me something, but I can see he is a bit hesitant. He says, "I love you, and you are one of my best friends, but I don't think I can be your boyfriend in the future. I'm worried. What if you die?"

Things get silent for a few seconds, and both our heads are staring at the basement floor. I nod my head and say, "I understand." I knew one day this would be a reality for me. I say, "Michael, I can't help that. No one can, but this is why I need IV antibiotics so I can try and be alive for as long as possible." I tell him that I understand his concern. I think about my possibility of dying also from time to time, but I can never come up with a solution to stop that from happening. It's understandable given my situation for people to think the way Michael does. My life expectancy as of now is only in the early thirties. Hopefully, the IVs will allow me to stay alive longer than expected.

I am a little taken back at what Michael said, but I am not too surprised. I completely understand where he is coming from, but I also know I won't just drop dead tomorrow from CF. It takes time to become so sick when one is compliant with their therapies and medications, but it's hard for people my age to understand. Many people think CF is a death sentence when they first research it.

It isn't fair to involve someone else into my life in the future, especially now at such a young age. I don't want others to be affected by my CF. He is the one who initially told me he liked me, and I can't change my situation as much as I wish I could. When I hear those who are older than I am say they don't need relationship issues, now I can sort of understand where they are coming from. Truthfully, I think this is a bigger issue than most adults face when in a relationship in their life.

As I clean up some of my Barbie dolls and reverse their clothing, I ask him if he is okay with us still being friends. He says, "Yes, you are still one of my best friends, and I hope you aren't mad at me." He apologized, and I told him there is nothing to be sorry about. It is what it is, and I apologized for the way things are. I am still waiting for my nurse to come and don't really even want to be around anyone at the moment. I need a minute to just relax. Michael says, "I don't want things to change with us."

I agree with him but also say, "How are things not going to change?"

He says, "I don't know."

I am not too sure either, but I say, "We are still friends." It is hard for me to see right now how things won't be different, but we can both feel the awkwardness between us. I am tired and hope my nurse arrives soon so we can start the medication. My big concern is my health.

We both go upstairs, and my mother asks me, "Jill, is everything okay?"

I am not exactly smiling and laughing the way I usually am when Michael is around. I say, "Yes, Ma, everything is fine."

Michael sits on the chair next to me, but he is pretty quiet. He is playing with Zach, and we both have a donut from Dunkin Donuts. We both love the Boston cream ones from there.

The doorbell rings, and finally, my nurse arrives. My nurse walks in, carrying a big bag which I would assume has everything he needs in it for tonight's visit. He is very nice and takes a seat right next to me. He asks who everyone is that is sitting at the table. I introduced him to my grandparents. He asks to see my PICC line, and I take the board off that is covering it. It is nice to let my arm breathe a bit and not be so stiff, but I am afraid the line will bend and kink if I don't leave the board on.

Michael is sitting at the table watching closely what is happening, and so is my family. My nurse asks if everyone is family at the table. I look at Michael and I say, "This is my friend."

Michael looks at me and says to my nurse, "She is so strong. I would have passed out by now."

My nurse looks at him and then looks at me. I am not sure what he is thinking, but it's obvious that Michael is very interested in what is happening. My nurse shows us how to unclamp the tubing and flush my PICC. He then teaches us how to prime and connect the antibiotic. He stresses how important it is for us to wash our hands before touching anything and how to use the alcohol pads to keep things clean. He explains that if we don't follow the steps that I can wind up with an infection in the line. He is going to be here for the next two hours to run both of the medications and to make sure I don't have any reactions. While the medications are infusing, he tells me I can go and watch TV if I want while my mother and father fill out a ton of paperwork with him.

Before leaving, Michael tells me to feel better and that he will instant message me over the weekend. I tell him thank you and that we will talk soon. Our company has left, and halfway through the infusions, he takes my vital signs and records them on a flow sheet.

The two hours pass by slowly and, thank God, all goes well. He tells me he will be back tomorrow to draw blood and change the dressing that covers my PICC. He also explains that the Amikacin antibiotic will be every eight hours, and the Tobramycin is once per day. He tells us to not start the Tobramycin tomorrow until after he draws my blood.

We are all exhausted and ready to get some rest. I am not looking forward to 6:00 a.m. tomorrow, which is when my next IV dose will start. As I lay in bed, I think about the entire day and how painful getting a PICC line was, but it was just as painful explaining what my PICC line was to someone who isn't familiar with CF. Today was a true reality check for me all around, but I hope to become stronger from all of this. I have to understand that not everyone is going to be accepting of what comes along with having CF, especially when I am older and I go on a date. I know my friends at school will be wondering why I am out of class for two weeks. I will have to explain to them what is going on, but I think telling them will be much easier. After all, they understood when I was out sick in the hospital a few years back, and they were all accepting.

*****

The weekend goes smoothly, and by Sunday afternoon, we are all exhausted, especially my mom and I. I am tired from the strong medications constantly circulating in my bloodstream, and Mom is tired from the vigorous schedule. It is a beautiful sunny Sunday, and I would love to be outside, but Mom and I both crash on the couch for a nap. The smell of Sunday marinara sauce is cooking in the kitchen along with some meatballs and sausage. I am looking forward to some delicious pasta later on. Having pasta on Sundays is a tradition in our family. We usually have Sunday dinners at home or at Nanie and Grandpa's with everyone.

Although I am not getting up for school this morning, it still feels as if I am. I can hear the sound of my mother's alarm going off down the hall. Today is day three of IVs. It is time to hook up the Amikacin which is the first medication. I stay in bed as Mom brings all of the supplies into my room. The hallway light turns on, and she is carrying a plate with the alcohol pads, saline flushes, heparin flushes, and the medication. Every time I smell rubbing alcohol, I now think of my PICC line and my hospital stay from three years ago. As the first antibiotic infuses, I roll onto my stomach and hug my pillow, and within minutes, I am sleeping again until it is time for my first chest PT.

Mom wakes me up around 9:00 a.m., and I can smell the delicious pancakes cooking downstairs. I am lazy in the mornings, and when I don't have school, it takes me a bit longer to get up. After ten minutes of lying here, wide awake, I gather up some energy and make my way to the kitchen. Mom greets me by saying, "Good morning, my little Jilly Monster."

I hate when Mommy calls me this, but it is her nickname for me. I don't really feel like smiling too much, but I say, "Good morning." Her eyebrows go up as she laughs, and she is looking at my hair in a weird way. I know she must be laughing at my wild bed head. I have very thick, curly, and frizzy hair, just like my aunt's. My hair is always a wreck in the morning, and before I leave the house, I must make sure I brush it very well and pull it back. I usually use gel or mousse to keep it tamed. The only way I can leave it down is if it is straightened or curled nicely without all of the frizz. If left naturally, it annoys me, and I look like a lion.

In life, most people want the opposite of what they have, and that couldn't be any more true when it comes to females and their hair. I wish I had straight hair, and my family and friends that have straight hair always wished they had curly hair. Sometimes I wish I didn't have CF due to how time-consuming it is, but I never heard anyone say they wished they had an illness. Then there are things in life that we don't want the opposites. I have heard people in life tell me they would trade their hair for mine but never that they would trade their health for mine.

The morning is going by slowly. I eat my breakfast and do my chest PT. Before you know it, it is time for dose number two of IVs for the day. Mom has taken both medications out of the fridge this morning. This way, they are room temperature. You do not want to infuse them at cold temperatures because it will be very uncomfortable. We infuse the first one in one hour. Once that is complete, we flush the line with saline and then hook up the second one.

As the second one is running, we have lunch and then take the IV with us to pick up Francesco from school. We park and wait in front of the doors where Francesco comes out of. As I look to the right, I see all of my friends coming out together from the main door. It is beautiful out today. The weather is getting warmer. I am wearing a lightweight jacket and my left arm is not in the sleeve part of my jacket. Leaving my arm out should help the PICC line tubing from kinking and stopping the flow of the medication.

We are happy to see each other. They ask me why I won't be in school, and I show them my IV. They ask me what the tubing is for, and I explain that it is a PICC line. I tell them that it is a long-lasting intravenous. I tell them I need strong medications that can only be done through the IV and that it is best for me to be at home. They are all very understanding and tell me that they miss me, and I tell them I miss them too. It's almost like I feel that I am missing out on what my friends are doing, but we all have our own lives and own journeys.

All of the cars are lined up and parked in a certain way so that no one boxes someone else in. Each day, someone directs the cars so that there are no accidents. This doesn't give me too much time to see everyone, but at least I saw my closest friends.

It is time for us to leave the parking lot, and I tell my friends that we can talk on AOL Instant Messenger and on the phone. Now that my friends know what is going on, I am sure word is going to spread quickly when the class notices I am out. I am not an extremely private person when it comes to my CF, and having this PICC line is making CF more visible. It is a pretty invisible disease, but I notice people are staring at my arm in the school parking lot. A couple of weeks go by with the same routine consisting of IVs, blood draws once per week, nursing visits, and once per week doctor appointments. I am still on three chest PTs per day along with extra nebulizers. However, while I am on IVs, I am told to hold off from the inhaled TOBI antibiotic.

We go weekly for a CF doctor appointment, and this is the end of week two on IV antibiotics.

I do my pulmonary function test, and thank God, my lung function has increased a little higher than its baseline. It is right where my doctor wants it to be. Dr. G listens to my lungs and tells me that I sound good and that I can now go back to doing my normal routine of two chest PTs per day and every other month of TOBI. I am told to complete another day on the IV antibiotics to finish a full two weeks, and then my homecare nurse will remove my PICC line tomorrow night.

I am happy and excited to go back to my normal life starting Saturday. My doctor is happy too, and she is smiling at me as she says, "Good job, Bella." She tells me to come back to see her in two months, which means I will be able to come during summer break.

After my appointment, my parents and I grab some lunch at the pizzeria near the hospital. It is Friday night already. The final infusion has ended. I can't believe it's been two full weeks. I have gotten used to the IV schedule and wonder how I will do without the IV. We flush my PICC line, and my nurse is here just in time to remove it. I am a bit scared of the removal process and hope I don't pass out like I almost did when they put it in. My nurse tells me to lay down on the couch. He puts a chuck underneath my arm; or as I call, it a wee-wee pad.

He puts his gloves on and removes the adhesive first as he holds the line in place. He uses alcohol pads and, little by little, peels off the dressing. It has been so itchy and feels good that the air is hitting my skin. One of the toughest parts about having this PICC line was showering. Mom had to wrap my arm really well each time with Saran Wrap and tape it tight to keep it dry. My arm was pretty much useless when showering, and I relied on my right arm and Mom's help.

My nurse asks if I am ready, and I say, "Yes." In a few seconds, the entire PICC line is out. As I lay there, I see inches upon inches of tubing come out of my arm. This line was over one foot long. Now I feel the spaghetti feeling the nurses told me about when they placed the PICC line in my arm. We hold pressure to stop the bleeding, and he uses another dressing to apply pressure around the site. My nurse brings the line over to the kitchen table and measures it with a paper tape measure. His eyes bug out of his head, and he tells me to not run around and just wait a few minutes while he figures something out.

My parents ask what is wrong, and he says the size isn't matching what the hospital wrote down on the paper. He immediately calls the nurses department that placed the line. They answer the phone, and he rambles my info off to them. I hear him say, "Oh, thank God." I see a sign of relief come over his face. He looked pale when he measured the line, and the coloring in his face has returned.

As he hangs up the phone, he says, "They wrote the wrong size down on this paper, but in their records, they have the same length written down that matches my measurement." He then explains that he can see that the end of the line looks normal and is pointed the way it should be. We are all relieved knowing a piece of the PICC hasn't detached from the line. My nurse also shows us the end of the PICC line and asks us, "Do you see how it gets pointy at the end?" He says, "That means it's the end, but I had to call just to make sure. Little mistakes can make for a big disaster, especially in the medical field."

This was a bit scary, but I am happy it is all over. I am so glad my nurse knows what he is doing. My parents both tell me that he knows his stuff and that he is the type of nurse you want.

My IV course finished just in time to begin playing on the AAU Diamonds travel team. This is my first year playing, and I am excited to meet my new teammates and get to travel and see new places. I have heard that sometimes AAU teams can travel across the country. Our first practice is next week. I feel energized and am pretty healthy for the start of the season. Being IV-free for the weekend gives me a couple of days to adjust back to normal life. I am supposed to return to school tomorrow and am a little nervous to see everyone after being home this long. My friends have been writing down the in-class assignments as well as homework assignments for me and sending them home with my brother each day. I have been keeping up with the workload as best as I can.

I get a good night's sleep, and 6:00 a.m. is here already. I hate the sound of my mother's alarm going off. I know I only have about twenty minutes left to rest, and then she will be in to wake me up. We start my nebulizers and therapy. The vibrating of the vest is relaxing for me, and I fall asleep with it going. Mom wakes me up to make sure I cough in between positions. Francesco is still sleeping and doesn't have to be up until another half hour later. He looked so comfortable wrapped in his blanket as I passed his room to go downstairs. I wish that was me right now.

My therapy is done, and Mom tells me to stay awake during my nebulizers. She hooks up my nebulizer and goes into the kitchen to make our lunches. Each time she doesn't hear me breathing in, she yells, "Jill, breathe!"

I jump up and my eyes open and I take a deep breath. The sound of her voice startles me and mostly scares the crap out of me. Back and forth goes the little blue rubber flap on the mouthpiece. When Mom doesn't hear the flap, she knows I'm not breathing deeply. The last thing I want to hear right now is her yelling at me.

After a few minutes, Mom comes inside and tells me I have to breathe. I say, "I am breathing or else I wouldn't be alive."

Mom laughs and says, "I know that, but you know that you have to breathe in deeply." She tells me to do so, and I do. She says, "That is the sound I should hear."

I have to readjust myself to these early times. Mom still doesn't hear me breathing deeply, so she uses another one of her secrets. She sits next to me and holds my nose, and involuntarily, I have to inhale through my mouth or else I will stop breathing. I get pretty angry when she does this, but later on, it makes me laugh. I am pretty cranky in the mornings and am not always nice to my mother, but when she tells me how I treated her later on in the day, I feel bad and apologize, but I was half asleep and not thinking straight. I don't remember most of how I acted. Holding my nose is a pretty clever idea, and she always finds a way to make me do my treatments properly.

I finish my therapy and quickly eat my favorite school day breakfast: cold cereal. It is not too filling, but I am not really a breakfast or morning person. Sometimes I have Eggo Waffles before school or eggs and bacon. I have about five minutes before we have to leave, and I have just enough time to brush my teeth and get my uniform and shoes on. Sometimes I tie my shoes in the car.

Francesco will be upset with me if I make him late. Francesco is waiting at the door and ready to leave, and so is Zach. Zach takes a ride with us and sits in the front passenger seat next to mommy. She always says that he is her little copilot. As we open the door that leads into the garage, Zach runs to the passenger door and waits to be picked up and put in the seat. Zach doesn't jump, so he relies on us to put him on top of things. As we pull up to the front door of the school, Zach wags his one-inch tiny stub of a tail and from the car window. He greets the janitor who opens the car doors for the students. We kiss Mom and give Zach a goodbye pet and tell them we will see them later.

Mom drives off, and you can hear Zach barking and crying for us down the street. I miss Zach already, but I am excited to get to see him and play ball with him later. He is such a lovable and sweet puppy. I still cannot believe he is mine. He is just the cutest thing ever.

I walk into the classroom with a smile, and my friends and I are happy to see each other. My teacher, however, doesn't seem too happy to see me. I'm not sure if she is ever happy. I walk in and say, "Hello, Mrs. C. I'm back."

She looks at me and says, "Oh, you are back. I moved seats round. You are sitting there."

I am a bit taken back by her response, but I find my seat and start to unpack my books. I think everyone else is taken back also. My friends raise their eyebrows and look at me in shock. I smile and shake my head, and so do my friends. Mrs. C doesn't really have a personality.

The school day drags by slowly. Each hour feels extremely long today, and I cannot wait to get out of here. Being in her classroom just puts you in a bad mood. The only enjoyable part of the day is lunchtime, and that went by way too fast. My teacher is a great teacher when it comes to school work and teaching us lessons. She doesn't get along well with the kids, and the parents aren't fond of her either.

The bell rings, and it is time for dismissal. I look over my homework list as I pack up my books that I will need for tonight. I cannot wait for third grade to be over. I have never hated school this much than now. My mom is waiting outside with Zach, and they are both happy to see my brother and I. My mom asks, "Was everyone happy to see you back?"

I say, "Yup."

Mom smiles and asks, "What did Mrs. C say when she saw you?"

"She said to me, 'Oh, you are back.'"

Mom is in total shock and says, "Jillian, that's what she said to you? I cannot believe that. She didn't even say, 'Glad you're back?'"

I say, "Nope, she is miserable."

Mom says, "I know she is, but still."

I am free from what feels like jail and ready to go home and relax. Luckily, my prior teachers have been very nice but not this one. I am noticing that not everyone at this school is very "Christian-like." I guess this is why she fits in and no one notices her behavior. They don't practice what they preach here. My parents decided to put me in catholic school when I was younger because they knew health-wise, I would be faced with many challenges. They thought having support in our faith would be best for me on a daily basis. I understood where they were coming from; however, I haven't seen this school practice our faith too well. Not everyone here is hypocritical, but as a whole, they aren't too "Christian-like."

I am happy to only have about two months left of third grade, but it isn't going as fast as the other school years. I am happy that my new AAU team starts this weekend. This weekend, we are headed to New Jersey, and luckily, the tournament is only about forty minutes away, so we won't be staying at a hotel. We have two games on Saturday with a two-hour break in between. This is going to be one of my longest basketball days so far, but it will be fun. I am playing the point guard position and splitting games with the other point guard. We are the shortest girls on our team.

In total, we have fourteen girls on the team. I have become friends with my teammates in just a few short weeks. It is nice to meet new people and that we mostly all get along. This is the first time all of the parents and siblings will get to meet. This is way more competitive than playing for my church.

It is Saturday, and we get to the gym an hour early. All of the parents are introduced to one another. A half hour before our game starts, we warm up. The buzzer sounds, and we step foot on the court. I am not starting today, but I am all ready to play whenever I am subbed in. Every point we score we have worked for. I use my speed to my ability and score a few points in both games today. Our games are split into two halves instead of four quarters, so there are less breaks. The court we played on was a college-sized court, and there was a ton of running.

Our first game we won, but the second game we lost. The second team was much bigger and better than we were. Our coaches shake all of our hands and say, "Great job today, girls." This is only our first year together, so in time, I think we will get better and more used to playing with one another. Our practices are held twice per week for two hours each.

Lately, I feel like my life consists of school, homework, studying, basketball, and therapies. This type of schedule doesn't leave too much time to hang out with my other friends, but we try to get together for a bit after school, even if it is only for a half hour to an hour. I spend a lot of time with my new basketball friends.

Speaking of friends, I haven't seen Michael in a while. Life has been so busy over here. It's our second tournament, and we are going back to New Jersey this weekend, but this time, our tournament is two hours away. We will be staying overnight on Saturday into Sunday since we have four games scheduled. After school, we come home and have a snack. It is time to start packing all of our stuff. We have a lot more to pack than the other families. We have to pack all of my medications and my nebulizer compressor along with my huge vest machine. Some of my medications are also refrigerated, so we can't pack them just yet. It is difficult to pack everything in advance because I need to use most of it tonight as well as tomorrow morning.

This just means that we will have to be up even earlier than usual. We do our best to prepare everything, and I have a hard time falling asleep due to being excited for tomorrows' games. I fall asleep with my Walkman playing on my headphones, and halfway through the night, I take my headphones off. The alarm sounds, and my mom wakes me up to get all of my medications and therapy done. It feels like a school day on the weekend. My dad goes to get bagels and coffee and packs the car for us.

We eat our bagels in the car and meet up with the rest of my teammates and their families on the service road. We follow each other since some of us tend to get lost. A couple of the families carpool, and before we know, it we are on the road. It is hard for everyone to stay close since we are on the highway and the other cars are switching lanes. The parents have fun trying to keep up with one another. We also have to pull over numerous times to make sure everyone is there.

Luckily, my parents have a cell phone in case they have to call another parent and ask them to please wait up for us. Our traveling track record isn't great, and we always get lost. Not everyone has a cell phone, so we all try to stay alert and be mindful of who is in front of us and who is behind us. Dad is checking his rearview to make sure the family behind us is keeping up. Cell phones have just started coming out and becoming more affordable than they were in the past.

We all arrive in one piece and start filling up the parking lot. One of my teammates is parked next to me, and when I see her through the window, I wave and smile. This is such a cool experience. This gymnasium is huge, and it is more of a complex than a gym. We enter, and my coaches hold the doors for everyone. I was right. It is a huge complex with about six full-size basketball courts.

My coach is told we are playing on court four, which is right in the middle. The court doesn't have wood floors or tile like I am used to but rather a mushier type of court, almost like a rubber. Hopefully it won't hurt as much when one of us falls or dives for the ball.

MOMENTS OF IMPACT

We warm up by shooting around and doing some drills on our half of the court. The buzzer sounds, and it's showtime. Our parents have their chairs set up together on the opposite side of the team benches. Many of the AAU gyms do not provide chairs for the families, so everyone has to bring their own fold-up chairs. AAU is very different from the other leagues I have played in. My parents have dark-green chairs to match the color of our uniforms. My AND1 sneakers don't match, but I loved these when I saw them and had to get them.

All of the teams in this tournament are much taller than us. We have a few tall girls, but we are mostly on the shorter end, and we have speed. The first game goes by, and we lose, unfortunately. I think our second game will be a bit better. I know for me, I was still waking up a bit. I don't function too well in the mornings.

We have about three hours until our next game. My team decides to get fast food, but my parents want something not so rushed, so we head to a Chinese restaurant after dropping our things off in our hotel room. This restaurant is beautiful with marble flooring and a stunning foyer. Dad says, "Let's see if they will even seat us looking like this." I am in my uniform, and my family is wearing comfortable clothing.

The restaurant seats us without a problem, and they explain that the other side of the restaurant is a catering hall, and right now, they are setting up for a big wedding. I am impressed and am sure the food is going to be delicious. This is the best Chinese food I have ever had. It is gourmet, and the wonton soup has real homemade wontons with a delicious broth. This is the Chinese version of fresh pasta. I am so glad we didn't have fast food like everyone else did. I feel energized and ready to run.

We win our second game and head back to the hotel. My teammates and I are all happy, and I played better this afternoon. I was much more alert, and so was my team. Our coaches are proud of us. We go to our rooms and then order food together. We play some games in the conference room together. It was a fun night, and we prepare for tomorrow's games.

We have a two-hour drive home. We hope to not hit much traffic. We fill the gas tank up so we don't have to stop on the way home. We enjoy some snacks from Wawa as we follow each other back. We didn't do too bad this weekend. Today, we won one game and lost one game. Next weekend, we have a couple of games in Philadelphia. School feels like it's going faster this week, but it is the longest part of the week. My reward for the long school week is basketball.

It is our final practice for the week, and my coach tells us to all play a game of Knock Out while he speaks to our parents. Both of our games are on Saturday, so we will get a little bit of a break on Sunday and not have to stay over. My parents decided to print the directions from MapQuest, and we are going to drive with only two of the other families. It was much easier to follow each other in a small group rather than my entire team. We arrive safely at the gym. I enjoyed listening to my Walkman on the way, and I waved to my friends behind us and in front of us every so often.

We enter the gymnasium, and it is pretty run-down, and most of the lights are out. Only a handful of them have bulbs. It doesn't bother me too much. I have played in old run-down gyms before. My parents aren't too thrilled, and I hear the parents saying to one another, "Did we really pay all of that money to come to this tournament?"

Being run-down wasn't the worst of it. The bathrooms don't have any toilet paper. Luckily, some of our moms have tissues in their purses, and my dad goes to the car to get napkins. We have to be a team on and off the court today. We are really rationing what we have today. Dad is holding the napkins and laughs as he says, "Jill, these will have to do."

I agree and am happy we had the napkins in our car. My teammates and I go into the bathroom, and we all say among each other how nasty this gym is. The home team doesn't seem to be fazed by the shape of their bathroom, and I can see having zero toilet paper doesn't seem to bother them. Somehow, they are still using the stalls. They have about ten girls on their team, and only two parents are in the bleachers on their end. Of course, there's no soap either, which is not good. It is disgusting to think that everyone will be touching the same ball today. I'm sure germs will be spread easily.

Today, my team and I realize how blessed we are to have essentials in our bathrooms, even if our bathrooms need to be redone. A lot of times, our gym is out of paper towels, but we realize that isn't such a huge issue after today. Our team won both games, and this made the trip worth it. The more games we win overall, the better the shot we will have in the playoffs. The number of wins we have in the regular season will determine what division our team will be in. This was one of our last tournaments, and in a few weeks, we will be playing in the regionals, which are the playoffs. I wonder, *If we win it all, what will happen next? I guess we will get some type of plastic trophy as usual.*

We have a couple of weeks to practice until the regionals and we will most likely be playing on Mother's Day. My birthday is this week, and my parents are giving me a birthday party at Fun Bubble, which is right up my alley. Fun Bubble is a big complex inside a dome bubble which consists of a rollerblading section as well as basketball courts and a baseball and soccer field. My party is this Friday after school at 4:00 until 7:00 p.m.

We arrive with the goodie bags and check in with the people that work there. My friends begin arriving. Of course, Ashley is here along with our other friends from school and some of my new and old basketball friends. I haven't seen Michael in a while, but I invited him and his brother. Francesco is happy to have a few friends of his come too. We start off by dividing everyone into two teams to play soccer. Followed by soccer is basketball, baseball, and rollerblading. Halfway through, we enjoy some pizza and snacks. We do some more playing, and then later, we will be having the cake.

My mom and dad are sitting with the other parents who they have become friends with over the years. They are talking, eating, and enjoying coffee together. As we are rollerblading, Michael comes next to me and asks me, "Who are all of the boys here?"

"They are my friends from school. Why?"

"I was just wondering. Are any of them your boyfriend?"

"No, but why should that matter to you? They are my friends, and I've known them longer than I know you." I don't know why he cares who my friends are.

It is time for the cake, and all of my friends are standing behind me and sitting on the sides of me. My mom has her camera out and takes a bunch of pictures. Mom is a picture person and tries to capture every moment that she can. I guess that is why I enjoy taking pictures also. My aunt gave me her old camera, and I love to take pictures with it. We now have throwaway cameras also, so when we get the pictures developed, the camera is then thrown away. It is a one-time use.

At home, Mom has containers full of photos from the day we were born. We all enjoy the ice-cream cake, and it is time to hand out the goodie bags. They are filled with candy, sports pencils, and sport erasers. I had such a great time celebrating with everyone and wish I could come here every day. I ask Ashley if she had fun, and she says, "Yes, but I am not really into sports. I hate sweating." I feel bad that she didn't enjoy it as much as I did, but I am glad she came.

The rest of the weekend we enjoy being AAU-free, and we celebrate my birthday with our family. This year's birthday is much nicer than last year. Last year, my parents still weren't fully back together, so I had to have two celebrations—one with my mom's side of the family and one with my dad's side. Francesco had to do the same. I remember his birthday feeling a bit more awkward. It was hard to have fun when you know there is war among your family.

There is only one more week of practice until the regionals. This week, in school, we have the plant sale where vendors are set up with different plants and flowers so that we can purchase them as gifts for Mother's Day. My parents give Francesco and I twenty-five dollars each which will allow us to buy roughly three plants each. Francesco buys three, and so do I. We give one each to our grandmothers, and Mom gets one each too. Francesco and I happen to get Mom the same kind of plant, and in the future, she says she will be able to replant them together in one big pot.

Nana is great with plants, and she truly has a green thumb. When plants aren't doing well, we send them to her, and she is like a hospital for them. She always brings them back to us looking healthy and green again.

It is Sunday morning and time for our first game, which is at 9:00 a.m. I had to get up pretty early to get my nebulizers and chest PT done. My team starts warming up at 8:30 a.m. Before starting the game, we have a small Mother's Day ceremony where all of the players bring a bouquet of flowers to our mothers. Mom hugs me and tells me, "Thank you." I can see this made her happy. I feel bad that my game fell on Mother's Day, but it is nice to be able to spend the day together.

In between the games, my family goes to the diner for lunch, and then we go home for a bit until the second game starts. Luckily, the gym we are playing at is only about five minutes from our house. It was nice that the regionals were held in our borough this year. We have teams that had to travel to us today. We win our first game but lose the second one. I scored a few points in each game, but the second one was pretty challenging. The other team was much taller and stronger than we were. The only way we got some points on the board was by shooting from the perimeter. That was our last game of the season, and I am kind of bummed that it is over. I am becoming more competitive, and I enjoy when we win, but it has been a great experience and a lot of fun.

My coach tells us that he wants to either have a pancake party or a pizza party to celebrate the end of our season. We have one more month left of school. The days are getting warmer, and we are sweating again. It is hard to concentrate in class when you are sticking to the chairs. We use cold water bottles and wet paper towels on our necks to try and keep cool. I have been wearing shorts since May 1.

Gym class is the worst part of the warm weather. My classmates and I enjoy playing the games, but we don't enjoy sweating bullets. I can't understand how our parents pay so much money for tuition and yet we still don't have air-conditioning. I have been in this school for five years now, and everything is still the same. The pink and blue bathrooms are falling apart even more than they were the previous years. The doors won't stay closed in the bathroom, and sometimes we have to use toilet paper and wedge it between the doors. Not to mention the toilets are leaking water when they are flushed. The janitors have been mopping up the puddles of water quite a bit. My friends and I hold the doors closed for each other.

I am excited it is the last week of school. My teacher has brought in a bunch of movies for us to watch, and we are finally enjoying this classroom. I would still rather be home in the AC. We received our report cards today. I did well in all of my classes except I did not score too well on the state English exam, which I knew would happen. My teacher speaks with my mom and informs her that if I don't go to a summer tutoring program for reading comprehension, I will be left back and have to repeat the third grade. I had a feeling I failed the exam since I didn't really read the passages. I wasn't interested in the stories, so I decided to bubble in anything and hoped for the best.

Part of the exam was made up of writing and the other part was reading comprehension. I scored a two out of four. My mom is a bit upset, but she doesn't know that I didn't read the passages. She really thinks that I have some sort of reading comprehension problem. My mind tends to wander a bit on such large English exams.

It is time for the pizza party with my AAU team tonight. My coach has it at his house, and we are all excited to see each other. It has been about one month since we were last together. We all hangout downstairs, and our parents are upstairs with our coaches. We are having fun laughing and eating. One of our teammates is wearing a strange pair of brown shoes that almost look like slippers. She is a bit strange and different from the rest of us, but she is a good and caring person.

One of my other teammates who I have become friendly with decides to play a prank on her and take her shoes. When she isn't looking, she picks them up and puts them in the recliner of the couch and closes them in it. My teammate comes inside, and she is looking for her brown shoes. I felt bad because she already knows who took them, and who else would take them besides the ball-breaker? Everyone is laughing, and I laugh a bit too, but I don't want to be in the middle of this.

As my teammate looks for her shoes, I quietly get up and head up the steps. I hear her telling my other teammate that she knows she took them. I can hear her begging her to give them back. I come back into the room where they are. My friend who hid them finally gives her a hint, and she finds them. She says, "That was really mean."

I have to agree, but I mind my own business, and afterward, I tell my friend that what she did was mean. She says, "It was just a joke. I meant no harm."

The pizza party is over, and on the way home, my parents tell me that my team has been invited to the invitationals in Orlando, Florida. My parents tell my brother and I we are going to Disney in a couple of weeks. I am beyond excited! I have never been to Disney before. Basketball is allowing me to travel and see a lot of places that I most likely wouldn't have visited this year. Our summer clothes don't fit from last year, so my mom takes Francesco and I shopping for some new clothes and bathing suits.

*****

The next couple of weeks we spend packing things and ordering medications to ensure we have enough for our trip. We also have to get a doctor's note to allow us to bring certain medical equipment onto the plane. We have also been given a note from my doctor that allows us to move to the front of the lines in the amusement park. With the heat and humidity that Florida has during the month of July, it will be difficult for me to wait in those long lines with my breathing condition.

It is the morning of our flight, and we drop Zach at Nanie and Grandpa's house. I am going to miss Zach so much, but I know they will take great care of him and give him lots of love. My parents have a taxi bring us to the airport in Long Island. We hit some traffic but arrived in time for our flight. This is my first time on an airplane as well as my brother's. I get to sit at the window seat, and I love looking at the clouds as we fly above them. Taking off was a bit scary at first, but before you know it, we were above the clouds. I didn't even realize we would be flying over the clouds, and it is peaceful up here. I wonder how far up the sky actually goes. My ears pop a lot, and we are all chewing gum to help keep them from popping more.

I listen to my Walkman and eat lunch. The lunches are small portions, but they are enough to hold us while we are flying. Before you know it, two hours later, we arrive in sunny hot Florida. As the plane lands, my dad says, "Here, take this."

Mom opens her hand, and in it is my dad's bridge from his mouth. He then says, "I feel like I am going to pass out." Dad says, "The pressure must have popped it out." Dad cannot look at teeth without getting squeamish and lightheaded.

Francesco runs to the back of the plane to ask the attendant for some cold water. My dad sits and has some water and begins to feel much better as Mommy is telling him to just relax and that everything is okay. My mom wraps the teeth up and puts them in her bag. My parents think it's best to wait until we return home to have his bridge replaced, but for the meantime, he is going to be careful when eating.

The airport is about twenty minutes from where we are staying. My parents rent a car, and when we check into the hotel, some of my teammates are already there. Some of them aren't coming until tomorrow. Our first game is in two days, so hopefully, everyone will get here on time. Tomorrow night, we have practice for about an hour. The complex has given all of the teams some gym time so we can get used to their courts.

Florida is beautiful. I love the palm trees, and it is relaxing here but too hot for me to live here all year-round. We get settled in and head to the food court, which is on the premises at our hotel. I am starving, and when we reach the food court, they have a drink package which includes unlimited soda for one set price for the entire stay. My parents purchase drink packages for Francesco and me. The resort gives us a huge drinking container each, and I am excited to enjoy my favorite soda, Coca-Cola.

My mother tells me that I am not actually going to have unlimited soda. She tells me that it's important I stay hydrated with water and Gatorade. On a regular basis, I am only allowed a certain amount of soda and only really drink it on special occasions. We sit with some of my teammates and their families in the food court. I am having so much fun already.

After we eat, we are tired and head back to the room. Mom unpacks our bags, and she says, "Oh no. Where are the enzymes?"

Dad looks at her and says, "How could we forget them?"

Mom looks again through all of our bags, and still no enzymes. We only have the ones that I carry with me at all times. I am lucky if I have enough for the next twenty-four hours. My parents call Nanie and tell her where the enzymes are, and she goes in the closet in our house and grabs two big bottles. She overnights them to us with FedEx. As far as tonight goes, we have to ration my enzymes. Mom picks out low-fat foods for me to eat. This way, I don't get a bad stomachache.

After dinner, we go back to the room, and I hang out with my friends outside of our room doors. The next day, my enzymes arrive at the hotel while I am at practice with Dad. Mom got them from the front desk, and they arrived safe and sound.

Practice was a lot of fun, but it was scorching hot outside. We took a lot of team pictures outside of the complex at Disney's Wide World of Sports (DWWS). I have never seen a place like this before. It consists of about ten basketball courts and numerous baseball and soccer fields. I am sure there is more that I didn't see. It is impossible to see the entire complex in just one hour.

As we come out of practice, it begins to pour. The rain feels so good, but we are all saturated. We run as fast as we can to our cars. When we reach the hotel, we wait in the cars for the rain to stop. I hope the rain cools things off a bit, but it seems to be remaining warm and sticky. I cannot wait to take a shower and be in the air-conditioning.

For dinner tonight, we decide to go off of the premises with two of the other families. When we get back to the hotel, we all hang out outside our doors again. All of our rooms are near each other. As it gets late, everyone goes back into their rooms. My friend, Ali, and I hang out a bit longer in our room. We laugh and imitate some of the movies we both enjoy. Our favorite one to imitate is *Big Daddy*.

We go to bed, and before we know it, it's time for breakfast, and then off to our first game we go. When we arrive at the complex, someone escorts us to the court where we will be playing on. It is very easy to get lost in this place. Finding the restroom is also a challenge, but with some help, we manage to find our way around. As we walk through the hallway, we see a big trophy made of crystal, and it is about two to three feet tall. It is shaped like a huge cup. I point to it and say to my parents, "I want to win that one."

My dad laughs and says, "Maybe you never know. Just play hard and smart, and maybe you guys will win it."

I know it will be almost impossible. We are the smallest team here and definitely not the strongest but possibly one of the fastest. There are teams from all over the country. I feel like I am in the Olympics. One of my teammates' parents has warm-up shirts and jerseys made with our last names on them. I love them and feel like I am a pro with my name on the back. My jersey reads Monitello with the number 00. I couldn't get number four, so I chose something that would make me stand out. I have never seen a basketball player wear 00 before, but I think it's unique. One of the other parents made us green towels with the AAU Diamonds lettering on it. It isn't a towel to use but rather a towel that we will put pins on. Each team we play against is supposed to bring a pin from their hometown, and before each game, we will be trading pins with our opponents. It is so cool to see where all of the teams are from. I think the towel will be a nice memory that I will hold onto forever.

We lost our first game, but I am excited to have lunch and go in the pool when we get back to the resort. I am scared to go down the big water slide, but my friend, Ali, is telling me to stop acting like a wimp and to go down it with her. I agree to give it a try and am really enjoying it. It isn't scary at all, and I cannot wait to get back in line to go down again. I was a bit worried because every time I go under the water, I always wind up clogging my ear and getting an ear infection, and I don't want that to happen while I am away.

The rest of our team is also in the pool. This pool is huge, and it is easy to lose each other, but Ali and I stay together. My parents and Ali's parents are also becoming friendly, and tonight, we are all going out to dinner. My parents aren't great with directions, and neither are Ali's, so of course, we all get lost. As we are driving, we see a sign that says Tampa. I hear my dad say, "Tampa!"

We pull over and look at the map to try and get back on the right path. We are at least a half hour out of the way, and since we are starving, we decide to eat at the Macaroni Grill. It is a chain restaurant, so we aren't expecting anything gourmet. We all order, and the food takes quite a while to come out. Ali, Francesco, and I are laughing and drawing on the paper that the restaurant has given us. Our waitress serves our food, and it isn't the best quality which is expected. The food is also cold and not very edible.

Before we leave the restaurant, Ali writes "Macaroni Grill Stinks" on the brown paper beneath her plate. She shows me the words she wrote, and I start laughing. She then uses the knife to cut the crayon in pieces. As we drive back, I feel a bit guilty. I helped her cut the crayon a bit, and it wasn't a nice thing to do. The writing was all Ali.

We have about an hour until we get back to the resort. As we drive, I tell my parents about the writing and crayons. They aren't happy to hear about this, and they tell me to not do that again. I hear Ali tell her parents too, and they aren't too happy either, but Ali is still laughing. We all agree the food was not great, but we shouldn't have done that. The sun and heat have exhausted me today, and I am ready for a good night's rest. As I lay down, I fall asleep almost instantly.

We arrive at the complex and head to the court that we are playing on. I see that trophy again as we pass it. I ask my coach if the first-place team will be getting that trophy, and he says, "No, only one player will be getting it." He tells us that an individual person will receive the trophy for how well they played. I know I don't have any chance at winning that then because I am sure that there are girls that are much better than I am. Our game begins, and our opponents are tall again, but we manage to keep the score close, and to our surprise, we wind up winning this game. They were pretty tall and looked like they could be a few years older than us. Before the game, we exchanged pins, and they are from Kentucky.

We have another game later on, but in between the game, my family decides to eat at the restaurant that is on the premises of DWWS. They serve mostly burgers, hotdogs, fries, and sandwiches here. I order a hotdog and French fries. My teammates start strolling in to eat here also. It is always exciting to run into one another. We all sit at our own tables, and before we know it, it's time to get back into the gymnasium for our second game. It is a bit of a walk, and all I can think about is the air-conditioning. It is like my skin just eats up the sun, and my hair feels like it is on fire.

Tomorrow, we have another game. I scored about eight points, and I had a couple of steals today. I realize it is better to shoot than try and get close to the basket. Mostly all of my opponents are much bigger than I am, and I will most likely get stuffed by them. I am happy to have scored a bit and that our team won our second game today. My teammates also had a few points each and most of the scoring came from the perimeter. The weather is beautiful after the second game, and instead of going back to the resort, we decided to go to Blizzard Beach with Ali's family.

Blizzard Beach is a water park. I have never been to one before, but I am a pool person, so I am sure I will love it. We enter the gates to the park, and we are given wristbands once we have purchased out tickets. The lady tells us that they are open until eight tonight, so we have quite a few hours to enjoy the water rides. There are so many things to do, but we head to the big, skinny, and long slides first. This slide uses a thin foam raft to go down the slide. We lay on our stomachs and race down the slides. It takes me a second to get going, but once I do, I fly down so fast. I am pretty skinny and don't weigh too much.

Ali is a tiny bit bigger than me, and Francesco and Ali are way in front of me. If I didn't get stuck starting out, I think I would have beat both of them. It's fun to race each other, and Francesco is enjoying it too. Our parents take turns holding everyone's belongings. My enzymes cannot stay in the car because they will melt, so we bring a small insulated bag to keep them cold. They cannot get too cold or else they will not work properly. We are tired from being in this heat all day, so we decide to relax and go around the lazy river a couple of times.

*****

The next morning comes quickly, and today my team has a by, meaning we don't have any games today. My family decides to drive to Universal Studios. I cannot believe how large this park is, and I am really looking forward to visiting NBA City. First, we go on a few rides, starting with *The Terminator* in 3D. It is more of a show than a ride. I take my 3D glasses off in the middle of the show to see how far away the stage is. I can't believe how far the stage actually is from us. My parents and Francesco keep their glasses on and enjoy the entire show in 3D.

Next, we go to the *Scooby Doo* ride which is also pretty cool. I get a bit dizzy on it. Everything is moving at once, and my seat is going up and down and side to side. These types of rides always make me nauseous. Yesterday, a few of my friends came to the game with their hair wrapped, and I asked them where they had it done. They said that Universal Studios has a kiosk that does it. My parents tell me that after NBA City, I can have it done too.

NBA City is so cool. There is a big basketball player statue outside the entrance. We take a few pictures and head inside to see what the hype is all about. Right inside the door is a regular life-size basketball hoop and a foul line which a lot of people are waiting in line to try. After we eat at their restaurant, my parents let Francesco and I do the foul shooting. They give you one minute, and you have to try and get as many foul shots in as you can. I get a lot of my shots in, and from behind, I hear strangers saying, "That girl's good."

In my head, I think to myself, *I better make them in because no one is defending me right now, but most of the people shooting aren't getting in anywhere near the number I am.* We spend about twenty-five minutes taking turns shooting, and then we leave NBA City and walk to the hair-wrapping place. The lady picks out a small section of my hair to use. She then tells me to pick out two colors. I choose green as well as white to match my team colors, and about thirty minutes later, it is all done. My head is a bit sore, and it is pulling toward the back of my head. I guess I just have to get used to it.

We go to a few of the other exhibits, and our last stop is the *Jaws* ride, which is on a boat. I am a bit scared of the fire, but I know the shark is fake. It acts just like a real shark, and you can tell a lot of work and money has been put into this ride. As the shark gets closer, it sprays us with water, and it feels refreshing. It helps us cool off a bit. I think the water was my favorite part of this ride. I didn't really care for the rest of it.

Dad uses his video camera and captures most of the week, and Mom took plenty of photos too. Tomorrow is our last day here, and we have just one game. Our game is pretty early, and I wake up as the sun is rising. We have a quick breakfast and get to the gym.

We wind up losing our last game in Disney. The team we just finished playing wasn't too feminine. One of the girls looked like a boy with very short hair, extremely long shorts down to her ankles, and she was huge and very strong. I asked my teammates if that was a girl or a boy, and they were just as confused as I was. My friend who is the ball-breaker on my team tells me, "It's a shim. You know, a she-him."

I look at her and laugh a tiny bit and say, "Okay. I got it. Well, that makes sense."

My friend was guarding "Shim" the entire time, and she said, "Shim played like a guy. I could barely guard her without climbing on her back." That would make sense why she fouled out today. Overall, I had an amazing time, and it was such a great experience. This may have been a once-in-a-lifetime type of experience. It was also nice to get a vacation out of this trip.

We decided to stay an extra day. As we are getting ready to leave, my dad's phone rings, and it is my coach informing us that I was nominated for an award, and I won it. I cannot believe this is happening, and I am in complete shock. My coach explains to my dad that each team was asked to nominate one player that they felt played well as well as someone involved in community service. Over eight hundred people were nominated consisting of both boys and girls from many different sports. After the nominations are in, then DWWS comes out to the games, and they watch the players that are nominated. They are the ones who pick the winner.

They ask if we can come tomorrow to receive the award because the newspaper will be present at the event along with the DWWS members. My parents reschedule our flight for later on so that we can attend. I am asked to wear my uniform. That way, the Diamonds will be represented.

My mom, of course, has her camera, and my dad has the video camera going as well. We arrive, and as we walk into the building, I see that large cup-shaped trophy again, and next to it is a smaller one with the letters reading Sears Excellence Award. The people from DWWS introduce themselves to us, and then they ask me to stand behind the trophy. I am asked to hold the trophy for a bunch of photos. Mom is snapping pictures as the newspaper is taking them also. Dad is taking a video.

After my pictures are taken by myself, my family joins in also. It is a beautiful trophy made out of crystal and a wooden base. My coaches are also here, and a couple of my friends from my team stayed to see me receive the award. I take pictures with all of them, of course. I have the biggest smile on my face and cannot believe I have won this trophy out of so many athletes. Some of my opponents and the older girls and boys are watching me receive the award, and they congratulate me. I think they are a bit shocked that someone as small as I am and as young as I am just won this.

I ask the people from DWWS who is getting the big trophy, and they respond, telling me that they aren't sure yet, but that I will be nominated for that one also. They will be presenting that award at a later time in about a month from now when the other sports finish up. I feel like I have won the entire tournament. I also got awarded two hundred and fifty dollars, but I have chosen to give the money to the PAL which is the organization that my team is a part of. I am excited to share this good news with my family and friends back home.

As we leave the complex, Dad is so happy and says, "That was great. This made it even more worth it." This sure was the icing on the cake. After receiving the award, we eat and get my second therapy done. We are all pretty tired since it was an unexpected busy day, so we take a rest before going to the airport. I wake up from napping, and for a minute, I forget where we are and why we are still here. A cab is here to pick us up, and twenty minutes later, we are at the airport.

As we get out of the cab and walk a few feet, my parents realize they forgot the video camera and the tapes we recorded in the cab. We call the car service and track down the cab. Dad takes another cab to get to the car service office, and luckily, he is able to locate the cab, and he got his camera bag back. Dad keeps saying that he doesn't care if the camera was stolen but he just wants the tapes. He makes it back to the airport just in time, and we board the flight. I am drained and fall asleep on the plane after we take off.

Before we land the, thunder and lightning wakes me up. Mom tells me that they are having issues landing due to the weather. We circle for about twenty minutes, and as we land, it is pretty shaky, but we reach the ground safely. Thank God we made it home safe. That weather scared me a bit. Every day while we were in Florida, it rained once per day and mostly in the afternoon. Just when I thought we escaped the rain, we came home to the same weather.

Grandpa has come to pick us up, and since it is so late, the ride back is only about forty-five minutes. Zach is extremely happy to see all of us, and he is jumping and running around when we walk in the door. I am happy to be home and am looking forward to sleeping in my own room.

*****

The next day, my parents put my award in our living room on top of the entertainment center. I love looking at it. It reminds me of all of my hard work that I do each day. I am reminded of the hard work that I put into caring for myself each day and how hard we work to raise money to find a cure. Not to mention how hard I work at becoming a better basketball player and student. Winning this beautiful award has made our trip so much more special and completely unexpected. I am proud to represent the PAL Diamonds and be a part of the CF community while achieving my dreams. Today, I learned that nothing is impossible.

As of now, a cure to CF seems impossible, but I know God hears my prayers, and I believe one day, it will be possible, but I don't think we are close to one yet. After all, when I was diagnosed, we didn't have many medications. Just eight years later from when I was diagnosed, we now have Pulmozyme and one more inhaled antibiotic. A week has gone by, and we have seen most of our family since coming home. We were able to develop the pictures and share them with everyone. We watched the videos that Dad took with everyone, and it was a lot of fun to relive those moments.

My family is happy for me, and they congratulate me on receiving the award. Over the weekend, my local newspaper, *The Staten Island Advance*, called us because they would like to interview us so they can write an article about the award. I have never had a newspaper article written about me pertaining to sports. My name has been briefly mentioned quite a few times in the sports section. My parents and I were once in the newspaper with two of the other families to announce the CF walk.

They ask if they can interview us tomorrow and if we can also bring some photos of me with my trophy. I am excited and can't believe this will be in the paper soon. We meet with the woman who is writing the article. She is very intrigued as she learns about all I have to do each day and how I manage sports and school. She is a biology teacher and knows a bit about CF and how genetics works.

Mom and I answer a bunch of questions that she has asked us pertaining to my experience in Disney and my experiences with CF. She tells us she isn't sure when the article will be in the paper. We get the paper delivered on a daily basis, but my parents plan to buy extra when the article is printed.

A few days go by, and today, I am going to Ashley's house to go swimming with her and her sister. Mom is also coming to hang out with Ashley's mom. Ashley and I love swimming, but it gets us pretty hungry. We order pizza for lunch and then enjoy one of our favorite snacks: tortilla chips with salsa. We joke around and call ourselves fat as we stuff our faces. It is a perfect summer snack, but I only put a little bit of salsa since too much will hurt my stomach and give me acid reflux.

Ashley looks at me and says, "You barely put any salsa on it."
I tell her, "I know, but I don't like spicy foods."
She laughs and says, "Look, it says mild."

I laugh too. She has a valid point, but I say, "I know, but it's still spicy for me."

We both go back into the pool for another swim. My mom keeps on reminding me to take more enzymes, and finally, I do. After swimming, we go inside, and Ashley plays a few songs on her piano.

"Wow, Ash, you play so beautifully." She has been taking piano lessons for some time now and is much better at playing than I am. She asks me to play a couple of songs, and I do. She is impressed by how I play the long version of "Heart and Soul." She then asks me if I can teach her how to play "Heart and Soul." I do my best to teach her, but I don't have any music notes for her to read since I play by ear. One day, when I have time, I hope to take lessons and be able to read notes like a real piano player.

Later in the week, I am going to have Ashley and our other friends come over by my house for a pool party and BBQ.

*****

The weekend is here already, and it was a lot of fun getting to see my friends after being away. I show all of them my trophy, and they think it is so cool. They tell me I am going to be in the WNBA one day, and I know that is nearly impossible. I now say that anything is possible, but as I have gotten older, my health is more time-consuming than in the past. My friend, Nicki, asked me if I can teach her how to play basketball, and I say, "Of course. The next time we hang out, I can teach you."

She is an amazing soccer player, and I tell her, "I have a lot to learn in soccer to reach your level."

She says, "I will teach you soccer, and you can teach me basketball."

That sounds like a good plan. Nicki and I plan to hang out next week, and I can't wait to swim and play some ball in the yard. Since starting basketball and travel ball, I have put soccer on the back burner a bit. I still enjoy playing, but not as much as I enjoy playing basketball.

MOMENTS OF IMPACT

It is Friday morning, and our house phone rings. My mom picks it up, and it is Michael's mom. She says, "What is Jill up to today?"

My mom says, "She is home."

Michael's mom tells us that he wants to see me to congratulate me on my award. My mother tells her that I have my therapy to do soon, but he can come over whatever time he wants since we will be home.

About a half hour later, Michael comes walking into the living room as I shake with my vest and nebulizer going. He sits next to me on the couch and says, "I heard the good news that you won an award. Congrats."

I smile and say, "Thank you." I point to the table as I say, "There is my trophy."

Michael gets up and stares at it for a bit. He smiles and says, "Wow, that's beautiful. Why isn't your name on it?"

I say, "Because we couldn't stay in Disney to wait for it to be engraved. My parents are going to have my name engraved onto it."

He reads the words and turns around. He looks at me and says, "Excellence, huh?"

I say, "That's what it says."

He says, "This is big. You're a superstar."

I say, "Not really." We haven't seen each other in a while, and being around one another feels like "normal," the way things were before I went on IVs. He asks me all about Disney, and I tell him about our trip. He tells me he wishes he could have come to Disney too and that he has only been there once.

My therapy is finished, and Mom has finished barbecuing some hotdogs and hamburgers. We enjoy our dinner and then go outside to play some basketball. He reminds me that we never had that one-on-one game to see who's better. He says, "I think after winning an award, it must be you that is better, but let's see." I get the ball first since he says, "Females first."

I say, "What a gentleman." I shoot and get it in the basket twice in a row and am up by two. When you play one-on-one, each basket counts as one point instead of two. When a person scores, they get the ball again. The third time, I take the ball and drive to the hoop, but he blocks me and takes the ball out of my hand. I know I have to play a bit harder. I cannot lose to him. I let him shoot and swish one point. I realize he may be better than I thought and that I should probably play some defense. He scores again, and on his third try, I steal the ball, and up I go for a layup. I am up by one, and it's my ball. As I am dribbling, he grabs my arms from the back and squeezes me. I drop the ball, and we both start laughing as I say, "My ball, that was a foul!" I tell him to not go easy on me because I want to win fair and square.

It is pretty warm out, and we agree to call it quits and jump in the freezing cold pool. The sun is already down, so the water is probably much colder than it was during the day. Under my shorts and tank, I have a bathing suit on, but Michael doesn't. I ask him where his bathing suite is. He laughs and says, "I didn't bring one. I didn't know we were going swimming." He is in the pool with his boxers, and I laugh as I shake my head from left to right. I tell him that he can borrow my brother's bathing suit and that he has extra clothes that he can borrow also. He tells me he will borrow clothes from him after drying off.

We both jump in, and it is refreshing, but it goes from refreshing to freezing within minutes. We are in there for about five minutes and are both shivering. Our lips are turning a bit blue. I grab some towels from the screen house, and those are nice and warm. He tells me that he didn't mean to act the way he did when I was on IVs. I accept his apology, and we agree to both let it go and just remain friends.

We dry off and have a snack. Michael's parents come to pick him up, and I hand him the bag of his wet clothing from the laundry room. He laughs and thanks me, and his mom asks, "What's in the bag?"

He tells her, "We were playing basketball and got warm, so we went in the pool. I didn't bring a bathing suit, so I wore my boxers."

Michael told me earlier that there is no difference between boxers and a bathing suit. I beg to differ on this one, but whatever; I am not the one swimming in my underwear. In my opinion, when underwear gets wet, they stick to you, and you can see everything that can't be seen when wearing a bathing suit. A few years back, I was with a few of my friends that are girls. We decided to go swimming, and I didn't bring my bathing suit. Mom told me to wear my underwear and to keep my long T-shirt on. It felt much different from a bathing suit, and I don't plan to wear it again. During the summer months, I try to keep a bathing suit in the car just in case.

He asks me, "When are we going to be hanging out again?"

I say, "I am not sure. I have plans with friends this week."

He says, "Okay, we will IM each other or talk on the phone."

I am glad that he apologized about the time I was on IVs.

*****

Nicki and I get together, and I teach her how to dribble the ball with both hands and how to do a proper layup. She is not very well polished with basketball, but with some practice, she can be good. Her athleticism makes it easier to teach her.

Tomorrow, I begin the reading comprehension classes since I failed the state exam. I don't want to get left back for a stupid mistake on my end. I walk in, and it is very quiet. My tutor introduces herself to me. I am getting one-on-one tutoring today. My parents chose for me to have private tutoring and not a typical summer school program, which I think is better. We start off by her assigning me a few pages to read, and then I have to answer the questions. This time, I decide to actually read and get all eight questions correct. I can tell the teacher is a bit baffled. She looks at me and asks if I guessed the answers.

I tell her, "No, I actually read the passages this time."

She gives me something a bit more challenging, and I do well on that one also. I only get one question wrong out of six. Wow, it is much easier to just read and answer the questions. I wish I didn't make the first time around so difficult. I read another passage, and an hour has gone by. She tells me to come back next week, and she sets up a time with my mom. I go twice per week until further notice, but my tutor expects that I will have to attend tutoring for approximately two months.

The teacher tells my mom that I don't have any reading disabilities and that I did so poorly on the state exam because I chose to not read. I knew that, but I am glad the teacher has confirmed it.

We are halfway through the summer, and today, the article about me is in the local newspaper. I open to the sports section, and there I am on the first page. The headline reads, "She's a Real Diamond on and off the Court." Wow! That is some title, and I am honored to be a Diamond. The article is beautifully written. It is a long article.

I let Ashley know that I am in the paper today. After reading the article, she says, "Wow, you are a star, Jelly!"

I laugh and say, "Not really, Hershey."

Ashley and I have nicknames for each other. We made these up a couple of years ago. I am Jelly, and she is Hershey. We chose these names because Jelly goes with peanut butter, but Ashley told me that she likes chocolate better, so Hershey and Jelly it is. I think to myself, *Who doesn't like chocolate?* I am sure there are people who don't like it, but I don't know anyone who doesn't.

*****

It is the last week of August, and Joe calls my dad to ask if we want to take a ride to the Seaside Boardwalk for the night with their family. My dad says, "Sure, the kids will love that. We will meet you guys there."

Seaside is about forty-five minutes away from our house. I have never been there before, but we always pass the exit on the parkway when we go to Nana and Grandpa's shore house. I hope we don't hit too much traffic. Francesco and I are looking forward to playing the boardwalk games and going on the rides. I am not a huge ride person, but I enjoy the Ferris wheel and the slower rides. Since I was young, my dad always took me on the Ferris wheel in Long Beach Island. It is amazing how much you can see from up there.

The first ride we go on is this mini roller coaster that is inside of a tunnel. The ride is pulling the seat in different directions as it goes up and down like a roller coaster. This one shakes the seats from side to side and pretends to crash into the walls. Just when you think you are going to crash, your body is jerked to the opposite side. I am a bit nervous and have a nervous belly feeling. As it goes up and down, my stomach feels like it's in my throat. I have never been this nervous on a ride, but other rides have made me much more nauseous, like the teacup ride at Fantasy Island in Long Beach Island.

Francesco and Michael's brother are sitting in front of us, and Michael and I are in another one. Halfway through the ride, I tell Michael that I am scared and can't wait to get off. He laughs and leans over to me and says, "You're fine, and out of everything you go through, you are the scared one? You are strong."

I say, "I may be strong, but not when it comes to rides. My stomach is tingling."

We are all yelling and laughing at the same time. As the ride goes up and down, it is pitch black the entire time. I don't know how Michael is finding this to be so much fun, but maybe for the boys it is. We play a few of the boardwalk games, and I think I have a shot at winning a stuffed animal. Michael asks me which stuffed animal is my favorite. I say, "The Tweety Bird one."

He says, "I'll win it for you."

I laugh and say, "Thank you, but I can win it on my own."

Michael only gets one of the shots in out of the three basketball shots, and I get in two out of three. I turn to Michael and say, "The balls are overfilled with too much air."

He nods his head and says, "Yes, that's nonsense." He then looks at me and says, "Balls."

Francesco is laughing about the "balls" joke too. I think to myself that girls are so much more mature than boys are. It seems that all the boys gathered from what I said was the word *balls*. I refuse to give any more money to the basketball vendors but try my luck with some of the other games.

Francesco wins a few pieces of candy as well as Michael and his brother. I guess it's better than nothing. I leave with a lime green rope bracelet, and Michael has an orange one. The Ferris wheel is the last ride we go on. They close in a few minutes but let us on. The Ferris wheel seats are closed in all around like a cage, and they have a small door that opens to get in and out of them. Michael and I get in the next available one, and our brothers take the one before us.

As we reach the top, we are looking down and admiring how high up this goes. We can see the entire beach and beyond. He asks me if I am afraid of heights, and I say, "Nope, how about you?"

He says, "Not really, but this is pretty high up." He doesn't really want to look down much, and neither do I. Our seats are swaying slowly from the motion, and it's a bit windy. We come to a complete stop. Usually, a complete stop means that others are getting on, but they are closing soon and told us we were the last ones on. There is no one else up there with us, and we realize something isn't right. We start yelling, "We are stuck. Help!"

To our surprise, we found out that we were stuck and that they were having some issues with the Ferris wheel. We hear our parents telling us to calm down and that they are working on fixing the issue. We are both nervous. I say, "I can't believe we are really stuck up here."

He says, "This is crazy and scary, but at least we are together." Then to scare me, he asks, "What if they leave us up here?"

I don't really want to think about being stuck up here any longer than we already are. Twenty-five minutes goes by, and we reach the ground. Our brothers are laughing and saying over and over, "Jill and Mike got stuck." They are pretty much singing it just to tease us. It wasn't too funny to us, but I am sure if it was the other way round, we would be the ones laughing. As we waited for them to get us down, we saw little by little everyone leaving the boardwalk.

Everything is closed now, and we say goodbye and head home. Luckily, we don't hit any traffic. My dad has work early tomorrow morning. Tonight was a lot of fun, and I am starting to like rides a bit more than in the past, but tonight, my favorite ride failed me.

*****

As the week goes on, I finish up the summer tutoring and am able to go onto the fourth grade. Tutoring was two months long, and the teacher told me that she had to make me attend since a certain amount of tutoring hours was required. The teacher tells Mom that I did well and that I really didn't need tutoring from a learning standpoint, but obviously, I had to do what I had to do to go to the next grade. All I had to do in the first place was just read. I also completed all of my summer reading and took notes on all three books.

I am ready to start the fourth grade and get back into a busy schedule. I did enjoy having time to relax and not rush around, but if I want to be productive, I have to rush to keep up with everyone else. There isn't enough time in one day, and each day, it feels like time is against me.

We are back at school, and my friends and I wait in the auditorium to hear our names called once again. There are about seventy of us going into the fourth grade. We are evenly split up, and I am happy to be with a few of my friends. Most of my friends wound up in the other class this year. After being around my AAU basketball friends, most of them tell me how nice their schools are. They say the staff is nice, and I hope to switch to a different school one day. I will miss my friends here, but I can see them the same way I see my basketball friends outside of school.

Ali and I have remained pretty close, and we still get together often and hang out on the weekends and when our schools have off. I also became friendly with Trina through Ali. Trina goes to the same school as Ali, and I would love to go to their school one day after hearing how much they love their school. My parents tell me that I can possibly switch schools when Francesco goes to high school, which will be in two years.

The fourth grade is divided up, and I am so happy to have my teacher that I had in the first grade. She is sweet and makes sure everyone is doing their work. I am happy that I don't have to explain my medical situation to her since she already knows. She pulls me out of class the first day to remind me that if I have to use the bathroom or excuse myself that I may do so without asking and that I can also snack whenever I am hungry. This makes me feel a bit more comfortable, and I am happy she knows that she can trust me.

Mom is there to pick us up from school, and she is so happy to know I have Mrs. S. I think a weight has been lifted off of Mom's shoulders as well as mine.

Fourth grade is pretty straightforward with a lot of work, but I am able to keep up without an issue, and I am actually choosing to read now, which is great. I don't want to spend any more of my summers in summer school English courses. I also found out who is going to be coaching my basketball team and am pretty excited. Tryouts are tomorrow, and I am curious to see who's trying out this year. As I lay in bed, the only thing I can think about is tomorrow's tryouts. The school day feels like it's dragging on forever today.

The bell rings, and I grab my belongings and head home. I have a snack, and it's time for my basketball tryouts. When I say I had a snack, I actually mean two slices of pizza from my favorite pizza place across from my school. They were delicious, and I feel all energized. The coach blows the whistle, and everyone goes to the baseline to run a suicide. After we run the suicides, it's time for layups and dribbling drills. We then go to some shooting drills, and now it's time to scrimmage.

Scrimmaging shows the coach how we would all play together if it were a real game. I am picked as one of the point guards. There are two girls that are younger that are trying out for our team. The other point guard is a year younger, and we know each other from another basketball league. Her dad is actually the coach this year. I think we will play well together and, hopefully, the coach thinks so too. I am having so much fun that I wish the tryout wasn't over already. Two hours have passed, and it only feels like we have been playing for half of the time.

*****

Two days later, the phone rings, and it is the coach saying that I have made the team. I can't wait until our first official practice. Next week, we start practicing, and next weekend will also be our first game. The week of practicing goes by so quickly. We have all gotten to know each other a bit so far. Today, we are playing in the

Halloween tournament. All of the A-teams in our age group are in the tournament. Their gym is huge and much bigger than ours. It is the size of a college court which is much wider than ours is. I like playing on larger courts. It gives us more room to run and spread out, but it can be much more tiring too. A few weeks go by, and our practices have been a lot of fun. We came in third place in the Halloween tournament, which is pretty good. We have never beat Ali's team yet. They came in second place.

Last year right before the playoffs, we beat the first-place team during our regular season. It is fun to play against your friends, but you have to exclude the friendship aspect and play competitively. It's hard to not smile at each other. To make things more fun, Ali and I grab one another's shirt when playing man-to-man defense and try to hold each other back. Grabbing shirts isn't allowed, but it is fun to do when the ref doesn't see you. It is also pretty frustrating when it's your shirt getting tugged on.

When you play against your friends, you don't just shake hands before and after the games, but you hug them. There is a part of you that is loyal to your true friends on the basketball court. Some of the girls cannot only be competitive but also play dirty on the court. I remind myself that it's just a game, and when the game is over, you will still be friends off of the court, even if it doesn't mean being friends on the court. It's funny because my parents are close friends with my friend's parents, and during the game, everyone sits with the parents of their kids' teams. Talk about a game dividing people, but it's only for one hour. After the games, most of the parents are friends again or rather I should say they purposely walk over to one another to say hello.

*****

I can't believe the winter is here. This school year is passing by so fast already, and I am looking forward to winter break. Tomorrow is Thanksgiving, and today we have a half day. It feels like just yesterday we were getting ready for the holidays. Today, we also have the Thanksgiving assembly as usual where the entire school donates nonperishable foods. I bring a few cans of vegetables and boxes of pasta. I place mine on the stage when it is time for my class to do so. Mom makes sure to send Francesco and I with a bag of goods each to donate.

Imagine not having food, especially on Thanksgiving. There is so much to be thankful for among all of the obstacles I face. I am thankful for my family, friends, a home, and, of course, food and shelter each and every day. I thank God for his blessings each day and ask him to protect my family. Before going to bed each night, I pray, asking God for his protection while we sleep.

The assembly was nice, and it brought the entire school together. For one day each year, it makes us feel united. During this time, we forget about any enemies we may have, and there is a feeling of peace. There is a sense of peace as we exit out of the school building. Nanie picks Francesco and I up from school. Our family is here from Florida, and my aunt shows me how to prepare the string beans and stuffed mushrooms for tomorrow's meal. We clean the mushrooms and then make the breadcrumb filling. I am dying to eat the breadcrumbs alone, but my aunt tells me I can eat whatever is left after stuffing them. She tells me to save the stems because we are going to cook them too.

I have never cooked the stems before, but it is cool to learn something new. I also help Nanie stuff the artichokes. I watch her prepare them as she cuts the pointy parts off and spreads them apart. She then washes them and soaks them. We stuff them with breadcrumbs and olive oil. Everything looks delicious, and I wish I could eat it all now. We don't feel like cooking dinner for tonight also, so we ordered in.

It has been a long day, and my parents are back from where they had to go. We go home and get ready to celebrate the holiday tomorrow. Nana and Grandpa are also coming to Nanie and Grandpa's house. It will be great to see my entire family at the same gathering. Both of my favorite holidays pass quickly, and it is New Year's Eve already. My parents, Francesco, and I are going to a New Year's Eve party at my school. A friend of Mom's is in charge of the party, and we have a table with some of our closest friends. My parents invite

Michael's family. My family usually doesn't go out on New Year's. We are usually at my grandparents' house with our entire family.

All day, I am busy getting my therapies and medications done so I can have fun tonight without any worries. We arrive, and there's a lot of familiar faces to say hello to. My parents show Francesco and I our table. Michael's family is sitting with us and my friend Kara's family. As soon as we arrive, we leave the table to hang out with our friends. I introduce Michael to my friends from school, and they tell me that he is cute. I just smile and don't really have much to say.

The DJ is playing some good music, and I dance a bit with my mom. My dad isn't one to dance. I am not a big dancer, but I will dance a little bit. The DJ hands out plastic hats and plastic glasses with 2000 written on them. Wow, I can't believe it's going to be the year 2000 in a few hours. This is the year that people say that our computers will crash. I think it's all a myth, but I don't really understand it all.

A guy friend of mine who is in my class asks my mom if she will dance with him, and she says, "Sure, Ant." He is a nice respectful boy, but unfortunately, next year, he is transferring schools because he needs some extra help that our catholic school cannot offer, which sounds about right. I see in class that he gets frustrated and needs a little more time to do things than others, but he is extremely bright and smarter than most in our class. It is nice to see him having fun on the dance floor tonight.

The music is blasting, and we can barely hear ourselves speak. The walls and tables are decorated with 2000 tablecloths, sequence, and signs. I wish the basketball hoops were pulled down and we can play while the party is happening at the same time. We can smell the food that was catered in. It smells heavenly, and I can't wait to eat. After I leave the dance floor, Michael comes over to me and asks, "Who is that?"

I say, "My friend from school."

Michael laughs and goes into the hallway.

I go into the hallway and say, "That's not too nice. You are making fun of a friend of mine, and he has issues."

He says, "No, I'm not. I am laughing at the way he is dancing."

I tell him to stop being a jerk, but I notice he does stupid things when he seems jealous. Jealousy isn't a good look. He tells me that I should go and dance with my friend. I ask him why he hasn't danced at all, and he says, "I hate dancing."

I say, "I don't enjoy it either, but I was dancing with my mom a bit."

Michael apologizes for laughing, and a couple of minutes later, the rest of my friends join us in the school hallway. Michael asks if we want to all play tag, and everyone says sure. I tell him we can play but to please be nice to everyone. I know what he is already thinking, and I tell him in his ear to please not tag one of my friends. My friend is overweight, and I know he will tag her every time and make her feel uncomfortable. She and I have always been close, but there was a time when she told me something that she shouldn't have which caused some hard feelings, but we are past that.

Michael knows about that time, but I have to remind him that we squashed all of that and that we are good friends now. He laughs and says, "No, I wasn't thinking of tagging her."

I nudge him in the arm and say, "Yes, you were, but please stop."

He rolls his eyes. I know this kid like a book after all we have spent a lot of time together and have had some interesting conversations. We have to be careful as we play tag since we aren't supposed to be running. Michael gets to be it since he's the only boy playing. Luckily, I am the first to get tagged. Mike laughs and tells me in my ear, "See, I didn't pick the fat one."

It's nice that he didn't pick her, but calling her fat wasn't too nice. I guess it is good that she didn't hear him. As we are running around, the bully is here, of course. She asks if she can play too. Michael says, "Sure."

I go over to him and say, "That's the girl that doesn't get along with me. Why did you say yes to her joining us?"

He says, "I didn't know that was her. I'll just tell her that she can't play."

I tell him since he already told her she can play, we can't say no now. I am now it, and I decide to tag her. Michael tells me let's hide on her since she isn't nice. He then says, "She is a sasquatch. She is taller than all of the guys."

I say, "Yes, she is."

Mike and I disappear into the back hallway and each time she gets closer, we move to another area. She is looking for us for quite a while. We are tired and both want something to drink, so we go back to the table and sit down. We laugh and agree that she deserves this after how she has treated me. I don't know why she would want to play with me and my friends since I am so different according to her. I notice she doesn't have any friends to hang out with which is very normal for her.

About ten minutes later, she finally sees us sitting down. She comes over to me a bit angry and says, "That isn't fair." We get up from the table and go back into the hallway. I tell her that not everything is going to be fair. She has on her face what I like to call her "pouting" face. She then comes over to Michael and tells him that he is cute. He laughs at her and says, "You're ugly, I don't like you." He comes over by me and tells her that he is with me. She has her pouting face on again, and it feels good to make her feel like the odd man out for once since she tries to make me feel like this on a regular basis. I always thought she had friends outside of school, but I am realizing she doesn't have friends in school nor outside of it.

I tell her to find her own friends and to leave mine alone. The bully also tells me she is going to tell everyone at school that I have a boyfriend. I respond with, "Go right ahead, I don't really care." After all, no one that she is going to tell knows Michael anyway. I try to be cordial, but she is always starting with me and makes it difficult to like her. I just want her to find her own friends and leave me alone, but I guess that's hard when no one likes you.

It's almost 12:00 a.m. As we go back into the gym and sit with our families, I tell Michael, "Thank you for being on my side."

And he says, "Of course, I got you."

I tell him, "I know we are only friends, but I appreciate what you said to her."

He says, "But are we?"

I shrug my shoulders. We get along well and have a lot of fun together, but clearly, CF has a way of getting into every aspect of life. It will only get more difficult as I get older. I don't really have much to say back, but I guess actions speak louder than words. They have a large screen set up showing Time Square. We count down and yell, "Happy New Year!" as the sixty-second timer hits zero. We hang out for about another hour and help clean up the gym. What a start to the new year.

*****

January is a busy month, and it races by. My team is doing pretty good this season, and we are in third place. Playoffs will be starting at the end of this month. My family's schedules are pretty packed out. We are already in February. It is a snowy Saturday, and my parents are going away for the weekend with Joe and his wife. Kids aren't allowed to go, so Francesco and I are staying at Nanie and Grandpa's house. All of my bags are packed with some clothes and my medications. I also bring my nebulizer and vest with me. Nanie always offers to do my therapy by hand if I prefer. She gives me a good therapy. I always cough up a lot of mucus at Nanie's house.

Nanie and I laugh a lot together as we do my therapies. Laughing loosens the mucus and makes me cough it out. My parents always feel comfortable leaving me at Nanie's since they know she takes amazing care of me. My parents drop us off, and as we walk in, Dad's phone rings. It is Joe. He says his mother-in-law isn't feeling well and can't watch his sons, so he doesn't think they can go.

Nanie overhears him and offers for Michael and his brother to come stay by hers for the weekend. Twenty minutes later, Joe and his wife drop off the boys.

I feel like I am on vacation with our friends too for the weekend. Nanie's house is always fun. We have dinner and play hide-and-seek as well as a couple of board games. It is getting late, and we are all getting tired, so we put a movie on as we relax in the living room. You can't stay at Nanie's and not have a snack, so we enjoy some snacks also. Nanie always has plenty of goodies to match your taste buds.

We are all getting tired. Francesco and Michael's brother are a bit more awake than Michael and I. They stay in the living room, watching TV. They decide they are going to sleep downstairs in the living room on the couch. Nanie has two beds upstairs in my Aunt D's old room. Michael and I are told we can sleep in there, and our brothers are told the same. It isn't easy falling asleep when someone else is in the same room. When I have sleepovers, it is always difficult to fall asleep. My friends and I usually talk until we fall asleep. I am pretty tired, but after laying down for a few minutes, we both start talking.

Michael asks me if I am still awake, and I whisper back yes. We don't want to wake my grandparents up or my great-grandmother who is right next door. Michael whispers, "I can't hear you. Move over and make room."

I move over and then ask him, "Are you crazy?"

He laughs and says, "Why? I am not doing anything bad."

Our door is cracked open a few inches. I look into the hallway, and it is very quiet. We are whispering back and forth the entire time, but I notice our voices are getting a bit louder. I tell him to keep it down. It is almost 2:00 a.m.

Mike asks me if I want to play Truth or Dare.

I ask, "Are we going to play this again?" This game always causes some type of disagreement or rather exposes the truth about something one of us doesn't want to talk about.

He says, "I promise I won't dare you to do anything stupid or ask any stupid questions."

I am hesitant but say, "Okay." I think to myself how strange it is to be in my pajamas in front of a boy. I then ask him, "Don't you wear pajamas when you go to sleep?"

He says, "Not really. I sleep in my boxers."

Here we go again, talking about boys' boxer shorts. I get that they look like shorts and all, but in reality, they are underwear. I ask him normal Truth or Dare things so that he stays on certain topics. We both agree this game is getting a bit boring. We decide to just lie here in silence for a few minutes. Mike brings up the topic of sexual things. I ask him where he learned all of this, and he tells me from his brother and friends. He says, "Don't you have these conversations with your friends?"

I say, "Not really. Girls talk about different things."

I ask him if he talks about these things with his friends normally, and he says, "Not really, just one time. That is what boys do."

Our brothers come running upstairs and into the room. Francesco looks at his friend, and they both say they are not sleeping in the same bed together. Francesco throws Michael out of the bed, and he goes into the same bed as his brother. Francesco asks me in an angry but quiet tone, "Why are you guys in the same bed?"

I told him, "We were just talking and didn't want to yell across the room, so Mike moved into my bed."

He looks at me in disbelief and says, "Yeah. Well, don't do that again. It doesn't look right."

I say quietly, "Okay, I know." I'm embarrassed, and all I want to do is fall asleep right now.

Michael asks the boys, "What happened? Why did you guys come running in and laughing?"

Michael's brother says, "We heard a noise, and it scared us. Why are you and Jill still awake? It's like 3:00 a.m."

Michael says, "We aren't tired."

Wow, it's actually been over two hours that we have been talking. I am now finally tired but mad I have to share my bed with Francesco. I like having the entire bed to myself, this way I can spread out and be comfortable.

*****

The next morning, we wake up, and Nanie is cooking pancakes and bacon. She asks if anyone wants anything else, but we are happy with the pancakes and bacon. Breakfast smells delicious and tastes even better than it smells. We had so much fun playing hide-and-seek last night that we decided to play it again. Francesco and his friend are counting in the bedroom that we slept in. We want to hide downstairs somewhere, but we don't have much time, so we hide behind the den couch.

MOMENTS OF IMPACT

My grandparents' house is pretty big, so it takes some time to find one another. As I lift my head above the couch to see if they are near, my face is turned to the right, and on my left cheek, I feel lips for a second. I sort of jump out of surprise. I am caught off guard. Obviously, it is Michael, and as I turn my head toward him, he is smiling. He says, "You didn't see that coming."

I am caught off guard and say, "Nope."

Francesco and Michael's brother come into the den, and somehow, they know our hiding spot. They come behind us and scare us. We run from behind the couch and sit down. When it is their turn to hide, we have a bit of a hard time finding them. Francesco is hiding in the shower, and his friend is hiding inside of the hamper. As he jumps out of the hamper, we all start laughing hysterically.

We decide to have some downtime as I do my nebulizers and vest. Michael sits next to me while I do my therapy and nebulizers. In the past, he has even tried to do parts of my therapy by hand. He asks me to talk or say something as my vest is going. I'll admit it is pretty funny to hear someone speak with the vest on. As I talk with the vest on, it makes my voice sound a bit robotic, and that makes everyone laugh. I have done this so many times for my friends and family that it doesn't make me laugh too much anymore, but I can see why people find it funny.

After lunch, Michael and I go into the piano room, and I play a couple of songs. I ask him, "What was that all about?"

He says, "I like you." He apologizes about his reaction to me being on IVs. I accept his apology, but I am at a loss for words. For the most part, we all had a fun weekend together.

*****

My team makes it to the semifinal game in the playoffs. We are playing against most of my friends from AAU. Today, we are playing Ali and her team. I am happy to see my friends, but today, we are opponents. I say hello to the opponents and I hug Ali before the game. Of course, I am guarding Ali who is their best three-point shooter. If I can keep her as far away from the arc as possible, then we will be okay. We are also doing our best to keep Trina from taking three-point shots. Trina also likes to drive to the hoop and draw the foul.

I like taking free throws as much as Trina does. We are tied the entire game, and with just three seconds left on the clock, we are up by one point. I think we have this one, but it isn't over until it's over. We are playing so hard, and my team isn't as polished as they are, but hard work is what is keeping us neck and neck. Our coach is also much better than our coach last year. The ball is inbounded under their basket, and it's their ball. It is in Trina's hands. I can't see how she will pull this one off. Her back is to the basket, and as the buzzer is about to go off, she throws the ball backward in the air and over her head without looking. She takes what I like to call a "Hail Mary" shot. You won't believe this one: swish! It goes in as the buzzer lights up red and sounds.

I am in shock and in disbelief. She got extremely lucky on that one, and I feel completely robbed along with my team. I am also pissed because that should have been our game. We didn't foul her since the chances of getting a blind shot in is close to zero, but she did it. It would have been much easier for her to get free throws in than that shot.

Ali's team is hugging each other and jumping up and down. Both teams line up to shake hands. I am upset a bit, but I still shake my friends' hands and say, "Good game" of course. One thing you will always see from my team whether we win or lose is true sportsmanship, except for the bully. She doesn't always show the best sportsmanship.

My coach and his daughter invite us to eat at Harold's NY Deli, and a few other teammates come with their families too. My family loves Harold's. They make oversize sandwiches which four people can share and still have leftovers. A slice of their cake is equivalent to an entire normal-sized cake. The food is delicious, and I am full.

I am exhausted. I go home and relax. As I lay down, I think about how I really thought that game was ours today. Anything can happen with just a few seconds left in a game. I guess anything can happen in this world also. Nothing is impossible and nothing is guaranteed either.

*****

A few weeks go by. I have more time now, so I am able to hang out with friends more and see my family more on the weekends. I also start back up with soccer, and that is a lot of fun. We only have practice once per week and one game per week. My AAU team will be having tryouts soon. This year, I feel I am even better than last year. I wind up having to miss some of the soccer games at the end of the season since AAU started and we are traveling. Luckily, my tournaments aren't more than a couple of hours away, which allows me to play soccer too when I am able to make it.

My team doesn't make it to the nationals, but we still enjoy ourselves this season. At one of my soccer games, an AAU soccer coach approached me to ask if I would want to play on a travel AAU team. I turned it down and told the coach, "Thank you, but I play AAU basketball and I don't have time for both."

The coach tells me if I change my mind to give him a call. He tells me, "I can make you a better player." He tells me that I have potential to be a really good soccer player. I love both sports but enjoy being indoors better than outdoors. Soccer is played regardless of what the weather is. Lightning is the only thing that stops a soccer game from happening. I have played outside in some crazy weather over the past five years.

It is almost time for the Cystic Fibrosis Great Strides Walk. Basketball has given me an outlet to spread more awareness about CF. The newspaper wants to do an article on me and share the walk details and ways that people can donate to the foundation. The article is going to be in today's newspaper. As Mom waits for me in the parking lot, I come out of the school building doors. I am so excited to see what is written in the paper. Mom hands me the newspaper.

Wow, I can't believe it! I am on the front page again. This is such a cool picture. It is me dribbling the ball at one of my games this year. My tongue is sticking out as it usually is when I am on the court. I am going up for a layup as I concentrate on the basket. The title of the article is "Something to Shoot For."

As I read the article, they talk about how I am shooting for my goals on and off of the court. The biggest goal mentioned is how I am determined to raise funds to cure CF. They are 100 percent correct. I hope a lot of people see this article and choose to join us at the walk or make a donation. We have been the top fundraising team at our local walk for quite a few years, and we aren't going to give up now.

My coach from CYO is outside of the school, picking up his daughter. He asks me if I will sign the article for him. I say, "Sure" as I take the pen and sign the bottom of it. He tells me I am a star and going to do something big. I hope so, but I am not sure. There are a lot of factors in my life that can make my dreams difficult, but I am determined to reach my goals and to never give up. Each year, we increase our goal a bit, and we have been thankful to reach it year after year.

The spring is passing quickly, and tomorrow is the Cystic Fibrosis Great Strides Walk. We have already raised about $23,000, and that doesn't include whoever comes tomorrow and walks with us. I am so excited about tomorrow that I have a hard time falling asleep tonight. Eventually, I do, and it's already time to wake up and start my therapy. It is a beautiful, warm, and sunny May day. My AAU team is joining us as well as our family and many other friends. My coach tells everyone to wear their AAU jerseys, and I put on my green and white jersey with the numbers 00 on it. My coach also has headbands for us to all wear with the words "Jillian's Team" embroidered on one side and PAL Diamonds embroidered on the other side. The headband is white with green embroidered lettering. Dad had a company make embroidered PAL Diamond shirts for all of the adults to wear.

My team and I choose to wear our uniforms. It is loud at the walk with so many of us walking with our walk teams. The music is loud, and it wakes everyone up. The CFF has put out bagels and coffee which were donated by local businesses. After we walk, there will be sandwiches for lunch donated as well. Mom helps the foundation prepare for the walk. She goes with the person in charge, and they go around to local businesses to see who would be interested in donating food and to see who is interested in doing pinups. A few stores and diners are more than happy to join the pinup campaign where they ask their customers to donate one dollar and to sign their names on the sneaker paper. They then hang all of the sneaker papers on their wall to show who has donated.

At the walk, we are given a band to show that we are part of the walk. This way, no outsiders will eat without making a donation. Our walk is at a public park. The foundation has to get permits from the city each year to hold the walk in this location. If we give food to outsiders, there won't be enough food for the walkers. Nana stands next to the food line and checks to see if everyone has a band on. The foundation hasn't asked her to do this, but she takes it upon herself to do so. She is pretty well-known with our NYC CFF chapter.

One of the men doesn't have a band on, and sure enough, Nana throws the man off of the line. She asks him if he made a donation, and he says, "No."

She then says, "If you want to eat, it will be a twenty-five-dollar donation to the foundation."

I am a bit embarrassed with how she is so straightforward with him, but the CFF coordinators tell me she is great and that they love her and appreciate having her help. Nana isn't afraid to approach anyone, and she has no problem speaking her mind. She is a tough woman. I guess when you grow up in a large family with seven other siblings, you have to hold your own.

My friends and I bring our Razor scooters, and we all scoot throughout the walk trails. It is a lot of fun but difficult for us to all stay together. Zach came with us this year, but before the walk even started, he was exhausted. He hung back with my family that didn't walk. I think it was too much excitement for him. He has never been around that many people at once. There were also a lot of other dogs here.

After four hours, the walk is over, and I kiss and thank everyone for coming. On the way home, I ask my mom what we raised, and she says, "About thirty-two thousand dollars." She tells me we are the top fundraising team again. I really do believe in everything the CF Foundation is doing. We seem to be getting closer, yet we are so far from a cure. I guess everything takes time and effort, and we have to be patient. Every year on the morning of the walk, I think to myself, *Could this possibly be the year we cure this thing?*

As I am getting older, I realize it isn't happening this year and that this isn't easy to do. There are so many aspects to CF and different severities. Not everyone has the same mutations. I have two copies of the most common mutation. I have DeltaF508. How could they possibly cure all of us? My entire life, I have been told we are trying to find a cure, but I only see a few medications have come out since I was born. I am not sure how the new medications are discovered, but I know in science class, we do science experiments. I guess experiments are what they do to create new medications and hopefully a cure. The only way to know if something works is to test it out numerous times.

It is Monday afternoon. I come out of school, and my mom shows me our local newspaper. It is a picture of me, Ali, and Trina on our scooters from yesterday's walk along with a bunch of our other friends. If this photo doesn't show my team and friends supporting me, then I don't know what will. There is also an article, and I can't wait to read it when I get home. Mom tells me that the article is all about the walk and how much has been raised.

I am excited to tell Ali and Trina about our photo in the paper together. Their school gets out a half hour earlier than mine, so they may have seen it before I did. Mom says, "I called their moms to let them know."

Over the past couple of years, it's really nice to see how close I have become to Ali and Trina. They are two of my best friends. What is interesting too is our families became very friendly before knowing that our families had faced difficult health situations that we can all relate to. Ali's brother has type 1 diabetes, and her mom is a nurse. Ali's family also lost her oldest brother to a car accident in front of my school when Ali was a baby. They are all very accepting of my situation, and when we hang out, Ali sits next to me on the couch as I do my therapies. We watch funny movies together as I inhale my meds and shake in the vest. She is the type of friend we all need in life.

Trina's family has also faced medical hardships. I can only imagine how her family felt when her little brother was diagnosed with leukemia at the age of four. Thank God he is in remission, and he looks amazing. He is a happy kid, and it is hard to watch him and not smile. He still gets tired quickly and needs to rest more than others his age, but he is full of life. I can only imagine the fear her family has, worrying if the leukemia will possibly return one day. Trina's family believes in Christ the way I do. Her brother's story is inspiring to me, and so is how strong her mom's faith is in Jesus's healing. I think to myself if Jesus got him through this, I have hope he will bring me through my struggles too. If there is one thing I learned from my friends, it's that nothing is too much for Jesus to do.

A few years back, their family went to Lourdes, France. Trina's mom explained to me that people go there for healing, and after she took her son there, he became cancer-free. He also did many rounds of chemotherapy, but leukemia is not easy to cure. She tells my parents to bring me there as well. I am a bit afraid to travel that far, but I appreciate her giving us that suggestion. I guess everyone has a story to tell, which is why I am sharing mine with all of you. Any chance I get to be in the newspaper I accept. I want to raise awareness about cystic fibrosis and hope to get others to join our fight. The more people that are aware of CF, the more people will want to contribute. My life may not be the most ideal or desirable life to read about, but these are the cards I was dealt, and my story is real. I can never write nor share in the newspaper exactly what I go through, but we try and give everyone a glimpse of what it's like.

I will continue to play my cards out until the end. I may even bluff a few times and tell myself my life is pretty normal, but right now, it does feel pretty normal to me. I have Ali's birthday party next week, and she is having a pool party in her yard. I cannot wait. Ali has invited a bunch of girls from our team. We have a great time eating together and swimming. We also fit in some basketball in between swimming.

*****

School comes to an end, and luckily, I don't have to go to summer school this year. This year, I chose to read and concentrate on my English class. I want to spend the summer doing fun things. It is a hot summer, and we spend most of the time in the pool and with our friends and family. I am looking forward to going to the Villa Roma in a couple of weeks, but today is my aunt and uncle's block party. My aunt and uncle tell me to invite my friends, and I invited a few of them, and my family invited their families too. Unfortunately, Ali couldn't make it because she is on vacation, but Trina and our other friend that I call the ball-breaker from our AAU is coming.

Michael and his family are coming also. Michael lives one block away, and he messaged me saying he will pass by earlier before everyone comes, and then he says he will come later on. He tells me he has something to show me. I go early and help my aunt and uncle set up the tables, coolers, and canopy as usual. After helping, I take a rest on the stoop while my aunt is getting food ready inside. My parents dropped me off and had to do a few things before coming. Francesco is in the basement watching TV.

Michael comes speeding by on his bicycle. After passing, he notices I am outside and comes to the curb. I walk to the street, and he says, "Come with me for a few minutes. I'll take you for a ride around the block."

I say, "I would, but I am helping my aunt."

He says, "Just for five minutes. No one will know you're missing."

I have my phone on me, so I agree and I tell him, "Sure, but only for a few minutes because my other friends are coming soon."

He tells me that he just got this bike for his birthday and shows me the pegs on the back of it. He tells me to get on the back. I don't want to walk alongside him, so I put my hands on his shoulders and jump onto the pegs. I hope I don't fall off.

As we ride down the block I hold on tight. It is not comfortable being the one on the pegs. It is about ninety-five degrees out, and I am drenched in sweat. That was actually fun. I tell him I am going to go back to my aunt's house, and he asks me to walk down the block and to come and say hello to his mom. He tells me she has been asking to see me.

We stop at his house and go inside for a couple of minutes. I say hello to his mom, and we grab some iced tea. She is happy to see me and says, "I feel like I haven't seen you in a while. You are like the daughter I never had."

I laugh, and a few minutes later, we both walk back to my aunts on foot. The block party is starting soon, so Michael is going to stay with me. My aunts are happy to see him, and Aunt T tells me quietly that he is a nice boy. I tell her he is. She smiles at me.

Everyone starts arriving, and a guy comes around to each house and lets us know that there will be a three-on-three basketball tournament for the kids later on, but you need four players. My friends and I agree to play, and we ask Michael to be our fourth person, and he says, "Sure, I'll play with the girls." I don't think he is thrilled, but he tells me he will do it for me.

Some of the boys are a bit physical, and they are fouling us a lot and pushing us. They are a lot stronger, but we are better than them. The boy guarding me pushes me a few times. It is their ball now, and Michael pushes the guy guarding me to the ground and tells him that he's a girl for being so rough with the girls. Michael is a bit protective of us. He isn't a great basketball player, but he is much stronger than I am. He happens to know these guys since they live in the neighborhood.

The referee tells Michael he is thrown out of the game for purposely shoving the opponent. A little fun just turned into a war. I shake my head in disbelief. I notice that he is a hothead sometimes.

My team wins the first game by a few points, but the second game, we wind up losing. It is too warm to stay outside, so we grab some water bottles and all hang out in the basement where it is freezing cold. Since the door upstairs is opening so many times, you don't feel the air-conditioning, but downstairs, it's pretty cold. Mike tells my friends and I that we are good basketball players and that we could beat his team. He then tells me that his next-door neighbor thinks she is good at basketball and that I can blow her away.

I say, "Why did you say that?" I pause for a second and say, "I mean, I probably can beat her."

He says, "Yes, you can." He smiles and asks me, "The next time you are over, can you please beat her in one-on-one for me?"

I am always up for a challenge, so I say, "I guess so."

The rest of the night, we all relax, talk, and eat. It is like a continuous lunch and dinner with plenty of snacks and cold drinks. The teenagers near my aunt's house are a bit of a handful each year, and they like to destroy things. As we are leaving, my uncle is arguing with them and their parents to keep their punk kids off of his property and away from his house. I can't blame him. They are all smoking and kicking around their empty glass bottles all over the street. They act like animals, throwing the bottles and breaking them. Of course, my uncle has to clean the ones in front of his house.

The police are called, and they are doing their best to get things under control as best as they can. Most of the troublesome kids aren't even from this block, but rather, they come here toward the end to make trouble. This is the way the south shore teenagers are around here. Of course, not all of the south shore teenagers, but a large group of them are. They all think their poop doesn't stink because they live in in pretty nice houses in good neighborhoods. They attend good schools, and their parents spoil them.

My brother and I have never been like that. I always think to myself, *Who cares what you have and what you don't have? It doesn't make you any better or any less of a decent person because of what you have, wear, and drive.* I am really looking forward to getting away and going upstate where it is peaceful, and we don't have to worry about the teenagers getting their way and destroying things.

For some reason out here, the teenagers have made the shopping center parking lots their hangout area. I can't figure it out because my friends and I would rather hang out at each other's houses or go somewhere to have fun. Upstate can sometimes be even a little too peaceful, but peace is just what I need to finish up my summer reading. School will be starting in three short weeks again.

*****

I can't believe I start fifth grade today. This is my last year in the lower grades. I still want to switch schools and go to Ali's school, but my parents tell me when Francesco starts high school, then I can switch. He will be starting high school next year. Just knowing I only have one year left in this school makes the year fly by even faster. I feel like I have to put my all into this year in order to achieve my goal, which is leaving this place.

October arrives quickly, and we have basketball tryouts tonight. It is great to be back on the court. I still have a lot to learn, but I am getting better each year. Tryouts go well, and practice starts tomorrow. We have a couple of new faces on our team this year. Of course, the bully is on my team, and her dad is one of the coaches. I don't pay too much mind to her and just do my thing. I enjoy all that life has to offer from the holidays to parties and sports. I even enjoy some of the events taking place in school.

My favorite part in class is passing notes under the desk to my friends. Sometimes, the notes make me laugh hysterically, and it is hard to not laugh out loud.

It is the very end of December, and right after Christmas, we get ready to move into our new house. It is huge and beautiful. I love my new room so much, and my new private bathroom is pretty awesome too. It's like having my own little suite. I won't be arguing with Francesco any longer over who owns the hallway bathroom since he will have his own suite too. His room and bathroom are even bigger than mine is. It is moving day, and Francesco and I along with Zach sleep at Nanie and Grandpa's. My morning therapy would have been too much for me to do at the old house while the movers go in and out. It is freezing and snowing a bit today. I feel bad for the movers, but my parents are determined to move everything today.

A few days pass, and we are getting settled into the new house. My dad has to get a few more things that he couldn't initially bring, so I take a ride with him. As I walk in, I immediately run to my old room. I stand there for a couple of minutes and feel sadness come over me. All of the memories in the house flash before my eyes, the good and the bad ones, but all of them are felt. It's as if my brain quickly plays a video of all the memories I had in this house for the past ten years. It brings a few tears to my eyes as I think about the many years I spent in this room and how it was transformed from a baby room to a kid's room.

I think of the nights that I lay awake and thought about the real-life things that impacted me and also the nights I had a hard time falling asleep due to the excitement I felt. Through it all, I remember speaking to God each and every night as I looked at these four walls and the streetlight piercing the vertices. I am going to miss this home so much. This is where it all started for me, and with nothing left in these rooms, it all feels so empty.

My dad yells, "Jill, come on! I got everything I needed!"

I don't think my dad misses this house much. He was the one who wanted a larger house in the first place. I also think that us moving signifies a new beginning for my parents and the differences they have faced over the past few years. As I head downstairs, I notice that familiar smell and comfort this house always brought me. What bothers me the most is knowing I will only be able to see it from the outside in the future. I am glad I took a ride with Dad today.

On the way out, I step foot in the living room and dining room once more and think to myself, *Now I can finally walk in here.* Mom only allowed us to use the formal living and dining room for special occasions, and on regular days, these rooms were off-limits. I flash back to all of the holidays and birthdays that took place here. What great memories we had, but all good things come to an end.

I quickly pull myself together and realize that many new memories will be made in our new home. There are a lot of new memories to be made in our new home. I'm sure I will enjoy setting up my new room and picking out things for my bathroom. The new home doesn't have a comforting smell just yet, but it does have a distinct new construction smell. The smell of fresh paint and new hardwood floors and cherrywood cabinetry. I want my new room and bathroom to be lavender, and I can't wait to go shopping for lavender bathroom accessories. Purple is my favorite color, and I also like green.

The house still needs some work, and our yard needs a ton of work. Dad says that it's best for the outside to settle along with the house before landscaping the yard and adding an inground pool. Our new yard is huge. It is one hundred feet deep and around seventy feet wide, which for Staten Island is a decent size. Most of the similar six thousand square-foot houses usually have a thirty-foot yard like our last one. I ask my parents if we can add a basketball hoop, and Dad says that he wants to put in a half court in the back of the yard. I am excited and look forward to seeing these visions come to life.

A few months pass since our move, and everything is starting to come together. The good thing about our basement not being done yet is that Ali and I are able to go in the basement and play kickball without damaging anything. The kickball is bouncing off the concrete walls every few seconds, and we can't stop laughing. I don't know if you would even call what we are playing kickball; it's more similar to a dodgeball game, but we are using our feet. I tell Ali that we should have fun before the basement is all finished.

She laughs and says, "Yes, this feels like we are in gym class." Then we decide to play actual dodgeball. I can't believe how much fun we are having with just the concrete walls and a kickball.

It is already April, which means spring break has just begun for the catholic schools. We are off an entire two full weeks. On Easter Sunday, we attend Easter mass at Ali's school, which I have applied to go to for sixth grade. Unfortunately, there are no openings, and I am on the waiting list. Ali's mom has written a letter of recommendation to the pastor for me. I am hoping there will be an opening by September. I can't believe there are no openings as of now. My school is practically advertising to get more students because their enrollment is low. Supposedly, one of the girls is moving, so that would allow a spot for me to take.

All of my friends, including Ali, love Ali's school, but I definitely can't say the same for my school. Some of my friends at my school know I want to switch schools, but I don't think they really believe that I am serious about switching. I am pretty sure if they had the choice to switch that they would also.

A couple of months go by, and I am enjoying this summer a lot. Ali's mom calls us to tell us she has heard from the school and I have been accepted. She tells me to wait until the letter comes in the mail before saying anything to anyone.

Next week, the letter arrives, saying I am enrolled for September. "Woo-hoo!" I am beyond excited. I can't wait to be in a new setting and have a fresh start. I am excited to meet new people. I will miss my friends a lot, especially Ashley, but this is something I wanted to do for a while now, and it's finally working out. I am still in disbelief that this is actually happening. I don't know how I am going to tell Ashley without her being upset. We always said we were in this together, referring to how we tolerated our school.

Right before school ends, my mom takes me to my new school for a tour, and we get to meet the staff. Everyone I met at the school tells me how much I am going to love it here. I finally feel like my parents won't be wasting their money. Granted, I received amazing education at my old school, but no matter how great the education is, my happiness is way more important.

The summer flies by, and for once, I am not dreading the start of a new school year. Ashley's birthday is in a few weeks, and I am not sure what she is doing to celebrate. Normally, I see her in school, and this year, her birthday falls on the weekend, so that will make it easier to see her. She always has a party with her friends, so I am sure she will be having one. Tomorrow, I begin school, but unfortunately, my uniform hasn't come on time. I ordered it over one month ago, so I should be getting it soon.

At my new school, the girls are only allowed to wear skirts, and we must have a school blazer with us every day. My old school allowed us to wear a skirt or pants, and we also had a sweater for the winter and shorts for the summer. My new school is a bit more old-school and more formal, so we have to look a bit more presentable. A friend that I know from basketball is going into the seventh grade, and she offered to give me her old uniform to borrow. This makes me feel more comfortable walking into a room made up of mostly strangers. I feel like I will fit in a bit more. It is so sweet of Kate to share her extra uniform with me. Just from this gesture, I can tell this is going to be a better place for me. She has no idea how much more comfortable I am now that I match the rest of the school.

My new school also has a school nurse who is here full-time, which is great in case I don't feel well. I am excited, and it is difficult to sleep the night before I start, but after lying here for a bit, I manage to get some rest.

*****

I am up bright and early, and I have to get up even earlier than 6:00 a.m. since school starts thirty minutes earlier. My new school is a bit farther from us too. As we arrive, my mom parks near the gym, and I enter into the main entrance around the block. I find Ali in the little gym with the rest of our friends. Ali also introduces me to most of the other kids. I am loving this school so far. Everyone is so nice and friendly. I truly feel welcomed. At my old school, they pick new classes each year, but at my new school, they pick classes every three years. This year, they are picking new classes.

Ali's name is called, and luckily, I wind up getting picked to be in her class. Most of my AAU teammates are in the other class, but we will still get to see them at lunch and recess.

The first few days are half days. My classroom is on the second floor. There are a couple of flights of steps to go up, and this school is much larger than my old school. It is also very old. Just looking at the woodwork and the brick outside, you can tell it was built many years ago. The radiators look like they are the original ones. As we enter our classroom, our teacher assigns us seats, and even the desks are old. You can smell the old wood, and the bathrooms are also a bit ancient looking. There is a welcoming cozy feeling to this school. I can't really describe it, but it's more of a feeling than anything else. Maybe it's because everything is older or maybe it's a combination of everyone being friendly and welcoming, but whatever it is, this is the school for me.

My teacher takes attendance, and everyone introduces themselves and says something about themselves and something special that they did over the summer. When it is my turn, I tell everyone my name and that I am new here and how I love playing basketball. I tell them about how much fun I had on vacation and that I went to the Villa Roma. I am happy that this school allows us to snack and drink if we get hungry. I know I won't have to worry about a teacher or nun embarrassing me when I need to eat or drink. I also won't feel so out of place around my new classmates. Having certain medical needs is much easier here.

This past winter, I started developing hypoglycemia, which is when your blood sugar goes low. I notice this started happening mostly after basketball games. After one of my games, I told my dad that I needed sugar, and I bought myself sugar straw candy at the concession stand. Within a few minutes, I felt so much better. I don't know how I knew that I needed sugar, but my body was telling me to find sugar and consume it. It didn't dawn on me that I had an issue until I explained it to my doctor after it happened numerous times. It started happening to me even when I wasn't playing sports.

We learned that a few hours after eating breakfast, I have to have a small snack or else I get jittery and my sugar drops. Being able to eat in class will make this less noticeable. The principal who is also a nun has spoken to my teachers about my medical situation. When I met Sister last week, she told me she had another student many years ago with CF attend school here. Unfortunately, the girl had passed away while in elementary school. I actually knew her when I was young. I used to go over to her house once in a while with my mom. I remember her being in a wheelchair all of the time and always doing a lot of nebulizers and therapies. This was before we learned that people with CF couldn't be around each other. It really is a small world.

This half day literally flew by, and I can't believe it is time for dismissal. On the way home, we stop to buy cold cuts and salads for lunch. Mom and I talk as we drive to the store, and she is happy to see how happy I am. We finish out the half day school week, and next week begins a full week. Over the weekend, we go to Staples and get some school supplies I will be needing. We attend church on Sunday as a family at our new parish.

At church, I see a bunch of familiar faces already. This feels like a true new beginning for me as well as my family. Francesco is enjoying high school so far, and he comes home pretty happy each day. My first full day begins, and I still can't believe that the entire room is full to the max and every seat is taken. I am not used to seeing a packed classroom. I hear there are waiting lists for every grade still.

It takes me some time to navigate the entire school. On the first floor is the main office and the younger grades, and on the second floor are a few other grades with my class being the oldest. Our lunchroom is down about four flights of steps and is in the basement. It is nice to have a gymnasium that is separate from the lunchroom.

MOMENTS OF IMPACT

My old school used the gym as the lunchroom, gymnasium, and auditorium. My new school has a small gym which is the auditorium and used for the younger grades' gym class.

The older kids have a gym across in the other building that is used to hold gym class. It's almost like a mini campus here. Another great thing about how the school is situated is when we go to church, we enter right through the school and don't have to walk outside in order to enter the church, which really comes in handy when the weather is bad. We also have a small chapel. I never saw a chapel before but have heard of it.

It is a beautiful morning. The sun is shining, and it's a bit crisp out. My mom drops me off at the main entrance, and I head upstairs to my classroom. We are all chatting and waiting until our teacher rings the bell she has on her desk and says, "Okay, quiet, guys."

Everyone gets quiet, and over the loudspeaker comes on the assistant principal for morning announcements, the Pledge of Allegiance, and our morning prayers. We pray together for many in our world and lives. Each day, she says, "Let's pray for all the sick, homeless, lonely, and people who have no one to pray for them and don't know how to pray." That is a mouthful, but if you listen to the words, there is a lot going into our prayers, things I would have never thought to pray for. This has opened up my eyes to those in need in the real world. I can see that everyone needs prayers.

After the prayers, we start each day with English and science. Later on, we will be switching classes for math and history. My teacher also teaches us religion class after science is complete. She tells us one of the priests will be joining us today to teach our religion class. She tells us that a priest will be in one day per week. As we are in the middle of our English lesson, my teacher excuses herself to speak with a few other teachers in the hallway. They all look upset and nervous. I think something has happened. As our class starts talking while we wait for our teacher to return, she comes in and just asks us to keep our voices down a bit. She tells us we can close our books and that we may whisper to each other.

We are told that everyone is going to the lunchroom. As the classroom empties one by one, Ali and I walk to the nurse's office so I can take my enzymes while I have a snack. We overhear that there has been an attack in Manhattan. We hear the other student saying that two planes crashed into the World Trade Centers. As each student hears the news, the entire school is aware of the situation.

As my class comes back from the lunchroom, we all sit in our chairs and talk quietly. We are all asking each other where one another's family members work. Luckily, my dad works in our town, and my mom is a stay-at-home mom. I start to think about both of my aunts since they both work in Manhattan. Come to think of it, my Aunt D works in one of the World Trade Center buildings. I am worried for her and cannot imagine the fear she must be dealing with right now after hearing the tragedy. I hope she is okay, and I can only imagine that not everyone will live that has been involved in this attack.

Aunt D is also pregnant with her first baby, and it must be difficult to get around, let alone in a building that has been crashed into. I get a glimpse of the TV, just as my teacher is turning it off, and it looks like such a disaster, something I have never seen before. My teacher has tears in her eyes. Over the next hour, one by one, my classmates are being picked up, and then my name is called to go to the office for early dismissal. I head downstairs, and my mom is there, waiting for me. She looks a bit shaken up by all that is happening, but everyone is. We drive about fifteen minutes away to get my brother. My brother's school isn't too close to our house, so it takes us some time to get there.

Normally, Francesco takes the train home with his friends, but under the circumstances, we are picking him up and his friend. As we drive, I ask my mom exactly what happened, and she tells me that both of the Twin Towers were crashed into. She tells me that one building got hit earlier and then the second one not too long afterward. She tells me that two people drove planes into the Twin Towers and that they aren't sure who did it and why it was done.

After picking up the boys, we go to the house of Francesco's friend to have lunch together. It is comforting to be with our friends. Their dad works in one of the Twin Towers, and luckily, they heard from him, and he is okay. He is trying to make his way home, but he is not able to take public transportation, so he is walking over the Brooklyn Bridge and hoping to be able to get home soon. I ask my mom about Aunt D, and she tells me that she happened to be late for work this morning and she wound up missing the ferry. I am happy to hear she missed the ferry today.

Mom tells me that she did get on the later ferry, but the ferry turned around when this happened, and she made it home safely. I think to myself how God makes everything happen for a reason. God works in mysterious ways. I am sure when my aunt left her house today, she was probably not happy to be running late. I'm sure she didn't know that God was looking out for her and her baby. We all sit in our friends' family room and try to process what is happening in what feels like our backyard. The TV is on, and as the news anchors are learning more about this tragic event, so are we.

Today is September 11, 2001, and on the TV, the news reporters point out of how 9/11 relates to the many phone calls that were put into 911. As you look at the TV, all you see is tons and tons of smoke and fire coming out from the tops of both buildings. I cannot imagine how these people feel and how scary this has to be. I know the fear I felt when finding out about this and thinking to myself what if where I live is next. I have never seen anything like this. The city that never sleeps is burning, and people are losing their lives while at work.

We head home, and my dad gets home at the same time as we do. My mom cooks some dinner on the BBQ. I can't say we all have an appetite, but we have to eat. Our conversation at dinner is much different tonight than any other night. We are speaking about things that you can only imagine when having a nightmare. The problem is this is real, and there is no waking up from it. I think of my friends from my new school, and most of them have parents and other family members that are police officers and firemen. I can only imagine what their dinner table looks like tonight. I am sure many of their loved ones are missing from their tables.

I am thankful that the four of us are together right now. I pray for all of the people involved in this tragedy. We are blessed that my aunt was late for work today and that she never made it there. What a sad time for our city and country. The next day, school is cancelled, and we have dinner at Nanie and Grandpa's house with our family. Everyone is not themselves and a bit on the quiet end. Aunt D tells us about friends of hers that haven't been found or located. Right within my family, we know of those involved.

After watching this over and over on TV, we turn it off and take a break from the sadness. A couple of weeks pass, and my dad's job has asked him if he will be willing to go down to where the Twin Towers were to help clean up and to try and find people. The fires are still burning where the Twin Towers once stood. He agrees to go and help. I am worried about him, but I know it is the right thing to do. My dad always helped whomever he could, and I know he will put his all into helping in whatever way he can.

There are so many people missing, and so many families want to know where their loved ones are. Mom has just finished cooking dinner, and Dad just walked in from his first day at what they are calling ground zero. He gets home late. We ask him how his day was and what it was like down there. He doesn't have many words besides saying it's a real disaster, and he tells us it's nauseating to share the things that he is coming across. He says he has found people's clothing and said then you wonder where these people are and how far under the debris they are. He tells us the air is extremely thick, and the smoke smell is unbearable. I know my dad had a tough day today along with so many other workers. All they want to do is rescue these people and hope they find them alive.

My dad winds up working down there for about a month, and each day, you hear more and more names announced of those who have passed. Each day, Dad has a similar story, but each day doesn't get easier. My dad looks tired. I am sure it is traumatizing. As the weeks go on, we find out that the planes that crashed into the World Trade Center were hijacked. These terrorists have caused pain and suffering in our nation forever, and we will never forget this tragedy and the ones we have lost.

*****

MOMENTS OF IMPACT

 We returned back to school the next week after 9/11, and each day, we had a moment of silence and our morning prayers as usual. It was a bit gloomy in school, and everyone was extremely nice to one another. I notice people are starting to respect one another everywhere you go in New York, which is unheard of here. It's sad to say, but I know this type of kindness won't last forever. We are all human and in this together, and we are all Americans.

 The weekend is here, and Mom has a few errands to do. She goes to the food store to pick up some things for lunch and dinner. I stay home and am on our computer, doing some homework. Mom reminds me it is Ashley's birthday today. I am surprised I haven't received an invitation for a party for her. I guess she chose to not celebrate with friends this year. Maybe with 9/11 happening, they didn't plan anything.

 Mom walks in the door and asks me if I called Ashley yet. I say, "Not yet, but I will in a few minutes." She tells me she ran into one of the moms from my school who works at the bank. I look at her and say, "Okay, what happened?"

 She doesn't look thrilled to tell me what she has to say. She then tells me the woman said, "I'll see you later at Ashley's party."

 I look at my mom a bit confused, and she says, "Ashley is having a birthday party, and you didn't get invited."

 I say, "Oh, that's interesting." I haven't heard from Ashley too much lately. I think she may be upset that I switched schools.

 Mom says, "Maybe, but that's not nice."

 I agree, but there isn't much I can do. I still call Ashley and wish her a happy birthday. I can tell she isn't excited to talk to me, so I make it quick and just wish her a happy birthday. She thanks me for calling but is very dull on the other end, which isn't like her.

 This weekend, I have basketball tryouts and try out for my new school's team. Later Sunday night, I received a call that I made the team. I am happy to be on a team with my friends. I am not sure about how much playing time I will get since they are already established, but I will play my hardest. My team practices two times per week, and our gym is one of the largest gyms, which means way more running during our practices. Practice is a real workout. This school is fair with the amount of homework that they give, and so I am able to balance school, basketball, health, and my social life much easier than before. Sister has a rule that the teachers must stick to a total of one hour each night of homework. Of course, studying is additional, but I was used to three hours each night of homework and then studying.

I feel like I now have a life and I am much happier and less stressed. Our first basketball tournament is the same Halloween tournament I played in last year. It is Saturday, and our first game is this evening. I am not one of the starting five like I was on my old school's team. It is so nice to be back in the gym.

The whistle is blowing and the crowd is cheering. You can hear the screeching of our sneakers on the hardwood floors. We all use the sticky pad to help make our sneakers less slippery. Before we had these sticky pads, we would spray hairspray on the bottom of our shoes. Sometimes the court can be slippery, especially if it hasn't been recently cleaned and polished. In today's game, I get some playing time and even score four points. We won the first game and we have another one tomorrow. I don't think I will play too much since tomorrow is against the first-place team. My old school has beaten the first-place team, but we still never came in first place. I think I could be a help to my team this year, but I don't know if my coach sees my potential the same way I do. Only time will tell.

Our team loses by only a few points to the first-place team. I only got a couple of minutes of playing time, but it was more than the rest of the bench. I am pretty much the sixth man. We are given a tournament T-shirt. I must have at least ten like these from prior tournaments.

Starting next week, we begin the regular season. My coach makes us work pretty hard in practice. After all, he played college ball himself. I come home pretty exhausted from these practices. With the court being larger than I am used to, it makes me more tired too.

It is a Saturday night, and it's the beginning of November. Tonight, I am going to a new friend of mine's birthday party. We are going to see the movie *The Santa Clause Two* and then have pizza and cake at her house. I am looking forward to hanging out with my new friends to celebrate her birthday. There are about eight of us going. We all enjoy the movie and have a fun night.

Watching this movie has put me in the Christmas spirit. I want to go home and put our Christmas tree up, but it's still a bit too early. School has also been enjoyable. Tomorrow is Friday, and it is the Christmas fair where the students get to shop and buy goodies and small gifts. We also will be able to take pictures with Santa. My friends and I plan on taking a group picture with Santa. Obviously, we all know he is fake, but it's still something fun for us to do together. We all plan on making a funny face and hold some type of prop each.

Our school is decorated beautifully for the holidays, and you can just feel when Christmas is near. It is in the air. There are also Christmas tunes playing on the stereo system. The first half of the day, we do schoolwork, and the second half is to enjoy the fair. We all take a photo with Santa and we have to take seven of them in a row since we are given Polaroids.

After the fair, we return to our classroom and put the gifts that we have purchased under our desks in plastic bags. I didn't buy too many things. I mostly just bought some little goodies. I did buy some candy for myself along with most of my classmates. We talk and show each other what we bought. Before you know it, it's time for dismissal. Before being dismissed, my teacher votes on doing a secret Santa, and everyone agrees to do one. She tells us that on Monday, we will choose the names from a hat.

As my mom picks me up, it is flurrying outside. What better time to have snow come down than after some Christmas fun? I am looking forward to a snowy weekend. We get to the train in time to pick up Francesco.

I am happy to only have one game this weekend. This gives us time to put up our Christmas tree and decorate the rest of our house. We never finish decorating in one day, but at least this will be a start. I love decorating and helping my mom with the tree, but she usually moves the ornaments around. She says my brother and I put them all in one spot, leaving the tree looking bare in many spots.

Our team is pretty good, and we beat the other team today. I am more excited about decorating tomorrow. I sleep a little later than I planned, but I am in time to help with the decorations. When I wake up, Mom is in the attic, taking things down. I can feel the cold air dropping as the attic stairs are pulled down. This feels like winter. Our attic is huge, and so we have a lot of space up there to look through everything before taking it down. The attic smells like the plywood that is on the floor. We put slippers on so that we don't get splinters.

As I look around, I imagine this whole area being an entire hangout room. My parents have mentioned that they can add a spiral staircase leading up to there in the future and make it another hangout area. I think they are a bit hesitant because we already have a ton of space to hang out. Maybe one day, this can be a two- or three-bedroom apartment for either my brother or I. Before moving here, my family looked at a house a couple of houses away from Nanie and Grandpa. That house had a huge apartment in the attic, and that attic was smaller than ours is.

We get all of our decorations down and sort them in the hallway. We put our old tree up, and it looks pretty lost in our living room, but we plan to get a new large one next year. My mom decorates the railings with garlands. We have two sets of staircases that lead to the upstairs—one in the back of the house and one in the front hallway. This means that we will need a lot of garlands to drape on the railings. Mom also adds bows to the garlands. It looks so pretty.

I am tired just watching Mom decorate that I doze off for a nap while I do my therapy. I love that our fireplace is on and you can smell it. I turn the TV on and put on the music choice holiday station. Now it feels like Christmas. I enjoy watching her decorate and seeing all of our decorations from our last house that makes this feel more like home. In between decorating, Mom starts her tomato sauce on the stove. The smell of garlic browning in the olive oil is mouthwatering. Mom isn't able to do her usual window scenes. Our old house had two large bay windows, and she would set up her elf workshop scene in one window and her Mr. and Mrs. Clause scene in the other window. We don't have bay windows in this house, but we sure do have way more windows. We are tired from decorating and I go to bed earlier than usual tonight.

*****

We are back at school, and it is time to pick our secret Santas. In a couple of weeks, we will be exchanging gifts, but we all agree to buy something small, like candy, each week leading up to the larger gift. I pick and I get someone I don't know too well, but I think I can buy things that she will enjoy. I think to myself, *What girl doesn't like Bath and Body Works?* I am going to get her a nice scented lotion along with a body spray and body wash. Our class came up with a twenty-dollar spending cap.

The good part about Bath and Body is if someone doesn't like the scent you buy them, they are allowed to go into the store and change it without needing a receipt. My favorite is cucumber melon, and that is the scent I buy her. My mom picks it up for me since I don't go near the mall during flu season, which is in full swing right now. I did most of my Christmas shopping a month and a half ago to avoid exposing myself to possible germs. I enjoy picking out my own gifts for my family and friends, so it was best for me to go shopping then. I also found out that my group of friends will be exchanging little gifts, so my mom is going to pick something up for each of them as well. I told her maybe different scents of the lotion for everyone would be nice. All of my friends and I are really into Bath and Body Works.

We have reached the last day of school before the Christmas break. I am so happy it is a half day, and we go into school to exchange gifts with our friends and our secret Santas. Our teachers give us a small party, and it is nice to see everyone before the holiday break begins. I have a basketball game tonight, and I am looking forward to that. We are playing against our friends who are on our travel team. We are playing at their gym, and it is pretty small, so I won't get too tired running up and down the court. This game is also a close game, and luckily, my coach rotated us all which helped us to remain strong throughout the game. We also remained in the lead.

We win the game, and now it's officially the last time I see my friends until after New Year's. We all wish each other a Merry Christmas and give our coach a gift from all of us. He had basketball ornaments made with our jersey numbers on them, which I can't wait to put on the tree when we go home.

*****

It is Christmas eve, and I am not feeling too well. I feel exhausted and feel like I have a fever, and I am having chills. We take my temperature, and it is one hundred and one. Christmas eve is Nana's birthday, and we are planning on going out for dinner. My mom tells me that I can't go, and Dad says he will stay with me. I am upset to be missing out on tonight. My family also goes to midnight mass afterward, and I won't be attending that either.

Mom and Francesco go with Nana and Grandpa along with some of our other family members. Dad makes me soup, and I rest as I watch *A Christmas Story* on TV for the hundredth time today. My fever spikes up to about one hundred and three, and I take more Motrin. We get it to come down a bit. It feels like I have some type of virus. I am angry and frustrated that my favorite time of year and holiday has to be ruined by a virus.

As I stay awake with my face and eyes burning from the fever, Dad falls asleep. I am upset that he isn't staying awake with me. I am sure he is tired from working all day. I miss my mom and feel like I am home alone tonight. If I really have an emergency, I know Dad will wake up, but I wish he was awake. Zach is sitting right next to me on the couch and keeping me company as he always does. I know he can tell I am sick because he hasn't left my side and hasn't brought any toys to me to play.

I change the channels on the TV and find another holiday film to watch. I doze off a bit but don't fall asleep for more than ten minutes. The time eventually goes by, and I hear the squeaking of the garage door go up. *Yay, Mom is back!* I ask her if they had fun, and she says, "Yes, it was nice." She gets me ready to go up to bed and tells me to go in her bed so that she can keep an eye on me and take my temperature from time to time. She makes sure I am drinking enough fluids so I won't dehydrate. I am glad I don't have to miss school due to being sick because I don't want to fall behind, but I would rather miss school than miss Nana's birthday and Christmas.

*****

It is Christmas morning, and Francesco is waiting to open presents. I am having a slow start but manage to get to the family room in time to exchange gifts. I feel much better, and even though I didn't feel too well yesterday, we decide to stay home today. Nana and Grandpa come over today.

The next day, I feel like myself again and am no longer running fever. It must have been a two-day bug. A couple of days later, we go to Nanie and Grandpa's, and it feels like Christmas day all over again. Nanie decorated her house so beautifully and tastefully as always. It must have taken her so long to do all of this, but she enjoys it so much, and Grandpa loves seeing everything decorated. We eat a lot and laugh and open presents together.

This year, my parents have our own New Year's Eve party at our house with our family and friends. We have a lot of fun. My dad is making all types of fried fish like we used to make every Christmas eve. The house stinks of fried food, and the oil smell is embedded in our clothes.

We celebrate the New Year and we all sleep late the next morning. It is a lazy day, and we sit around, relaxing and watching *The Honeymooners*. I get my things together since school is resuming tomorrow. Zach's birthday is on January 3, and he will be turning three years old. I can't believe we have him this long already. He was only two months when we got him. We couldn't have asked for a better dog. He is so well-behaved and he doesn't destroy our home or bark a lot. He is so loving, and I love relaxing with him on the couch. He keeps me company during each and every therapy. He enjoys the rattling of the vest and sometimes sleeps on top of my lap while I do my therapy. It is comforting to have him around.

We celebrate his birthday quietly since life is busy and back to normal. We give him a new toy, and he is so happy.

*****

School starts up again, and it is a busy weekly schedule. School and basketball feel more busy, and there isn't too much free time to just relax. The weeks go by, and we are into February, which is my dad's birthday month. For Dad's birthday this year, my mom is going to cook and have everyone over for dinner and cake. My mom likes to celebrate everyone's birthday. She says, "Even if it's just a cake, we have to do something." Birthdays are not only fun for whoever the birthday is for, but to me, it's celebrating another year of them being alive. Most people don't want to get older, but as a person with CF, getting older is a goal of mine. We fight for our lives on a daily basis, and our birthdays are a victory to kicking CF's butt for another year. Majority of the world, especially my age group, don't think about when their last moment will be. This is why I chose to not attend one of my games in January. Grandpa's birthday dinner happened to be at the same time as my game, and we thought it was best to not attend my game. Plus, as the season went on, the starting five were playing the entire game, and attending felt like a waste of my time. I am very committed to my sports teams, but this basketball season hasn't been anywhere near as much fun as in the past.

My dad's birthday celebration comes and goes so quickly, and it is time to play the first-place team again. I wish being with my family could have lasted even longer. I have been moved into the starting position since Trina is hurt. I am happy and a bit nervous to be starting since it feels like forever since I stepped foot in an actual game. The ball is tipped, and our team gets possession of the ball. The ball is passed to Ali, and she hits a three-pointer. We start the game in the lead. We go back and forth, being ahead and tying as well as being behind by a couple of points. I am doing well in this game, and I have scored eight points so far.

It's the end of the fourth quarter, and my team is playing well and moving the ball around the court quickly. I notice when Trina is on the court, our teammates all become ball hogs, seeing who could score the most, including Trina. She leads in being a ball hog. With a few seconds left in the game, we are up by two points, and the buzzer sounds. We have won the game. Today was truly a team effort, and everyone pulled their weight. We are all ecstatic, and now we see there is a possibility to win in the playoffs or rather the championship game. I can see Trina isn't too happy. She actually seems a bit mad that we won without her. When my teammates play well, I always tell them how well they did, but Trina doesn't say a word to me. Trina and I are best friends, but right now, things just feel awkward.

I am hoping this shows my coach that I can keep up with our team and fill the shoes of his starting lineup. With me playing, we actually beat the first-place team. My parents are happy to see that I am finally given a chance to show what I can do on the court. I work hard on the court, challenging the starting five at practice each week, and so it is nice to be given an opportunity, even if it is because of an injury.

Ali and I played really well together, passing to the open girl and sharing the three-point line today. I have a feeling that after Trina comes back that I will be benched for most of the games again. No one wants to see her or her parents get angry. They will truly make a scene over this. I get that an injury isn't the way to get a spot on the court, but the least they can do is take a little time from each of the guards and give me some playing time. If I couldn't perform, then I understand keeping me on the bench, but that isn't the case.

For the first few months, I kept thinking that I wasn't as good as my team, but after today, I am confident I can do just as well as the starting five. If you were an outsider watching today's game, you would have no idea that I am not a starter. Everyone tells me what a great game I played, and I even made it in the paper, which it's been a while since my name has been mentioned. As we drive home, I ask my parents, "Are there any coaches that look at the players for their abilities rather than who they know?"

My father laughs and says, "I know what you mean and wish they did, but these catholic sports programs are all about politics and who you know."

I know sometimes my parents can overreact a bit like the rest of the parents, but this time, my parents have a valid point. We saw this type of favoritism on my other team where coaches play who they know best and not who are the best players. This can all become a bit frustrating. Although I like my new school better, besides the discrimination situation a couple of years ago, I can honestly say I enjoyed sports much better at my old school. My coaches over there did show favoritism in certain aspects, but they played myself and my teammates according to what they knew and not who they knew.

A couple of seasons ago at my old school, my coach gave his daughter the MVP award and told my dad and I quietly that I deserved the MVP, but his daughter's confidence had been down. He told us that he wanted to build up her confidence with this award. I could not believe what he had told us. I get that she got yelled at the most on our team, but I had been robbed of this award. My teammate's dad told me, "Jillian, you just got robbed." I have to admit that many others agreed as well.

I let it go quickly because not having a physical award doesn't matter to me. Knowing in my heart who truly deserved that award is what mattered. I never felt like I should be in competition with my teammates, but these favoritism situations make you want to compete. After receiving the award that day, my coach's daughter had the biggest smile on her face. She really thought she was actually the MVP. She even went around bragging about it, and I just ignored what she had to say. It was hard to keep my mouth closed and not tell her the truth, but I didn't want to make her feel bad. After all, it wasn't her fault.

I tell my parents that I love the new school as far as school goes, but I don't think I want to play basketball on their team next year. It is only right to finish out the season, but there is too much nonsense, and I no longer want to be involved in it. My dad says we can see about other leagues. He tells me he is going to look into it, and maybe there's one in New Jersey that I can play in.

Whoever wins the championship game will get to go to Dunwoody which is where the state championships will be held. My team doesn't lose the championship by too many points, but Trina is back, hogging the ball as one of the starting five. I am put in for about twenty-eight seconds throughout the entire game which is a bit of an insult. I am neither angry nor happy that we lost today. I am actually happy that this season is over. You would think he would have at least rotated me in a bit more since I was part of the win last time we played this team. My friends on the first-place team ask me when I will be going to their school, and I tell them to stop joking around. They are actually serious, and when I had first told them I wanted to switch schools and leave my first school, they kept on telling me to go to theirs instead of the new school I chose. I explain to them that their school is a long drive for me and that I didn't switch schools for sports but because I didn't like the environment.

My coach tells us all after the game that it was a great season. I guess for the starting five it was, but I am ready to do bigger and better things than just ride the bench.

We are starting travel AAU ball a bit earlier and going to a tournament in north Jersey. We have a few new players on our team, and one of them is two years younger than the rest of us. She must be pretty good to be moved up by two years. Her name is Anna, and I am getting along with her well already. My parents have just met her parents, and they are already hitting it off. Anna is a pretty good shooter and is great at dribbling. I think I may have some competition with her, but she isn't as fast as I am. I hope we both get to play at the same time together. She's better than most of the girls our age and is more polished than I am.

A few minutes into the first quarter, Anna and I are put in together. I am playing point guard, and she's in the two position as one of the shooting guards. I am fast and able to get the ball in her hands quickly, and she makes most of the shots that she takes. I can see we are going to be a great duo. We give each other a few high fives. Her dad loves the way I play, but he says the rest of the team is too slow-moving and not polished enough for his daughter. He tells me to think about leaving the team and trying out for a better team. He knows a lot about the game and says that I am athletic with a lot of potential, but I won't get better with the coaches I currently have on this team.

A couple of weeks pass, and I tell my dad I agree with Anna's dad, and he does too. Anna's dad invites me to come and try out for a Brooklyn team in Coney Island called "Team Marbury." I am nervous to go to a new team, but I am simply just bored of the teams I play for, and I feel that I have outgrown them. I need a change and need to be challenged more by girls who are better and stronger than I am. I need more training to brush me up on my skills.

Tryouts are today, and right after I get home from school, I have to eat, change my clothes, and off to Brooklyn we will be going. We hit some traffic but make it there in time. I am the only one trying out today since the team is already put together. The coach is giving me one shot to see if I can keep up with these girls. As I enter the gym, Anna's dad is here, and he tells me he wants to show me a few things before it starts. He said he noticed that when I take a layup on the left side of the hoop, I go off of the wrong foot. Come to think of it, many of my teammates back home do the same as I do. He tells me I have to be like a puppet with strings. If my left arm goes up, so does my left leg and vice versa for the right side. I practice a bit and learn quickly how to switch feet.

Ten minutes go by, and the girls start coming in. It is loud and warm, and as soon as I see these girls, I am not sure I can keep up with them. I am not prejudiced or anything, but Anna and I along with two other girls are the only white girls here. The rest of the team is colored and Spanish, and they are much bigger and faster than we are. This area of Brooklyn and the people around here are known for basketball, unlike where I am from.

The coach comes walking in, and we all stretch and introduce ourselves. It is hard for me to remember everyone's name as there are over twenty of us. Just by watching them warm up, I know my work is cut out for me. Anna tells me to just play hard and treat everyone nice because they don't play around here. She wasn't kidding.

The coach starts out by dividing us into two teams. He says, "Ladies, let's see what you all got." Within a few minutes, he is already yelling at me and correcting all of my mistakes along with everyone else's. If you are shy and don't like criticism from strangers, this isn't the place for you. I can take criticism from a coach that knows what he is doing, but not a coach that has their favorites. This coach has zero favorites today, and his daughter is getting the brunt of everything that goes wrong. I actually feel bad for her. Even when it isn't completely her fault, she still gets yelled at.

MOMENTS OF IMPACT

Practice is for about three hours; or rather, tryouts for me is about three hours. Although they were more polished than I was, I held my own. I did better than I thought I would when stepping foot into this gym. The one thing I know I need to do is become stronger. One of the older girls was dribbling the ball and I stole it, which was great, but two seconds later, she threw me to the floor. If it were a real game, it would be considered a flagrant foul, and to be honest, it was a cheap shot. Pushing someone from behind as they dribble is a no-no. The floor is tile at this gym, and so it hurt much more than a wooden floor would have. I am pretty achy and black and blued on both of my knees and elbows. My left hip is sore and bruised as well.

As I went down and flew into the cement wall, my coach blew the whistle and told me to get up and to not cry. I held back the tears, but it was painful getting thrown on the tile and flying into the wall. I got back up, limped a couple of steps, and walked it off. I finished out the scrimmage and held my own.

After my opponent saw I didn't cry, she did in fact help me up, and she apologized to me. However, she only apologized after my coach told her that was an intentional foul. When it was over, my coach said, "I will see you all on Friday night at 7:00 p.m." He told us to be ready to work hard.

I go over to Coach J and ask him if I am also coming back, and he says, "Yes. If I didn't want you to come back, I would have asked you to leave after a few minutes."

I can see that my new coach is pretty honest and doesn't pull any punches. He told me that I have potential and that he is going to make me a better player and that I have to listen and work hard. Although I am bruised, I will be returning back on Friday.

As we drove home, my dad asked me how I liked it, and I said, "I am enjoying it, but it's tough." It's really tough, and the competition is on another level. I also believe if you play with better players, then you too will become better. I had to use every bit of energy I had and strength to hold my own today.

My dad tells me to please give it a shot and that he sees me being a better player in the future. I agree with Dad and am determined to be my very best with some help. Maybe I can even become a lot better with my coach's help.

On the way home, we stop at Nanie's, and she asks me why I am moving so slowly and why I have so many bruises on me. I tell her what happened, and she turns to my dad and says, "Are you really having her go back to play there again?"

My dad says, "Yeah, Ma. She will be fine. She is just banged up a bit, but she will get stronger and be fine."

Nanie looks at me and says, "Don't go, Jillian, if it's too much for you."

I tell her I know and to not worry.

As I go home and get ready for school, I think to myself, *How did I ever think that what we did at practices in Staten Island was exhausting? This is on another level.* I took a warm bath to help ease my achy muscles. Then I ate dinner, completed my homework, and studied for a bit. I could have never played for this team if I still went to my old school. Their homework load was overkill. I am exhausted and sleep like a baby.

*****

I get up and go to school. As I walk the hall, I am so achy. My muscles are burning. I tell a couple of my friends about where I am playing, and they think I am crazy. Thinking about my next practice makes Friday come even faster. I also gave up soccer this year since I wouldn't have time for any other sports besides basketball. The new team practices three times per week for three to four hours each practice. We have games on both weekend days from what the upcoming schedule shows. Now I really feel like I eat, sleep, and drink this game.

A month goes by, and our first game is today. It is Saturday, and our game is at 2:00 p.m. According to Anna, they aren't too organized when it comes to the game schedules in this league. Anna's right. Our game was supposed to start at 2:00 p.m. We are supposed to be playing on one of the outside courts, and due to the rain, the games are being moved indoors at the gym that we practice on. My game has been moved to 6:00 p.m. While we wait, we get food in between.

Today is opening day for the tournament, and so Stephon Marbury, who is an NBA player for the Phoenix Suns, is here to help kick off the league. It is his league, and I think it is really cool that he will be here. I brought my camera to take some pictures, and Anna's dad is going to introduce me to him. He will be the first professional basketball player that I will be personally meeting.

The games are running a couple of hours behind and so we go to L&B Spumoni Gardens for some delicious pizza and Spumoni ice cream. This is my first time having their pizza and Spumoni. Let me tell you there is nothing like it. We head back to the gym, and before my game, I am introduced to Stephon Marbury. I don't have many words, but I am in shock to be standing next to an NBA player that I watch on TV and look up to. Just being here to meet him is exciting, plus he got to watch our team play.

My team is the only girls home team playing tonight. He was very nice and signed a couple of things for me and took some photos with me. He also welcomed me and told me that he is happy to have me playing on their family team. It was a very welcoming experience, and later on, Anna explained to me that all of the people that I have met over the past few weeks are family members and close friends of his. It is so cool to be coached by the same coaches that taught him growing up, especially Mr. L who coaches the boys' team. He occasionally helps with our team too.

On Friday night, we split the gym with the boys' team, and they stay an extra hour to scrimmage against us. If we can play against the boys, then we can definitely handle the girls. Today was an amazing experience, and I am thankful to have met Anna and her family. They are showing me a whole new basketball world.

Our team won our first game today, and I know I have to do a bit better next time. I scored some points, and the main thing is we won. I am happy Team Marbury is giving me a chance to learn and develop into a better basketball player. Anna also tells me about Marbury's cousin who is in his sophomore year of high school. He is projected to be an NBA player too. She points him out to me and says, "You will meet him too."

He is amazing to watch and learn from. I am looking forward to attending one of his games soon. We were supposed to watch him on the opening day, but his team's game got moved since there wasn't enough gym time that day.

*****

As the weeks go on and the summer continues, my coach continues to make each and every practice more challenging. I have never been this tired from sports before, but after practice, it feels good to rest on the car ride home. My team practices three times per week from 4:30 p.m. to 7:45 p.m. I feel like I have moved to Brooklyn. My dad and I laugh, saying we are here more than we are at home, but we are enjoying every minute of it.

It is a Wednesday afternoon and since school is over, I enjoy our pool, and my Aunt D and baby cousin who is only about four months old come over to enjoy the afternoon together. My baby cousin, Marie, was born in March, and she is the cutest thing. I love hanging out with her, and it is a lot of fun being an older cousin to her. Marie is wearing the cutest little bathing suit that I have ever seen.

I hold her and sit with her on the steps of the pool. She is smiling, and I don't want to leave her, but I have practice in an hour. My dad calls me as he is driving home from work and tells me to be ready for when he pulls up. I get out of the pool and get dressed for practice. I quickly add water and Gatorades to a small cooler with ice, and I add a rag to soak in the cooler to help cool off my head. It is ninety degrees, but luckily, we practice by the water, and it gets a bit cooler as the day goes by.

We arrive, and there is nowhere to park. Luckily, Anna's dad found a spot, and he tells us to double park next to him. I notice double parking in Brooklyn is a very common thing but not where we live. I jump out of Dad's truck and grab a ball and begin warming up. I start with layups and some dribbling and then onto shooting.

We have already learned that my coach is going to be a few minutes late. He picks up a few of our teammates after he finishes work so we don't ever start on time.

His daughter decides to meet him there, and she arrives on time. She tells us that she tries to never be late, especially since her dad is the coach. He wants her to set a good example for the rest of us. We already know if she is late, all hell will break loose.

Our team is a mix of a couple of different age groups, but our coach has signed up the younger ones, such as myself, to play in two age group divisions consisting of two leagues. We have three games each weekend, and it is getting pretty hectic, but the exercise is great for my lungs, and I am staying very healthy right now. Mom and Francesco join us at all of the games, and it is nice to be together on the weekends. After the game, we usually get something to eat together.

Francesco also started playing on the boys' team over here. At my practice, Mr. L saw Francesco shooting and asked if he would like to play since they needed a shooter, so he accepted the invite. Practice is pretty exhausting today.

My coach has brought these huge foam pads with him that are used to push into us. This will teach us how to draw a foul and finish the layup. Let's be real; he is literally beating the crap out of us, and we are all getting slammed to the concrete. Each time I get up, I feel my adrenaline rushing and want to try and be stronger each time. The slam to the tile floors a month ago was just a foreshadowing of what was to come playing outdoors with this team. The number of scrapes and bruises I have within the first fifteen minutes is insane, and a part of me enjoys building up my strength. We are all laughing as we go up for a layup.

My coach tells us that if we don't get stronger, we won't stand a chance in the "land of the giants." When Coach says the "land of the giants," he is referring to players much bigger and stronger than us. I am the second smallest on my team, and so every game and practice feels like I am in the "land of the giants." My coach has also brought a parachute running vest to train us with which pulls us back and gives us resistance as we run. This vest is used to help us build up endurance and speed. Coach J has thought of everything. When the vest is taken off, I feel weightless, and it's like I am flying down that court.

Marbury's cousin named Bassy, who is projected to go to the NBA, runs on the beach in the sand to get stronger every single morning before school begins. I watched Bassy play last week, and I can see why everyone thinks he will go pro right out of high school. Three long hours pass, and we all can't wait to go home. I am drenched from head to toe in extremely salty sweat. I can taste the salt on my lips. The amount of salt that I have sweated out puts the amount of salt in a Gatorade bottle to shame. I can probably provide the salt for an entire case of Gatorade.

On the way home, I eat salty pretzels and drink some more Gatorade to replace all that I lost tonight. It's already Thursday, and I enjoy having a break and just relaxing in the pool and enjoying some summer snacks poolside. As I do my nighttime, therapy I listen to my Walkman that is playing the newest CD that I purchased. It's 50 Cent's first album called "Get Rich or Die Trying."

My Brooklyn basketball friends introduced me to rap music, and I don't want to not know the songs they sing to and listen to. To be honest, this type of music is growing on me a bit, and it's not what I am used to listening to. I am an Eminem fan and enjoy hearing him rap with 50 Cent. My team doesn't just enjoy playing ball together, but we have all become pretty close. We enjoy just sitting down and laughing and talking to each other. I have made a lot of new friends since joining this team. Before each game, we huddle together and yell out, "Family!" We do feel as if we are like a family, even more so than friends.

*****

It's Friday, and it's another scorching day outside. It takes everyone about a half hour to arrive by the time almost all of us are here. My coach's daughter isn't here yet, and she told her dad that she would be meeting him at practice. He asks us if anyone has seen Maria, but we all shake our heads and say, "No." Coach tries to call her phone, but he gets no answer.

A few of us know where she is, but we keep it a secret. She texted and instant messaged us earlier, asking us to not let her dad find out why she is late. She told us she is hanging out with her boyfriend and that she will get to the practice as soon as she can. When our coach tells us that she isn't picking up her phone, a few of us look at one another with our eyebrows raised. We start to smirk a little bit when he asks Anna, "Where is she? I know you know."

Anna says, "No, I haven't spoken to her."

Coach calls his wife, and she tells him that Maria will be there in a little bit. If there is one thing about our team, we are loyal to each other, and we will do whatever it takes to have each other's backs. We start practicing, and Maria arrives fifteen minutes late. She is already breathing heavy from running here, and her dad isn't happy with her. He tells her, "Before you think you are just going to join in, drop and give me fifty push-ups!"

She responds by saying, "Damn, are you serious?"

He says, "Yes, I am, and just for that, give me another fifty."

This wasn't the first time we saw someone drop and do fifty push-ups. He uses Maria as an example to show our team why we should be on time and why she should have at least called to let him know that she was going to be late. He is trying to teach us responsibility and discipline, but that punishment was a bit too harsh in my opinion. Of course, I have done many push-ups along with everyone else here for missing layups or shots such as free throws. I have done more push-ups within the last couple of months than I can keep track of. If we practice indoors, we also are punished by getting put on the wall. When I say put on the wall, I am talking about standing with your back straight against the wall in a defensive stand with your heels off of the ground and all your weight on the balls of your feet for about ten to twenty minutes straight. This is when you really feel the burn. It is exhausting, but my coach is trying to teach discipline to those who need it.

I grew up being taught respect and discipline, but many of my teammates did not. In the beginning, they thought they could arrive late and speak to Coach in a disrespectful way. A lot of the girls I play with are street kids, and they aren't taught too much at home. It is more the boys that are rude rather than the girls. Coach has the boys practice with us from time to time, and it is the same rules for everyone. Coach is trying to keep everyone off of the streets. Basketball seems to be the way to keep everyone out of trouble around here.

My coach's newest rule is if you fail any of your classes in school, you don't play. My coach collects report cards during the school year. As tiring as these practices are, this is what allows us to outrun every other team until they run out of energy first.

After about forty-five minutes of practice, we finally are given a water break. We all sit on the concrete and talk quietly to Maria. We ask her what happened, and she says that she was at her boyfriend's house and lost track of time. She tells us that her parents don't know about them being together. They think that she was at one of her other friend's houses. She tells her dad that she lost track of time and had to go home to get her shoes before coming here. If she continues to sneak around, I think she will eventually get caught.

Maria is eleven years old like I am, and her boyfriend is thirteen. He is actually on the boy's team that her dad coaches. She knows him from being in the same school. Maria isn't having a good practice at all, and she keeps messing up. She is turning over the ball a lot and missing easy layups, which isn't like her at all. She is one of our best players. She just isn't here today. I am not sure where her brain is, but I think she left it at her boyfriend's.

Coach yells at her for the thousandth time tonight, and before we know it, he tells her to go home. He asks Anna's dad to give her a ride and to make sure she goes into their apartment building. Anna's dad tries to reason with him, but he doesn't want to know anything.

Maria grabs her things and leaves practice. Her head just wasn't here tonight, and that is okay; it happens at times to all of us. I feel bad for her and hope she gets over tonight quickly.

Being it is Friday night our practice continues until 8:30 p.m., we are still somehow playing in the dark, and it's getting hard to see. The park lights have come on for the night, but there is nothing like the sunlight. My coach ends practice, and all I can say to myself is, "Thank God."

It's been a long day. I am happy I did my chest PT before coming. Before you know it, we will be back here tomorrow and Sunday again for our games. It's Saturday morning, and my team is arriving for our afternoon game. All of us are here, and even Maria is back with a smile on her face. We are all so happy to see her. I ask her, "What happened last night with you?"

She tells me she isn't sure and that her head wasn't in it. I joke around and tell her, "You were still thinking about your boo, weren't you?"

She laughs and says, "Yeah, I guess I was."

I can tell she loves being with him. Every time she tells us about him and sees him in front of us, her face lights up. She is happy when she is with him. I know she loves playing basketball and being with us, but I am not too sure how she feels about her dad coaching her for her entire life so far. She tells us that she and her dad don't have the best relationship and that he is very hard on her. She also tells me he is a bit abusive too. I am not sure to what extent she is referring to, but I don't think she is happy about going home each night. I think her boyfriend is her sweet escape. I can see what she is saying. He shows her a lot of tough love at practice. I hope she doesn't get herself into any trouble when she is with her boyfriend, if you know what I mean.

*****

The weeks go by, and my summer consists of basketball, barbecuing, swimming, and hanging out with friends and family. It is the middle of August, and it is our championship Team Marbury game. We won the Nike League championships in both divisions. We played in the twelve and under and the fourteen and under division. I got to play almost the entire twelve and under game and half of the fourteen and under game. My team is making a name for ourselves in New York City, and if we win this game, we will have beaten one of the top travel teams in Brooklyn.

I get up bright and early and get my vest therapy out of the way. A couple of girls have dropped out of our team, including Anna, so we only have five players today. We don't even have one substitute. My coach informed us that the league will be providing lunch for all of the teams today, and I am glad I don't have to try and fit lunch in before the game. My parents drive me, and we park the car a block away. We are playing on a different block today which we aren't too familiar with. You can hear the music blasting from around the corner. It is hot but also windy today.

There are hundreds of people, and I search through the crowd to find my team. There are only five of us, and I hope no one fouls out. The chance of our forward fouling out is pretty high. She is very powerful when blocking opponents, and she tends to slap them on the arms and back rather than block the ball.

My coach introduces me to the rest of the Marbury family. I have become good friends with Bee who is Steph's cousin; however, today, she is playing on the team we are playing against. She was on my team in the Nike leagues, but she plays AAU for the other team. Our game is the next one, and the boys' team is playing first. One of my teammates points out the coach of the boys' home team. As I look closer, I say, "He looks familiar."

My friend says, "That is the rapper Fat Joe." She tells me that his new song was released today.

As we get in line for lunch, the DJ introduces Fat Joe and tells us all about his new song "What's Luv?" and how it will be playing throughout the day. I realize I know this song and am pretty impressed that a famous rapper is here and that he is coaching our friends on the boys' team.

As we eat and listen to the music, Steph pulls up with his wife in his Escalade truck along with about three other Escalade trucks.

The boys' game ends, and we are warming up. On the wall facing us is a mural of a man wearing a basketball jersey, and it says "Juice." I ask my friends who that is, and they say he is a Coney Island legend. He was killed. I stare at the mural for a few seconds and realize he was young when he was killed. As I shoot around, I realize just how windy it is, and the wind definitely isn't in my favor right now. Bee's team has a starting five and an entire bench of substitutes. I hope I don't get too tired because I will be playing this entire game.

The whistle blows, and my coach tells us we better outrun them today. As much as I want to outrun them, we may run out of steam first. I hug Bee at half court, and we both wish each other luck. It is so strange to play against her today after playing with her all summer long.

I also know a couple of other people on her team, and I shake hands with them also and say, "Good luck." My teammate tips the ball to us, and we race down the court and score. We are immediately in a full court press, trying to pressure them to turn over the ball. We don't steal it this time, but after a couple of minutes, you hear the announcer say, "With the apple turnover."

My team has stolen the ball, and we get our first-minute jitters out. It is extremely loud, and tons of people are piling into the park. When playing in front of such a big audience with such loud music and an announcer, you have to blank out all of the noise from your head and just stay focused. If you have never played with this much noise before, it can be difficult, but my team is used to this sort of thing.

My team steals the ball again, and we draw a foul. Drawing the foul is great, but with this wind taking the ball in different directions, free throws will be tough. The wind isn't in our favor, and both attempts are missed. Half of the game passes, and we are up by quite a few points. We are exhausted and drink plenty of water and Gatorade. I try to keep cool by pouring water on my head.

The second half begins, and I decide to take a three-pointer. My dad yells, "No! Jill, what are you doing?"

I cringe as the ball leaves my hands. I shoot an airball, which has been completely taken by the wind, not sure what I was thinking. Just as I was getting comfortable playing in front of such a huge crowd, my confidence goes down pretty quickly. My coach is screaming, "Jill! What the hell are you doing? Use what the good Lord gave you!"

Coach J has a way with words, but his yelling has woken me up. One minute he is screaming at me with some vulgar language, and the next minute he is telling me to use what the good Lord gave me. I look at him in agreement, and he yells even louder at me. All of my teammates have been screamed at already.

At this point, the crowd isn't making us nervous, but our coach is. Coach calls a time-out and yells at me a bit more along with screaming at Maria and everyone else for something they did. Our opponents have scored some points by capitalizing on our mistakes. We get back on the court and smirk at each other. He tells me that if he had a sub, he would have pulled me out already. Everyone has been told this at least once today, and we are all in the same boat. This lights a fire under my butt, and I make sure to use what the good Lord gave me. I use my legs and, more importantly, my brain. Hard work and smarts is what wins games.

My coach isn't happy if we win by a couple of points. He always wants us to run the other teams to the ground until we are winning by a lot. Luckily, a couple of the other girls were able to score and keep the momentum going.

It's the fourth quarter, and we are still up. Maria passes the ball to me, and I dribble closer to take a shot. I am about ten feet from the hoop. It goes in, and I have gained some of my confidence back. My team continues to score and keep the other team from scoring. Our forward has fouled out with four minutes left in the fourth quarter. Our worst nightmare came true.

Our next tallest girl is a bit taller than I am. We are a pretty short team, but we are strong and haven't run out of energy just yet. It is hard to cover under the boards, but my coach puts me in the forward position because I can jump high and hopefully get some of the rebounds. I am just under five feet, and the other players are well over five feet. Some of them are closer to six feet tall. I do my best, and unfortunately, I start fouling too, but I manage to not foul out. I manage to get a few rebounds too.

We are up by fifteen points, and we waste the last minute of the clock by passing the ball around. We are exhausted, but they are even more tired. I get fouled and get one out of two free throws in. I am happy the wind is in my favor for at least one of my foul shots. The buzzer sounds, and my team jumps up and down, hugging each other. We shake hands with the other team and tell them, "Good game."

They are pissed they lost and even more annoyed that we beat them with just five girls when they had about fourteen. Bee doesn't even want to look at me as she has tears in her eyes.

The announcer announces for my team to line up and get our trophies. These trophies are beautiful. Each trophy is taller than I am, and it is made out of wood and metal. When you play in Coney Island, in the Marbury Classic league, and win the championship game, you can't help but look forward to that huge trophy. The other teams in the different age groups are walking around, carrying their trophies all the way to their apartment buildings.

Before leaving the park, I see Bee and tell her, "Good game."

She smiles and says, "Good game" and congratulates me on winning.

I say, "Thank you" and hug her and tell her she belongs on our team.

She agrees but says, "That's my original team. I play travel ball with them. I can't leave."

I smile and say, "I know. Don't be upset you lost. You played a good game."

My parents help me get the oversize trophy into the car. It is so large that it has to go sideways in the trunk of our Explorer truck. Today was an accomplishment, and now I am looking forward to going away with my family for a week before school begins again. I will be starting the seventh grade in a couple of weeks. Throughout the summer, I did a bit of reading each day, and I have already completed my summer reading. Usually, I finish the night before school begins.

*****

As we load up Dad's truck, my mom runs through the list of what she has packed to make sure we have all of the necessities. We are in charge of packing our clothes and what we want to take, and my mom packs all of my medical equipment that I will need for the next eight days. Mom has also ironed all of our clothes. Half of the bags we need to take are medically related. Mom confirms that we have everything.

Francesco and I are more worried about having the snacks and drinks we enjoy packed up. Dad is in charge of the cooler with the drinks and refrigerated medications, and those are all packed up too. We are ready to make our three-hour trip up state. I have my Walkman on my ears, and my parents have the music they enjoy playing on the car's speakers. After a half hour, I take my headphones off and listen to what my parents have playing. I love how music can set the tone, and I am one that remembers certain times in my life due to the music I am listening to. I am not sure if others can relate in the same way, but music is a big part of my life. It makes me forget about reality the way basketball and soccer do.

The drive is long and relaxing at the same time. In the front of the car, I hear my parents say, "Wow, look at the cows and horses over there."

I open my eyes, and I know we are getting closer as we pass all of the farms. There are acres and acres of farmland, and it is so scenic. It is beautiful in its own way. I can tell that I am out of New York City, and it's pretty peaceful here, maybe even too peaceful. It is always nice to visit here, but I couldn't see myself living here all year-round. I think I would get bored.

As we get off the main road, there are many hills, twists, and turns. We are in the middle of the Catskill Mountains. My ears are popping as we drive up to the resort. We pull up to the main building. Dad checks in as we wait in the car. As he opens the door, you can smell the air. It is thick, and there are no bus fume smells like the city, but it is more humid here. There are a few people leaving the pool area.

We get our key to our time-share unit and unload our truck and carry our bags up to our rooms. Francesco and I are excited and happy that we are here. I get my therapy done, and then we get dressed for dinner. We go to the main dining room, and it is packed. Everyone that has a time-share is here. Our time-share is the most popular week at the Villa Roma. Each year, the regular hotel rooms sell out. From coming here each year, we know a lot of the people, and our friends are here too.

As we are seated, we see our friends and tell them we will meet up in the lobby after dinner. The lobby is huge and has tons of couches. I am looking forward to going to the game room after dinner. The game room has a nice-sized arcade section, and it also has pool tables, ping-pong, bocce ball, and shuffleboard. There are a lot of activities, and we try to do as much as we can throughout the week. We spend most of the week sitting at the pool and enjoying eating out.

The week flies by, and before you know it, it's time to check out and get on the road again. Zach is at Nanie and Grandpa's house, and I can't wait to see him. I miss him so much, but it was also nice to get away and live at a slower pace this week. While being away, I still hit the basketball court and shot around a bit before heading in the pool.

Another favorite part of going away at the Villa Roma is eating lunch and drinking virgin pina coladas poolside. The live music is pretty cool too. If this week's vacation had a taste, it would be pina coladas and chicken fingers with French fries.

*****

As we drive home, I think about all the fun we had throughout the week and wish we could stay longer, but it's back to reality. Although we went on vacation, once again, CF didn't go on vacation, but it came on my vacation. CF makes the mornings difficult while being away. We can't just jump out of bed and head to eat breakfast at the coffee shop the way everyone else can. For my family, we get up and do my therapy as my mom cooks breakfast in the room. I am happy that we have a full-size kitchen, but we do our best to not use it too often. The only way we go out for breakfast is if my therapy is done after eating. This only happens if I am not coughing my brains out when I wake up.

When I eat before my chest PT, I am not too hungry. This is because I usually cough during breakfast and wind up swallowing the mucus. If I cough it out of my lungs before eating, then I won't fill up on it and will have an appetite. I feel bad that I hold my family up and wish that for at least one week on vacation that we could wake up and just skip my therapy. I don't think that will ever be my reality, and I am okay with that.

As many of the families stayed longer at the pool this week, my family left earlier to get my second therapy done before dinner. I am tired, and after breakfast, I fall asleep in the car on the drive home. Zach is running around and beyond excited to see us. We hang out a bit by my grandparents and then go home. We are all pretty tired and take the rest of today to adjust.

The next week consists of unpacking our bags and relaxing. Basketball starts back up the week that school begins. My coach decided to give us a couple of weeks off. This year, I have the same classmates as last year. It is nice since this is only my second year in this school. I am happy to be with Ali again. I decided to not play basketball for my school. I am going to play ball in Brooklyn again.

This year, my coach has signed our team up for a couple of new leagues. One of them is called BCBA, and the other is a travel league in New Jersey. My team is signed up under the parish we play for.

Our gymnasium is pretty old. It still has tile instead of hardwood floors, and there is no air-conditioning. In the winter, the heat is rarely put on, so it's always an ice box. Weeks pass, and we are back to practicing. My coach tells us that we have a few new girls coming to try out tonight. As I shoot around, the new girls walk in. I can't believe my eyes. It is my old teammate from my first school who I have remained good friends with and two of the other girls that I know. There is another girl with them whom I don't know. I say to myself, "What are they doing here and how did they find out about my team?"

My wheels are turning a bit, and just when I thought I escaped Staten Island, I realized Staten Island had followed me. I have nothing against these girls, but it was nice to be around all new people. There are three of us from Staten Island already, and now another four. I go over to say hello and ask them what made them come over here.

They say, "We heard how good you have gotten and how good they have become." They point to my other Staten Island friends. They say, "We wanted to come play and train where you were."

My eyebrows go up, and I say, "Welcome. It is not easy here. You guys better enjoy running and working hard because that's all we do here."

They smile and say, "We will do our best."

Coach walks in and blows the whistle. He asks me if they are my friends, and I say, "Yes, but I didn't tell them to come here."

He says, "Okay, well, let's see what they got. They have one day to prove themselves."

We do a lot of running and drills, and you can see they are already exhausted a few minutes in. My old teammate, "V" says, "Wow, this is a lot of running. I don't think I will be coming back here."

The other girls I know seem to enjoy the challenge but are tired too. They are twins, and so my coach starts referring to them as such. They do okay at the first tryout, and my coach invites them back a second time. He says to me, "They have potential, but they all need a lot of polishing."

The other girl whose name is Brielle is holding her own too, but she has the most difficult out of anyone keeping up with us. No matter what I do, I can't seem to escape my hometown, but maybe it will be nice to add more girls to our team. I tell V and the twins about the summer league that we just finished playing in, and I tell them that we played for the family team in the Marbury Classic. They think it's the coolest thing, and we can't wait for summer to come around again. I am happy to be playing with V. We were very close over the years, but since switching schools, we lost touch a bit. I knew her since I was five years old.

Another month passes, and we have our first travel game in Jersey. As we arrive, I see the rest of my teammates getting out of the cars. The twins and V have become pretty close over the years. They played for a different AAU team than I did in the past. I am becoming close with all of them too. It's nice that they joined our team. They are all a lot of fun on and off the court. We hang out a lot at each other's houses. Years ago, when the bully, Barbara, grabbed me by the neck at one of my basketball practices and threw me to the ground, V stepped in and threw her to the ground. V and I always had each other's backs, and she told Barbara to never grab me by the neck again. V is much taller and stronger than I am, and the bully met her match that day. Since then, Barbara hasn't bothered me and has actually been friendly when we occasionally see each other.

We warm up and are ready to outrun our opponents. Even V and the twins are ready to run. They have come a long way already. From the get-go, we are up by about ten points, and we continue to run the other team to the ground. We won our first game. I played the majority of the game and scored twelve points. My coach is happy but mad that some of my teammates missed their free throws. At practice, if someone misses free throws, we get punished by doing pushups and getting put on the wall. Our team gets along well, and we call ourselves the United Nations since we are made up of many different nationalities. We also get to learn about each other's cultures and traditions.

It is interesting to see what one another enjoys eating, especially when we bring home-cooked food to eat before practice. It is nice because we can all be ourselves around each other and still be friends. On this team, we get to be individuals. We tease one another and constantly joke around, but at the end of the day, we have everyone's backs. I love these girls as if they were my family. They have become my second family.

It is Friday, and tonight, we have practice, and the older boys are going to be helping out and challenging us tonight. Coach tells Drew, one of the boys, to play defense and push us around a bit. He tells him to not go easy on us and to make us work hard. We look at each other and whisper to one another that we will get stuffed and get our butts handed to us. It is my turn, and as I drive to the basket, I am a bit hesitant to crash into him and make body contact, but he says that he won't hurt us. As I go up for a layup, he pushes me away from the basket, but surprisingly, he catches me, and I say, "Thank you." I am glad to not be picking myself up off of the tile floor again. I have spent plenty of nights on it.

Maria smiles at me and says, "That was so sweet that he caught you."

I agree and tell her he's a really nice kid. The other boys that are our age usually knock us down and don't usually offer a hand to help us up. We know they aren't trying to hurt us, but Coach tells them to go hard and to not make it easy for us. They sure do take his words seriously.

A couple of months pass, and my everyday life consists of games, practice, school, and hanging out with my friends and family when I can. This school year has been a lot of fun. Our teachers are nice. This year, we switch classrooms each period and we have lockers to keep our things in. This is a little taste of what high school will be like.

It is the week of Christmas. It is such a nice time of year. We have our annual Christmas fair at school, and we are doing secret Santas again. The day before Christmas break, we have a Christmas party again. I know my classmates much better this year, and it is nice to hear what everyone's plans are for the holidays. My friends and I exchanged gifts again. Giving my friends things they will enjoy puts a smile on my face. I enjoy giving more than I enjoy receiving. We don't spend a lot, but we get each other something small.

I am happy to not have schoolwork over the break. As the bell rings, we all grab our bags and head outside. I can't believe my school bag is empty. At my other school, I practically had to pack my entire desk anytime we had a day off. My mom is with the other parents, and we all get into our cars to head home. It is freezing out, and so we can't stay outside too long. Mom stops to get me pizza for a snack, and then we head home to get some things ready for tomorrow.

Tomorrow night is the Christmas party with my basketball team, and the boys' teams will be joining us as well. A lot of the boys' and girls' parents aren't around and don't attend the games, so my parents and some of the others agreed to take care of the food. Mike, who volunteers at the gym, cooked a bunch of food as well, which is so nice of him and his wife. They both volunteer their time for this parish by running the gym kitchen. My friend's dad is also a chef, and he has sent some delicious food too. My parents cater trays of fried chicken and French fries.

We bring the trays into the gym and say hello to everyone. There are a lot of people to say hello to since there are three teams here along with some of the parents. Christmas music is playing, and everyone is running around. It is a happy time in this gym tonight. Half of the court isn't being used for the party, and so we take out a few balls after eating dinner.

I decide to shoot around a bit while everyone is on the other side of the gym. We aren't dressed in basketball clothes, but that doesn't stop a bunch of us from ballin'. Drew comes over and asks if he can shoot around with me a bit. I say, "Yes, sure. The court isn't mine."

He laughs and says, "Thanks" and grabs a ball. We decide to share one ball and take turns shooting and rebounding for each other. I excuse myself for a minute and ask my teammates if they are going to play too. Maria, Anna, and the twins laugh and say, "No, you guys are cute together. Go play with him."

I look at them as I turn around and walk back onto the court. They are still staring at me as they smile, and they say, "Have fun."

I wave my hand at them and gesture for them to join us.

Anna says in a loud tone, "Go shoot with him. You guys are cute together." As Anna runs over to me, she whispers in my ear, "Stupid, he likes you."

I roll my eyes and walk away from her and start shooting again. The twins join us for a few minutes, but he keeps passing the ball to me. He asks me if I want to play one-on-one with him. Out of the corner of my eye, I see Anna and Maria watching us, and they are smiling as they pick on some more food.

I say, "Sure, I'll play. What is the winning point?"

He smiles and says, "Whatever you want to play until. How about eleven? It's your ball first."

I tell him that he can have the ball first, and he says, "No, ladies first."

We are both scoring back and forth and are pretty much tied the whole time. I can only score by taking jump shots. Going in for a layup would be me entering the "land of the giants" right now. I think he is letting me score because I know he can play much harder than he is right now. I am not playing my hardest either. It is hard to play a sport when you aren't wearing the proper attire, especially for a girl. It's just a friendly laid-back game.

I decide to drive to the hoop, and he stuffs me. Coach J says, "Jill, what are you doing?"

I am in shock and had no idea anyone was watching besides my friends. He says, "Sorry."

I tell him, "You don't have to go easy on me."

And he says in a sarcastic tone, "Okay, so I will beat you up."

I start laughing and know he is joking. He takes a jumper and swoosh. I say, "Nice shot."

Then I score, and he says, "Nice."

A few minutes later, we both agree to get some water. As we go to sit down by the tables, we hear commotion in the hallway. I go to check out what's going on, and Maria and her boyfriend are playing dodgeball with one of the basketballs. I shake my head, laughing, and I sit down at the table where my parents are. Drew is quiet and a bit shy off of the basketball court, but he is sitting at our table. He tells me that this party is really nice and that it's nice that my parents could be here.

I ask him where his parents are, and he tells me that they couldn't make it. I notice that Drew stands out from the rest of the boys and is very respectful. Not all of the boys that play ball here are respectful. Drew tells us he is going to head out and that he is going to let his cousin know it is time to leave. I didn't know he had a cousin here. As he goes over to his cousin, I now realize that his cousin is my teammate and that I have become friendly with her. I did not see that coming at all.

As she says goodbye to everyone, I say, "Drew is your cousin?"

She says, "Yes." He has been playing here for a few years, but she only started coming here a couple of months ago. Now it all makes sense.

I focus my attention to where Maria is. Maria's boyfriend is a couple of years older than her, but I honestly don't see that ending too well in the long run. I think he has different interests than she does right now, but from having conversations with her, it seems like she is eleven going on thirty. I think she is growing up a bit too fast.

Let's just say she has more experience than the rest of us. I know age is only a number, but it is visible when people are on different pages.

We head home, and tomorrow is Christmas eve. My parents always have Christmas eve with our entire family most of the time. We make the seven fish Italian Christmas Eve dinner. This year, Nana and Grandpa are coming too. Most of the time, Grandpa takes Nana out for her birthday, but this year, they are joining us. On Christmas, we are going to Nanie and Grandpa's.

*****

Christmas morning is here. Francesco and I get up midmorning and wake my parents up. We head downstairs and sit in front of the tree. My mom puts the gifts in front of us that are from her and Dad. The gifts I wrapped are under the tree. They don't look anywhere as nice as the ones Mom wrapped. I grab my parents' gifts and Francesco's and place it next to them. I open up my first few gifts, and I get two pairs of Jordan kicks. My teammates have the same shoes which they got months ago, but I wanted to wait until Christmas to ask for them since my parents ask for a list of things that I would like. My parents always ask Francesco and I for a list each year. They are always generous, but we don't expect them to buy us anything. They also get me my first Phoenix Suns Stephon Marbury jersey. I am excited to wear it and have him sign it the next time I see him. It is so cool to get a new NBA jersey, let alone a jersey with the name of a player that I know. They also got me the shorts to match and a bunch of other awesome gifts. I am so thankful and love watching the rest of my family smile as they open their gifts.

This week has been a lot of fun. Seeing my family and friends has been the best part of it all. My parents had New Year's Eve by our house with our family and friends. I cannot believe how fast this week off went.

We are about halfway through the school year already and we go back tomorrow. I am not looking forward to the schoolwork, but I am happy to see my friends. The bell rings in school, and we kick off the next few weeks and months ahead. I go back to my normal routine.

We are in full swing with school and basketball in our house. Francesco plays high school basketball for our church. He isn't as competitive as I am but enjoys playing, and I love going to watch him play. Watching him have fun makes me happy. Although he criticizes how I play in each game, I know he is one of my biggest fans. His way of cheering involves some critiquing. Life is great right now!

I haven't seen Michael in a pretty long time. We are still friends and talk once in a while on AOL Instant Messenger, but we aren't close the way we used to be. I have even sort of forgotten about him a bit. I am too busy making new memories and enjoying new experiences. My memories with Michael have shaped the way I think about my future a bit and our friendship has left an impression on me. These times were also a learning experience for me.

It is February, and Michael and his family are coming to see our new house. Michael's mom says she has a housewarming gift for us. I'm not sure how to feel, but I am not excited to see him the way I used to be. As we show them around the house, Michael asks if I saw the gift they got my family.

I say, "I saw my mom open it, and it is beautiful."

He says, "It's from Lenox. It's expensive and it smells good."

I tell him, "Yes, they aren't cheap. Thank you, guys. I will have to smell it."

I show him my bedroom, and he says, "Wow, Jill, this is sick! You have your own bathroom. This is a suite."

I laugh and say, "Yes, it's pretty cool. I really do love it." Then we talk a bit about life as we sit in the living room.

He asks me why I am playing basketball in Brooklyn, and I explain that it's better for me. "I needed a change, and the competition doesn't compare to out here."

He laughs and says, "Okay, but you are a really good player already." He asks me if I am dating any guys.

I say, "No, I am focusing on basketball and school. I don't have any time for anything else right now."

He tells me he has a new girlfriend from his school.

I say, "That is good. I am happy for you." We really have grown apart so much, and it is for the better. Our conversation hits a dead-end, and Mike is asking me questions about the house instead of sitting in silence. He comes off a bit cocky tonight. I tell him that he has changed a lot, and he says that he has and that I have also. I can't debate that, but I think I have changed for the better. He is not the same boy that I sat across from in the pizzeria and became friends with that night. It's like the sweet kid in him has vanished. My brain hurts and I am happy it is bedtime.

The weekend goes by fast, and I am back in school. I am in English class, and a bunch of my classmates and friends have been out sick lately. I think something is going around. As I finish taking my English exam, the boy next to me starts throwing up. I immediately get up from my seat and move toward the door. There is definitely a virus going around, at least on our floor.

A few days later, I am home sick with that same virus. The virus is affecting my lungs, so I have an appointment with Dr. G, my CF doctor. We do PFTs, and my lung function is down. I was also completely exhausted for weeks, even before I got this virus. Dr. G tells me that I need IV antibiotics and that she will schedule me for a PICC line placement tomorrow with the radiology team. My mind immediately goes back to four years ago when I pretty much passed out due to the PICC line placement. I am a bit nervous, but I am feeling yucky and know this is what I need.

We go home and get some rest. The next morning, we wait for my name to be called inside of the radiology waiting room. I head inside, and they ask if I am a righty or lefty. I tell them that I am righty, and they decide to place it in my upper left arm. A half hour goes by, and we are all set. That wasn't too bad. It was much easier than the first PICC line.

This time, they looked at my veins and chest using an X-ray machine to see where to place the line. Halfway through the procedure, I felt some blood drip down my arm to the back of my elbow. The radiology team told me that it is normal. I am sure they have to cut my skin in order to get the line in. I am completely numb due to the injections. Last time, they only numbed my skin with topical cream, but this time, they injected the numbing medication into my vein. My entire arm is numb all the way down to my fingers.

A half hour later, the procedure is all done, and the doctor leaves the room. I thank him for his expertise. The nurse cleans my arm with alcohol and wraps it up nicely in a cloth. I come out, and my parents ask how it was. I tell them it wasn't bad and that we are all done. They are happy to see that I am not in pain or crying this time.

We drive home, and the nurse arrives a couple of hours later. The medications also arrive, and Mom puts them in the refrigerator. They are taking up almost the entire fridge. The nurse refreshes our memory on how to flush the IV and infuse the medications. We catch on quickly and are confident we can do this for a second time. I am also older and learn how to do it too.

Six days pass, and my mom wakes up at 6:00 a.m. on Sunday to start my first IV infusion for the day. I lay in bed, asleep. This IV runs for an hour, and then Mom will be back in my room to hook the second one up. Mom sets her alarm for one hour later. I can hear the alarm buzz, and she comes into my room. As she unhooks the first medication, she notices the line is all clotted with blood. She tries flushing it, and she cannot get it to flush. The blood is solid.

I wake up from hearing her tell Dad what is happening. My dad came into my room and gave it a shot, but no luck. They call the homecare company, and the nurse on call shows up a half hour later. She tries a bunch of times to flush it with both saline and heparin. She cannot clear it. She tells us she needs something called TPA, but we cannot get it from the homecare company on the weekend. We are told by Dr. G to come to the ER in Long Island as soon as we can.

We pack a few things in case we get stuck there and head out into the snowy streets. We arrive, and I am brought into the ER immediately after checking in. As Dr. G comes walking down the hall, there is a cute little boy following her around. She says, "This is my youngest son. He is three years old." He is shy but so adorable as he carries his teddy bear around with him.

Dr. G puts the medication orders in and we wait. Nanie came with us, and we are in a private room within the ER. We have a little TV in here. Nanie and I are watching the movie *Happy Gilmore*. We can't stop laughing, and it takes our minds off of what is going on. For a few minutes, I even forget why I am here. Every hour or so, the nurse and Dr. G come in to see how it's going. It's been a few hours since the TPA was put into my PICC line, and nothing is moving. We wait and continue trying to bust up the clot. This medication normally breaks up the clots quickly.

Dr. G also orders a ton of bloodwork on me while we wait. My dad is back from getting us some popcorn to snack on. We are all enjoying the popcorn and laughing at how it is stuck in our teeth. After a few minutes, Mom cannot stop coughing. She tells us that a kernel is stuck in her throat near where our tonsils are. Dad opens the medical drawer and finds a wooden stick that is used to hold down the tongue. He uses one to hold down her tongue and tries to grab the kernel with one of those long cotton swabs. They are both laughing hysterically, and Nanie and I are hysterically laughing too. This is funnier than the movie that is on. For a minute there, my dad thought he was a doctor.

We are in the perfect place if you need medical help. Dr. G hears the laughing and comes running in, thinking the line has cleared. When she sees my dad, she looks at him funny and says, "What are you doing?"

He says, "Diane is choking on a popcorn kernel, and it's stuck where her tonsil would be. I thought I could get it."

Dr. G grabs the things from Dad's hands, and within seconds, she grabs the kernel using a long cotton swab as she holds Mom's tongue down. We all laugh and thank her. She laughs, and from knowing her all of these years, we know she really got a kick out of that. Watching Dad was priceless, and it is funny how serious and focused he was.

Twenty minutes later, Nanie and I are still laughing about the popcorn kernel. I wish I had a picture or a video of my dad. We all wait and take a rest. We are eager to see what the bloodwork shows.

Over twelve hours pass, and we are still in the same ER room. A new nurse comes on, and he thinks he can help us. He tells us his daughter has CF, and she is older than I am. He has cleared her PICC lines many times. He puts more clotting medication in a syringe and also brings a bunch of empty syringes. He begins by hooking up the clearing syringe and gets some of the medication in the line. He takes an empty syringe and continuously pulls back. Eventually, he pulls very thick, almost solid blood out into the syringe. I am so amazed and thankful. This is a miracle. It brings a tear to my eyes and my parents too.

Nanie watches in disbelief and says how amazing the nurse is. He is a Godsend, and after working continuously for about twenty-five minutes, he gets it completely cleared. I am so happy that I don't need another PICC line. I am still wondering how it clotted so quickly in the first place. We did everything we were told to do, and somehow, it still clotted. We just can't figure it out. In order to make sure it is fully cleared and working properly, Dr. G decides to admit me to the hospital so we can run both of the IV antibiotics. I am resting in the bed, and my parents and Nanie rest their eyes a bit while they can. It is so much quieter in my hospital room than in the ER.

The nurse infuses both of the antibiotics, and all goes well. My PICC line is flushing normally, and Mom gets our things together. We are happy to be leaving. It has been an adventure. As we are getting ready to head out, my parents are looking over the discharge papers. Dr. G comes into my room and says, "You are not leaving." I look at her in shock and ask if something went wrong with the infusions. I thought everything seemed to go well. She says, "Jillian, you are diabetic."

My parents almost fell off of their chairs. I ask myself, "Would God really give me diabetes on top of Cystic Fibrosis? Don't I already have enough to do each day?" I am a bit sad and quickly start thinking about all the things I have coming up with school and travel basketball.

Dr. G says, "Jillian, your blood sugar is eight hundred, and you will be staying and getting your first insulin injection in a few minutes." She tells me it will be one unit of Humalog.

I look at her and nod my head in agreement with her orders. My parents are both standing up, and I can see that they are taking all of this in. In just one minute, my entire world is turned upside down yet again. The thoughts of everything I have planned for when

JILLIAN MONITELLO

I finish IVs has diminished so quickly. All I can think about is how the other kids in the school nurse's office feel when they prick their fingers each day while I swallow my enzymes right next to them. I am now one of them.

About the Author

Jillian Monitello is a new author who has a passion to share her inspirational story with the world. She was born with a genetic terminal disease called Cystic Fibrosis (CF) which causes a buildup of mucus in her lungs among other organs.

In 2017, she and her husband Rosario started a YouTube channel to spread awareness about CF and to share what living with a terminal illness looks like from their perspective. There is much more to Jillian's life than all of their videos can ever show, so she wants to share her story from the very beginning.

Jillian hopes to inspire and encourage her audience by allowing everyone to relate to the real-life challenges and victories she encounters. She writes about much more than battling an illness and hopes you will all join her on her writing journey.

CPSIA information can be obtained
at www.ICGtesting.com
Printed in the USA
FSHW021743210122
87843FS